LEAN AUDIT

THE 20 KEYS TO WORLD-CLASS OPERATIONS
A HEALTH CHECK FOR FACTORY AND OFFICE

BY JOERG MUENZING

Part of the Series
"Navigating to Results"

LEAN AUDIT

THE 20 KEYS TO WORLD-CLASS OPERATIONS
A HEALTH CHECK FOR FACTORY AND OFFICE

By
JOERG MUENZING

Copyright © 2015, Leanmap, All rights reserved

First Edition
Published by Leanmap
Switzerland | United States | Hong Kong
For more publications by Leanmap, visit www.leanmap.com

Printed and bound in the USA

Disclaimer

This book is presented solely for educational purposes. The author and publisher are not offering it as legal, accounting, or other professional services advice. While best efforts have been used in preparing this book, the author and publisher make no representations or warranties of any kind and assume no liabilities of any kind with respect to the accuracy or completeness of the contents and specifically disclaim any implied warranties of merchantability or fitness of use for a particular purpose. Neither the author nor the publisher shall be held liable or responsible to any person or entity with respect to any loss or incidental or consequential damages caused, or alleged to have been caused, directly or indirectly, by the information or programs contained herein. No warranty may be created or extended by sales representatives or written sales materials. Every company is different and the advice and strategies contained herein may not be suitable for your situation. You should seek the services of a competent professional before beginning any improvement program.

Copyright

No part of this publication may be reproduced or transmitted in any form or by any means, mechanical or electronic, including photocopying and recording, or by information storage and retrieval system, without permission in writing from the author. Requests for permission and further information should be addressed to audit@leanmap.com.

ISBN-10: 1514817829
ISBN-13: 978-1514817827

Layout and book design by www.abcmediasolutions.com

*"Perfection is not attainable,
but if we chase perfection we can catch excellence."*
Vince Lombardi

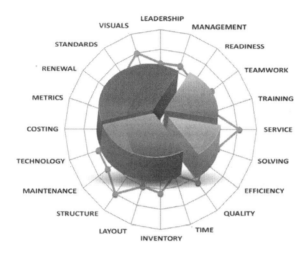

THE 20 KEYS TO WORLD-CLASS OPERATIONS

*"And the pursuit of perfection starts with the Lean Audit,
measuring where you are today to create a better tomorrow."*
Joerg Muenzing

CONTENTS

Preface xiii
Introduction 1
   Filling a Void 1
   For Whom This Book Is Written 2
   What It Is and Is Not 2
   Why You Should Read This Book 2
   How to Read This Book 3

1. Concept 5
   Creating a Competitive Advantage 6
   Theory 6
   Tool 14
   Scale 19
   Process 25

2. Keys 29
   Costing 32
   Efficiency 36
   Information 42
   Inventory 46
   Layout 54
   Leadership 59
   Maintenance 65
   Management 71
   Metrics 76
   Quality 80
   Readiness 92

- Renewal 98
- Roles 103
- Service 106
- Solving 112
- Standards 119
- Structure 125
- Teamwork 130
- Technology 135
- Time 139
- Training 145
- Visuals 148

3. Audit 153
- Enterprise Questionnaire 157
- Factory Questionnaire 189
- Office Questionnaire 213
- Lean Audit Templates 233

4. Results 235
- Step-1: Assessing Maturity 236
- Step-2: Calculating Balance 240
- Step-3: Identifying Opportunities 243
- Step-4: Estimating Agility 245
- Step-5: Projecting Impact 248
- Step-6: Defining the Plateau 251
- Step-7: Setting the Goal 254
- Lean Audit Journey 255
- Next Stop: World-Class 258
- The Leanmap Performance Cube™ 262

5. Certification 267
- About Lean Certification 267

Conclusion 273

References 275

Questions & Answers 277

Author and Company 279

PREFACE

Two days after handing me the 400-page annual report, the CEO of a large manufacturing company asked me how to optimize the manufacturing network—where to consolidate and where to invest. Although the information in the report was quite detailed—delineating past sales, inventory turnover, service levels, labor efficiency, overtime hours, defect rates, overhead costs, operating margins, and more—I did not have a good answer.

All the analysis and sophisticated charts represented snapshots in time; they were an accurate reflection of the past but inadequate indicators of future potential. A much clearer picture emerged when visiting the sites to see firsthand how work is accomplished and performance is managed. Talking to people and listening to their comments completed the picture. These observations and interactions allowed me to see clearly which sites were destined for success and which would be struggling in the near future, even though budgets were still in line for now.

Without exception, they all had embarked on improvement programs with varied success—Lean, Six Sigma, Total Quality Management, Flow, or Total Cycle Time. Despite their efforts, less than one quarter of these companies were truly advancing, while the majority showed signs of faltering in their competitiveness, which was not at all apparent from looking at the annual performance reports.

For example, one financially strong site had been run down due to local management deferring maintenance over several years to offset eroding margins. A few other organizations were struggling because they did not respond quickly enough to changing market conditions or they had overlooked the emergence of new, game-changing processing technology. But changing customer demands or outdated hardware was never the real cause of the original trouble; rather, it was the "software" in their minds. This was a common theme. All those teams were unable to escape from a successful past; they were burdened by a legacy mindset that hampered their ability to see a changing reality. They were holding onto practices and product features that customers appreciated years ago, but totally "missing the boat" on what the markets demanded now.

> We studied more than a 100 companies across multiple sectors to identify patterns shared by the most successful, and patterns repeated by the least successful. The product of our research is the Lean Audit, a comprehensive diagnostic system.

By contrast, the teams that were truly advancing did so primarily because they were proactive and performed multiple tasks differently: they took the broader trends into account and adapted accordingly. They frequently engaged with customers to understand their true needs (instead of looking inwards), they had a well-crafted strategy that provided guidance to make clear trade-off decisions (what to give up in order to achieve something else), and they invested heavily in developing capabilities in those areas that gave them a clear edge over competitors. Another common theme was this: they were using *velocity* as the key metric to drive change across the entire organization—thus shortening end-to-end cycle time from demand to delivery.

All management teams—regardless of how successful they were—felt they had to do something more or different to close performance gaps and strengthen their competitive position. But not everyone was clear on where to begin and how to proceed. Despite the extensive amounts of data they had available—like the 400-page annual report—the existing assessment and reporting systems were simply not able to provide visibility on the real issues, much less pinpoint them in the first place. As I traveled from site to site, this story repeated itself again and again, client by client.

There was a glaring need for a better way to analyze operations and transform the organization into its optimal state. The tools and techniques to address that need—all embodied in the Lean Audit—are the topics of this book.

Many people contributed to the Lean Audit concept and to the system itself. Their suggestions and ideas have been incorporated in the assessment criteria and checklists. I owe a lot to my many collaborators, fellow colleagues, clients and consultants, who all provided valuable input and critical feedback. I also want to acknowledge all those teams who used the results from the Lean Audit to kick-start and accelerate their own lean journey, and those who lived through the scenarios described in this book. I give special thanks to Sandy, my wife, caring about our family while I was on a mission away from home. Thank you all for your contribution and support, which has made the Lean Audit a reality.

INTRODUCTION

Today's global marketplace demands that companies become faster and more productive—on a consistent basis. To succeed and prosper in the long run, companies must drive the changes necessary to reach a level of health and maturity that make them invincible to attack by competitors.

Filling a Void

To improve competitiveness and prepare for the future, business leaders must base their decisions on more than traditional reports, which typically provide a snapshot in time, i.e. a view of the past that is not an effective indicator of future performance or how well a business is configured to meet future challenges. As such, a significant void exists in the information map available to business leaders. The Lean Audit fills this void by providing a simple and effective method to diagnose operational health and maturity in manufacturing and service companies—all in less than four hours!

For Whom This Book Is Written

The Lean Audit is written for senior executives, line managers, business analysts, scientists, and investors. The Lean Audit allows managers to determine the baseline before introducing changes; it helps engineers design better systems; it allows consultants to quickly identify improvement potentials; and it provides insights that owners need to make optimal investment decisions. For best results, readers should have some awareness of the concepts that comprise the 20 assessment parameters ("keys"), several years of managerial experience, and the determination to complete the audit and commit to an improvement plan.

What It Is and Is Not

The audit is generic enough to fit almost any manufacturing and service operation, yet specific enough to pinpoint areas of excellence and opportunities for improvement. It offers a clear view on how well a business operates relative to world-class benchmarks, and the visibility on areas that need an intervention. The Lean Audit is not intended to be a comprehensive guide to business transformation; rather, it is a practical user manual you can use to quickly uncover blind spots and value-creation opportunities. In just four hours, the Lean Audit delivers insights that lead to actions—actions that in turn lead to an increase in health and maturity that will ultimately give the factory or office a real competitive advantage.

Why You Should Read This Book

If you currently rely on traditional reports to manage your business, your view is limited because that information is static, outdated and ineffective. You need more powerful tools for the extra insights required to stay competitive in the changing global marketplace. This book gives you a simple—but highly effective—method to diagnose operational health and maturity in your manufacturing and/or service organizations.

You will gain the following benefits:

- a clear, documented reference point indicating where you are now,
- an understanding of what "better" looks like, and
- the fact base to develop effective improvement plans

How to Read This Book

This book is organized in five independent parts, so you don't have to read it from cover to cover; instead, you can focus only on what you need, and when you need it. Chapter 1, the *Concept*, introduces assessment principles and processes, helping you understand universal benchmarks and how to calibrate on maturity levels. Chapter 2, the *Keys*, explains assessment categories and includes examples and background information. Chapter 3, the *Audit*, is the heart of this book and the core of the Lean Audit process; it contains the questionnaires and scoring tables. Chapter 4, the *Results*, offers guidelines on how to analyze the data and turn scores into benefits. It also describes, via case studies, how companies have used the Lean Audit to accelerate their journey to world-class. Chapter 5, the *Certification*, explains the certification process, which gives the improving company an objective method to measure, verify, and certify performance over time.

Experts can jump to the questionnaires in chapter 3 and proceed with the audit. Beginners should first learn the theory in chapter 2 to get a thorough understanding of the concepts before undertaking the Lean Audit process. In any case, you should perform a trial audit to test your knowledge and look up terms that are less clear. Chapter 4 provides guidelines for the post-audit stage and chapter 5 covers supplemental information on the certification process.

Now let's get started.

1. CONCEPT

The Lean Audit is a structured framework that measures the strength of 20 enablers, or "keys", that are required to successfully operate and sustain a manufacturing and service business. A rating process measures the strength of each key on a five-point scale. These scores are then reported visually on a radar chart. The average score of all 20 keys gives an overall measure of the organization's health and maturity level relative to established benchmarks. The audit also identifies the gaps between current methods and best practices. The following chart shows a silver-qualified operation (level 3) with an expected improvement rate to qualify for Gold (level 4) within two years.

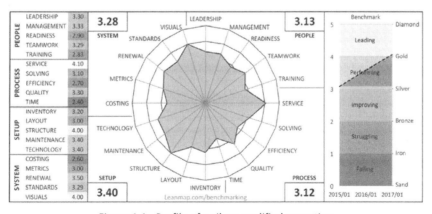

Figure 1.1 - Profile of a silver-qualified operation

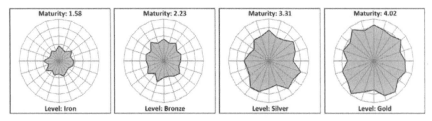

Figure 1.2 - Improvement journey from "Iron" to "Gold"

Creating a Competitive Advantage

The Lean Audit is an effective goal setting and feedback tool. It gives teams an accurate measurement of their own performance, allowing them to measure progress against established targets. It provides the means for senior management to set high expectations, such as improving maturity by one level every two years. It also helps to bridge the age-old gaps between operations, commercial, and product development—groups that traditionally occupy separate silos. The Lean Audit is not only a measurement and feedback tool; it also creates awareness and nudges teams into the right direction, and encourages individuals standing on the sidelines to join the journey. While people go on with their daily work, they are investing a small amount of time and energy toward systematic, continuous improvement that will make a huge difference over time. Those efforts also help them gain a deeper understanding of what customers truly value and how to deliver it efficiently. This enhances their ability to contribute to their fullest potential and gives more meaning to work by aligning the company's strategy and goals in a coherent way across the organization. Over time, the combined effect of hundreds of these actions is to create a significant competitive advantage, which is the primary goal of the Lean Audit.

Theory

Definition of Terms

Business entities and concepts can be referred to in various ways and there are subtleties in these references. I will set the foundation of the discussion by providing a definition for some of the more common terms about business entities and the concepts surrounding them.

A *Company* is an independent legal and financial entity that operates in the open market to satisfy customers and both internal and external shareholders. A company has a defined vision, mission, and values that form a specific culture. One company may consist of multiple organizations operating under various divisions.

A *Lean Enterprise* is comprised of all companies that cooperate and share the same strategy and value stream. Together, these companies specify value from the standpoint of the end customer, remove wasteful activities from the joint value stream, and generate those activities that create value in a continuous flow, at a balanced load, pulled by the customer, in sync with actual demand.

A *Lean Operation* describes an integrated socio-technical system with the primary objective of eliminating waste by concurrently reducing the variability stemming from suppliers, customers, and internal processes to dramatically reduce the order-to-cash cycle.

An *Operation* transforms inputs into sellable goods and services that deliver value to customers.

Operational Performance refers to the effectiveness of an organization in converting inputs into outputs.

An *Organization* is an individual manufacturing or service operation that has its own identity, management, independent control structure, inputs and outputs, but that operates as part of a group of similar organizations within one company.

A *Site* is the largest single segment of an organization that can be overseen by one executive team. It is organized around a plant, office suite, campus, or service center that contains one discrete unit of the organization. For organizations with operations in several locations, each operation in each location is a site.

A *Value Stream* consists of all activities across the entire process chain; from order entry to delivery in operations, request to fulfillment in service, or concept to launch in product development. The value stream covers all core activities required to generate the product and service, as well as information flow and administrative tasks.

Operations Configurations

Before we can analyze factory and office operations, we need to get a good understanding of how operations are configured. To create a competitive advantage, companies need to select one or two strategic priorities out of eight basic choices:

(1) low-cost operations, (2) high performance design, (3) consistent quality, (4) fast delivery, (5) on-time delivery, (6) development speed, (7) product customization, (8) volume flexibility. Once the strategic decision is made, the operation can then be configured to best support the competitive priorities of the enterprise under consideration of process choice, vertical integration, resource flexibility, customer involvement, and capital intensity. For the purpose of the Lean Audit, understanding *process choice* is critically important as it defines the flow of work. The nature of these processes are discussed next and summarized in the configuration matrix for manufacturers (figure 1.3) and service companies (figure 1.4).

The 5 Process Choices

Companies configure their operation according to the demands of the markets they serve and the characteristics of the products they produce and the services they provide. There are five models:

1. Project operations (flexible flow) perform work on a single item, like constructing a house, consulting work, planning an event, running a campaign, delivering training, developing a new product, or implementing a new software. Each project is unique, demanding a high degree of flexibility from people and equipment to create highly customized products and services; many interrelated tasks require close coordination. A project process is based on a flexible flow strategy. Workflow is redefined with each new project, so that project firms sell themselves on the basis of their capabilities rather than on specific products or services.

2. Job shops (jumbled flow) deal with low volumes and high variety, like a print shop, auto body repair, plumbing, catering, electrical work, a tooling shop, or photo studio. As each item is done by hand, one at a time, there is very little or no standardization. Many jobs are in various stages of completion, demanding very flexible employees and equipment. Job shops usually bid for work as they make items to order and not ahead of time. The specific needs of the next customer are unknown, and the timing of repeat orders is unpredictable (like patients in a doctor's office). Each new order is handled as a single unit (patient). Job shops use a flexible flow strategy, with resources organized around processes (like x-ray equipment). The flow pattern is jumbled, with no standard sequence of work, so that processing steps are adjusted specific to each job.

3. Batch operations (disconnected line flow) fall between job shop and mass production, such as bread baking, shoe production, grading exams, processing loans, university registration, license renewal, routine medical examination, manufacturing garments, furniture, heavy equipment, or components that feed an assembly line. Batch operations produce a regular mix of familiar items in a disconnected line setup, requiring equipment and processes to be adjusted specific to each batch. Some of the components for the final product may be produced in advance and variety is achieved more through an assemble-to-order strategy than the job shop's make-to-order strategy.

4. Repetitive operations (connected line flow) are characterized by a low variety of products and services, like fast food, automotive assembly and manufacturing of appliances, computers, or toys. Equipment is purpose-built and employees are trained on specific, narrow applications. Repetitive operations focus on the flow of items rather than a discrete set of activities, allowing resources to be organized around a product or service. Items move linearly from one operation to the next according to a fixed sequence with little inventory held between them. The line is either machine-paced or worker-paced, and production orders are not directly based on customer orders due to a make-to-stock strategy.

5. Continuous operations (continuous flow) produce a steady stream of a single product or service, like petroleum, chemicals, steel, beer, food, coal, cement, gas, paper, telecommunication data or electric power. Continuous operations demand a high degree of specialization from employees and equipment at a low degree of flexibility; making process segments tightly linked and flow rigid. The process industry is very capital intensive and operated round the clock to maximize utilization and efficiency rates.

Operation	Project	Job	Batch	Line	Continuous
Volume	One	Low	Moderate	High	Very high
Variety	Custom	High	Moderate	Low	Single
Flexibility	Very high	High	Moderate	Low	Very low
Orientation	Function	Function	Mixed	Item	Item
Example	Construction	Repair	Bakery	Assembly	Brewery

In the next section, we classify manufacturing and service companies according to their process design.

Product Companies – Assessed by the Lean Factory Audit (LFA)

Manufacturers design processes according to volume and variety, conforming to the needs of their customers and the characteristics of their products. For example, when a company makes a highly standardized commodity that caters to the mass market, the process is geared for repetitive, high-volume, lowest-cost production. On the other extreme, when the market demands a highly differentiated product, then the process must be designed to maximum flexibility. Like the industrial design principle "form follows function", the workflow pattern defines the structure of the operation to be configured as a (A) job shop, (B) flow shop, (C) line flow, or (D) continuous flow. The Lean Audit is applicable to all five setups, including projects, but delivers best results for the configurations A-D.

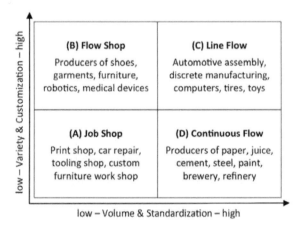

Figure 1.3 - Manufacturing process matrix

We have classified manufacturing configurations by their flow pattern and need to look now how resources are triggered—making products *before* or *after* a customer order has been received.

Make-to-stock (MTS) environments create products before receipt of a customer order. Orders are then filled from existing stock, and those replenished through production orders. The decoupling between demand and production allows batching orders, balancing workload and minimizing costly changeovers, but it adds the risk that the wrong items are kept in stock. These risks limit MTS to simple, low-variety or commodity items whose demand can be readily forecasted.

Assemble-to-order (ATO) environments make products from components after the receipt of a customer order. Common components are planned and stocked in anticipation of customer demand, initiating the assembly of the customized product. For complex items and those with unpredictable demand, ATO manufacturers usually hold subassemblies or products in a semi-finished state. The final assembly only starts when a customer order is received—like assembling a customized hamburger in a fast food restaurant.

Make-to-order (MTO) environments make products entirely after the receipt of an order. They are more prevalent when customers are prepared to wait in order to get a customized product with unique features, such as a specially engineered luxury car or a six-course meal in an elegant restaurant.

Engineer-to-order (ETO) environments require customer specifications, a unique engineering design, significant customization, or newly purchased materials. Each customer order results in a unique bill of materials and process routing to meet customer requirements, such as developing an application-specific machine or software, a tunnel or oil platform.

Most manufacturers utilize more than one flow pattern and more than one mode of resource allocation, so they are able to meet different demands in parallel, such as running an engineering trial or making customized products in parallel with their main flow of standardized goods.

We have now classified manufacturers and will move on to service companies. The Lean Audit helps classify service companies, addressing some of the specific challenges they face.

Service Companies – Assessed by the Lean Office Audit (LOA)

Service operations are characterized by customer participation, so that service delivery involves some contact between the consumer and the provider. Services are intangible and perishable, and therefore cannot be stored for consumption at a later date (an accountant's report is a snapshot in time and only valid now). A simple classification of services is by capital intensity and labor skills, grouping them into *equipment-based* and *people-based* services. Equipment-based services can then be subdivided into automatic services such vending machines and services monitored by unskilled labor, such as dry cleaning, and services operated by skilled labor, such as airlines and computer services. People-based services are subdivided into those utilizing unskilled labor, such as lawn care, security guards, and janitorial service; those utilizing skilled labor, such as appliance repair, car maintenance, plumbing, catering, and electrical work; and professional services such as law, medicine, accounting, and consulting. For the Lean Audit we will focus on people-based services and classify them according to customer interaction and labor intensity; low-touch environments like (A) mass service and (B) service factories, and high-touch environments like (C) service shops and (D) professional service.

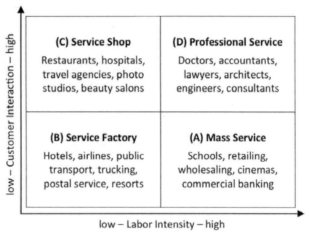

Figure 1.4 - Service process matrix

Mass Service as provided by schools, retailers, or commercial banks is characterized by high labor intensity and low degree of customer interaction and customization. Mass service organizations have a limited service mix and usually compete in price and choices. The service process is rigid and it has limited ties to equipment. The common challenges are scheduling of workforce, managing a rigid hierarchy with standard procedures, managing growth, and developing methods and controls.

Service Factories, like hotels, airlines, public transport, trucking, or postal service are characterized by a low degree of customer interaction and low labor intensity. Service choices are limited and new offerings are introduced infrequently, making service shops a very stable environment. The competitive advantages are price, speed, and personal touch. Capacity decisions, load leveling (avoid peaks and promote off-peaks), and on-time delivery are main challenges, together with hierarchical structures and policy constraints.

Service Shops, like restaurants, hospitals, auto repair shops, travel agencies, or photo studios provide a high degree of customer interaction at low labor intensity. They consider a high mix of services offered as a source of competitive advantage. The main challenge of a service shop is that demand is difficult to predict and bottlenecks occur frequently, making the service operation hard to schedule, standardize, and mange.

Professional Service refers to firms that rely on the specialized knowledge of a few individuals, such as doctors, lawyers, accountants, architects, engineers, and consultants. A high degree of interaction and customization, combined with high degree of labor intensity, characterize this segment. The common challenges of professional services are balancing administrative with value-adding activities, matching the skills required with the skills available, as well as complications of stochastic service time, dependent events, and probabilistic activities.

The Lean Factory Audit (LFA) and the Lean Office Audit (LOA) provide insights that managers need to address the challenges they face, helping them to transform manufacturing and service operations respectively.

How The Lean Audit Was developed

The Lean Audit is a structured framework that measures the strength of 20 enablers, or "keys", that are required to successfully run and sustain a manufacturing or service business. It provides a better understanding of operations and allows business leaders to make informed decisions to improve profitability and competitiveness. It is a reliable diagnostic tool that is easy to use and applicable to many industries.

In 2006, the Lean Audit came into existence as an Excel spreadsheet that was created to evaluate the efficiency of manual assembly stations. In its earliest form, it was not much more than a long checklist—useful but very narrow in its application. Over the next two years, we extended the assessment criteria to include automated processes, and in 2008 we released the first commercially available version of the Lean Factory Audit (LFA).

As our user base grew, a limitation surfaced: the LFA worked well for batch operations but it was not suitable for analyzing projects and continuous operations. Eliminating those weaknesses became a priority, and the assessment criteria were again expanded to cover all five operating environments—project, job, batch, repetitive, and continuous mode.

In 2010, the second version of the LFA was released and well received. As it gained in popularity, more clients asked for a tool that goes beyond manufacturing and includes checklists applicable to the service sector, which would eliminate several blind spots in the diagnostics. We spent the next two years broadening the scope to include office processes and business administration. The Lean Office Audit (LOA) was released in 2012 to work in tandem with the well-established LFA, allowing now a comprehensive diagnostic of the entire business. Taken together, this third generation of the Lean Audit was then tested in a controlled study to measure the reliability of the entire framework, including the relationship between audit score and operating performance. Feedback from the auditors allowed us to further optimize the questionnaires. This fourth generation, released in 2014, improved the repeatability and reproducibility of the Lean Audit results.

After eight years of development, the Lean Audit has become a highly effective, comprehensive diagnostic tool that allows even less experienced auditors to produce consistent and reliable results.

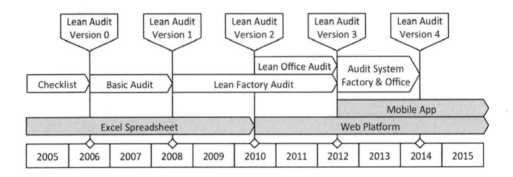

Figure 1.5 - Development of the Lean Audit system

Tool

The 20 Keys to World-Class Operations

A doctor does not limit his diagnosis to checking a patient's pulse and then conclude: "There is a heartbeat, so the patient is fine". Likewise, evaluating an athlete solely on his weight-lifting capacity would not yield an accurate assessment of fitness, while measuring strength, speed, pulse, endurance, balance, and coordination will produce a much more accurate result.

There are several vital signs to consider when conducting a health check for a business. Generally speaking, the accuracy of the overall assessment improves as the number of individual measurements increases, but there is a point of diminishing returns where the incremental gain is not worth the extra effort required to take more measurements. We found that it takes 4 to 8 checkpoints per parameter and 10 to 20 parameters to perform a comprehensive audit—10 parameters for a quick scan and 20 for a full diagnostic. For the Lean Audit we have selected only those parameters that have a proven impact on business performance and overall competitiveness. We refer to these parameters as: "The 20 Keys to World-Class Operations".

Audit Parameters

During the development phase of the Lean Audit, we tested nearly fifty assessment parameters, or "keys", and selected only those that are easy to understand and strongly correlate with operating performance. This makes the diagnostic system more reliable and the audit scores more meaningful.

The assessment parameters are *Costing* and budgeting, resource utilization and *Efficiency* management, *Leadership* and policy deployment, *Information* management, *Inventory* management, *Layout* and ergonomics, repair and *Maintenance*, performance *Management* and *Metrics*, *Quality* level, *Readiness* for change, *Renewal* through innovation and continuous improvement, *Roles* and responsibilities, problem *Solving*, *Service* level, policies and *Standards*, organization and *Structure*, *Time* management, cooperation and *Teamwork*, the use of *Technology*, *Training* and skill building, and *Visual* management.

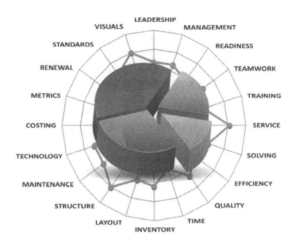

The 20 Keys to World-Class Operations

Types of Variables

The assessment checklists are based on two types of variables: manifest and latent. *Manifest variables* can be directly counted or observed; some examples are delivery, yield, attendance, inventory, or uptime. *Latent variables* are not observable and instead are inferred through a model from other variables that can be observed; some examples are attitude, leadership, teamwork, accountability, or readiness.

To illustrate, consider the latent variable "discipline", which can be assessed by considering multiple observed behaviors such as punctuality and attendance (manifest variables). "Success" in business is a latent variable that is often inferred by the manifest variables "sales" and "profitability". Besides assessing latent variables, the Lean Audit also gathers data on the three operational performance measures: quality, delivery, and cost, taken directly from the operations performance report.

Mega, Macro, Micro Level

The Lean Audit is a health check on multiple levels. In a similar fashion, a doctor measures a patient's health on multiple levels: temperature and pulse on the micro level, the response to a recently prescribed medication on the macro level, and the long-term implications of lifestyle and behavior (sports, smoking) on the mega level.

The Lean Audit mega level encompasses strategy and long-term planning (yearly), the choice of business to be in, the market types to serve, how to rationalize, and with whom to form strategic partnerships. Good decisions on the macro level improve competitiveness, while bad decisions lead to instability and decline. Macro level topics include tactics and medium-term planning (monthly); they include make-versus-buy decisions, degree of vertical integration, type of organizational structure, and the definition of processes, products, services, standards, interfaces, and value streams. The micro level refers to short-term planning and continuous improvement (weekly), as well as scheduling, processing, and problem solving (daily). The following table gives examples of assessment keys and management focus areas by level and time span, respectively.

Level	Focus Areas	Keys Examples	Time Span
Mega	• Strategy • Partnerships • Rationalization	• Renewal • Leadership • Technology	years
Macro	• Organization • Make vs. buy • Products, services	• Roles • Quality • Standards	months
Micro	• Scheduling • Processing • Controlling	• Management • Teamwork • Solving	days

Figure 1.6 - Assessment on mega, macro, and micro levels

Audit Scope

Every team is different, operating in its unique way and at its own level of maturity. This raises the question of audit scope, i.e., *Can a single score be a valid indicator for an entire organization?* The answer is yes and no. For example, suppose department-A is well organized at level five but department-B is chaotic and scores only one point at the audit. The average rating of three points would be unfair for department-A and it would also suggest that things run reasonably well for department-B despite of all the gaps and deficiencies. Here is a simple rule to set an appropriate scope for the audit: When an organization is small and homogeneous, and led by the same leader or leadership team, the variations between departments are expected to be small enough that a single score accurately reflects the maturity level of the organization as a whole. When, however, a company is split into divisions or sites, each entity must be audited separately to accurately assess the differences between them.

It is best to first perform an "umbrella audit" for the entire organization. This broad-scope audit gives the managers an opportunity to learn the assessment principles and benchmarks before they attempt to measure their site or function. Auditing on a smaller scope has the advantage that people connect to "their" score and develop a sense of ownership and pride when taking actions that improve their rating. At the other extreme, auditing every single work center within the same entity will not be very efficient since ratings will overlap, varying little when led by the same group or manager. In conclusion, measuring an entire organization as one entity is usually sufficient to identify gaps and initiate actions, especially when the organization is small (fewer than 100 employees) or its maturity is below Silver (level 3.0). For larger and more mature organizations, an assessment by function or value stream is the preferred method to more accurately pinpoint improvement opportunities.

The basic rule for the audit scope is 10/100/1000: it takes an organization of at least 10 employees to be large enough for the Lean Audit to accurately reflect its state of maturity. On the other hand, splitting an organization below 100 employees into smaller audit clusters is usually not worth the extra effort, while it is recommended for large organizations with more than 1000 employees to narrow down the improvement areas. Here are two points to remember: (1) start with a high level assessment first and only go as deep and granular as it is beneficial to scope the intervention, and (2) don't spend too much time dissecting scores and overanalyzing results. It will not change what needs to be done; rather, spend the effort on executing the improvements. It is the *change* initiated by the audit that delivers the benefit and not the audit scores alone.

Weight of Keys

The Lean Audit score is calculated by averaging the individual scores of the underlying twenty keys. This method might not seem very sophisticated because no weight is given and all keys are treated equally, but it is practical and effective. Some people for example believe that leadership is the most important factor, since nothing will happen without leadership. That may be the case but other keys are just as critical, like service and quality. If you don't serve your customers or you do not deliver the required level of quality, sooner or later you will go out of business. For the Lean Audit, simplicity and speed is more important than excessive precision because (a) the keys are all interrelated and interdependent, (b) weighing would add unnecessary complexity along with introducing endless opportunities for discussions, and (c) if a key is mission-critical but receives a low score, the corresponding performance must be improved, regardless how it is weighted relative to other keys. For this reason, the grand average is a simple and yet effective representation of maturity, and sufficient to pinpoint areas of excellence and deficiency.

Auditing the Factory and Office

The Lean Audit includes two types of questionnaires:

The Lean Factory Audit (LFA) questionnaire is for companies that produce a tangible product, such as a bakery or an automotive assembly line.

The Lean Office Audit (LOA) questionnaire is for companies that produce information, such as a call center, travel agency, or accounting firm.

Each audit has 12 common keys and 8 specialized keys of which two are unique to factory and office settings, marked with asterisks (*):

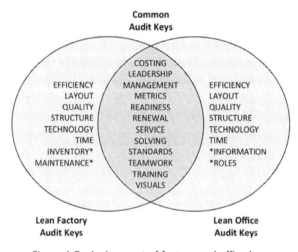

Figure 1.7 - Assignment of factory and office keys

Scale

Assessment Structure and Logic

The Lean Audit is conducted using a numeric scale to indicate the strength of each assessment key. It uses the average response values from indicator variables—as determined by the checklist answers—to construct a value for each key. This approach simplifies the analysis without compromising the measurement model because indicator variables, in the form of audit questions, are measured on a standardized numeric scale (1 to 5), which enables the scores to be aggregated. In this fashion, the average value becomes the response value for the key. Additionally, each key is clearly defined in the audit questionnaire, establishing an explicit relationship between the indicator variable and its corresponding key. Analysis of 106 datasets of our case study confirmed that our checklists accurately measure the values for the corresponding keys they were designed to measure, see more details in chapter 4 *Results*. The diagnostics questions are designed to act as reliable measures of the underlying key.

The Need for a Stable Reference

The Lean Audit produces a measurement by assigning a score to an observation according to a rule, which is defined by the different checklist levels. This measurement is only useful in relation to a reference that gives it a meaning. When those references are widely accepted as best practices or well-established standards, we speak of it as *benchmarking*. Those standards can be internal, external, global, or universal. Internal benchmarking compares performance to best results achieved within the same company; external benchmarking measures performance against practices established by an industry; global benchmarking uses best practices that are cross-industry; and universal benchmarking compares performance to the law of nature or to an indisputable physical limit.

Measuring Against Universal Benchmarks

The Lean Audit as an assessment tool is only as good as the quality of reference it measures against. Comparing scores against those from other companies is not effective because it's like chasing a moving target. A robust assessment requires a fixed reference point, derived from an ideal, a universally accepted truth, or a physical limit. Examples are inventoryless flow production, zero defects, and real-time response. Using ideals as references however is not always motivating, as the state of perfection can actually never be achieved. This means that on one side we need a reference that is stable; on the other side we want a reference that is motivating by being achievable. To solve this conflict, we select globally accepted benchmarks that are close to the ideal but still achievable; they represent the maximum score of five points on our rating scale.

Here are some examples of good and bad references:
- » *Lack of references*: going faster, doing better, as soon as possible
- » *Local benchmarks*: 10% better than last week, best local output
- » *Global benchmarks*: 24/7 service, 6 Sigma quality, 90% efficiency

» *Universal benchmark*: lossless, instantaneous, zero defects

Assessment Levels for Individual Checkpoints

Each key has distinct levels of performance, from one to five. A single sentence describes each level within each checkpoint with very specific criteria. The rating scale starts at one, because a level of zero would indicate total failure of vital functions, like a company on subsidy or a patient on life-support. On the other extreme, the maximum score of five points for the entire audit is nearly impossible to attain, as even leading companies excel mainly in those dimensions that define their competitive advantage. It's like a long-distance runner who is training for a marathon will never outperform a good sprinter in short distances. Top companies qualify for "Gold", scoring 4.0 to 4.5 over the entire audit and only a few keys at "Diamond" level (score 5.0). McDonald's for example is not excelling in making burgers but in supply chain management, attaining a top score in the Inventory dimension. Here is a generic description of the five assessment levels used in the Lean Audit framework:

» *Level-1:* undefined and unstable, no evidence of improvement
» *Level-2:* first steps taken, visible improvement, issues contained
» *Level-3:* practice fully implemented but performance not yet stable
» *Level-4:* practice sustained over 12 months with traceable impact
» *Level-5:* automatic excellence and culture of continuous improvement

Qualification Levels for the Entire Organization

The benchmark score of 5.0 qualifies for "Diamond". It is a state of automatic excellence where performance is near perfection and approaching a natural or technological limit. Flow is seamless and transparent. Decisions are value-driven, and focus is set on partnerships and transplants, extending the company's strategy and structure to its customers and suppliers to create a "Lean Enterprise". Exceptional performance makes owners and managers confident that strong results will be delivered now and in the future. Such a level-five company compares to an Olympic athlete who sets a new record or a sports team winning a world championship.

→ The phase between 4 and 5 is characterized by "Leading".

A score of 4.0 qualifies for "Gold", a level where capabilities are well established and deliver consistent results. Processes are connected and quantitatively managed as one stream rather than individual departments. Performance is robust, but not yet automatic. Adjustments and correcting minor glitches are still required to maintain desired levels. Customers and employees are consistently satisfied. Focus is on changing operating concepts and on growing market opportunity. Such a "Lean Corporation" has been optimized within its boundaries; it is leading an industry or a specific market segment within its region. Level four compares are like a local champion, closely supervised by a trainer to maintain his or her title.

→ The phase between 3 and 4 is characterized by "Performing".

A score of 3.0 qualifies for "Silver", a level where basic structures and capabilities are in place. The overall system is fully functional and processes are confirmed as standards. Performance is on target most times but requires extra effort to compensate for instabilities and unforeseen events. Problems are well understood and root-causes are being addressed. Focus is on customer support excellence and operating efficiency. Level three corresponds to a capable swimmer who steadily travels through the water but requires continuous effort to stay afloat.

→ The phase between 2 and 3 is characterized by "Improving".

A score of 2.0 qualifies for "Bronze", a level where people are aware of the issues and have taken the initial steps to contain problems and build basic capability. Conditions have been visibly improved, but the lack of discipline and weak standards cause breakdowns, major inefficiencies, and unreliable, inconsistent output. Focus is on cost reduction. Level two corresponds to someone who started with a therapy or a fitness program to improve health.

→ The phase between 1 and 2 is characterized by "Struggling".

A score of 1.0 equates to "Iron", representing the starting level, where processes are undefined, output is unstable and performance is out of control. People work in a reactive mode and are struggling to meet even basic demands. Conditions are sometimes chaotic and firefighting is considered normal. Focus is on responding to requests in a timely manner. Level one is like someone with serious health issues that make it difficult to breathe, eat, or walk.

→ The phase between 0 and 1 is characterized by "Failing".

A score of 0.0 equates to "Sand", involving the failure of vital functions. Operating below level one requires subsidies and grants to stay afloat. Level zero is comparable to a patient on life-support, requiring intensive care to stay alive. Focus is on survival. This state is a hypothetical one and not within the scope of the Lean Audit, because an organization must be operational (alive) and reasonably healthy to be assessable, scoring one and above.

Overview of Qualification Levels and Improvement Phases

5	DIAMOND	Invincible
	Phase 4...5: "Leading"	• Integrating suppliers and customers • Flow is seamless and transparent • Automatic excellence achieved
4	GOLD	Competitive
	Phase 3...4: "Performing"	• Systemizing and standardizing • Processes linked, interfaces optimized • Strong results but not yet automatic
3	SILVER	Controlled
	Phase 2...3: "Improving"	• Reducing waste and variability • Processes getting under control • Meeting targets requires extra effort
2	BRONZE	Contained
	Phase 1...2: "Struggling"	• Fire-fighting and de-bottlenecking • Hot spots contained, breakdowns fixed • Reactive mode to "make the numbers"
1	IRON	Critical
	Phase 0...1: "Failing"	• Target for turnaround "rescue mission" • Chaotic conditions cause major losses • Rapid interventions to "stop bleeding"
0	SAND	Down

Figure 1.8 - Qualification levels and improvement phases

World-Class Improvement

Improvement is always possible but not always easy. Moving from level one to two within two years is relatively easy, as many "low-hanging fruits" can be harvested. It's harder to move from level two to three, and even harder to progress to level four; so most companies level off between level three (Silver) and four (Gold), depending on their ambition, capability, and leadership. The incremental effort required to reach the next level increases with growing maturity, but the capability of people and processes also increases proportionally, so that the ratio between effort and capability ideally remains the same. With this linear relationship as a base, we can assume it will take the same amount of time to climb each step, from

Iron to Bronze, Bronze to Silver, and from Silver to Gold. Under optimal conditions, the entire journey to world-class takes less than one decade, or one step every two years, or a half step per year. The rate of improvement is limited by the ability of an organization to learn and implement required changes, as each step demands a new way of thinking and working. It's like a baby that needs two years to crawl and walk, before it can learn to run.

Measuring Small Steps, Celebrating Successes on the Way

Attaining a certain qualification level (Bronze, Silver, Gold) marks a milestone on the journey, but it also means it will take years to get to the next level. When progress is measured solely in qualification levels, feedback is too infrequent to have a positive impact on motivation. Another possibility is tracking improvement with *numbers* instead of *levels*, but moving from 2.69 to 3.04 does not seem quite the achievement as attaining another level does, like from Bronze to Silver. Receiving positive feedback for incremental improvements is a powerful recognition and feedback mechanism. In practice this means splitting qualification levels into quarters and handing out "stars" for each one quarter increment: one star (*) for one quarter (+0.25), two stars (**) for two quarters (+0.50), and three stars (***) for three quarters (+0.75). This way, the team has a reason to celebrate small successes on their journey toward world-class. Gaining a new "star" every 6 to 12 months encourages the right behaviors and fuels the motivation to continue.

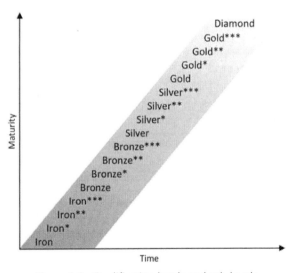

Figure 1.9 - Qualification levels and sub-levels

Process

This section provides an overview of the steps and time required to assess any manufacturing or service business.

Figure 1.10 - Auditing process

1. PREPARATION: getting ready for the audit (2 hours)

Driven by an actual business need, it's usually a member of the C-suite who initiates the assessment with a focus on the manufacturing (LFA) or office operation (LOA), or both. An executive steering committee is then formed, nominating the members of the audit team. It informs stakeholders about the purpose of the audit, whether it will be benchmarking, self-assessment, progress measurement, or opportunity discovery. For an effective evaluation, the audit team should include representatives from all key functions that make up the assessed site or value stream. A typical audit team consists of five to ten people who understand the target area best. Members should be open-minded, outspoken, able to take new perspectives, and willing to challenge conventions. For preparation, each member receives a copy of the Lean Audit or at least a detailed description of the assessment keys and rating scale, to be read before the audit. The team is ready when everyone understands how the audit process works, support from an external auditor is confirmed, and the audit date is scheduled on the calendar. You might wonder if external support is really needed. The answer is that it is not a requirement, but it is extremely helpful. This is because even strong teams benefit from the support of an experienced external auditor, who will guide them through the process, keeping people focused and honest, all the while challenging assumptions and identifying new opportunities from an outside perspective.

2. AUDIT TOUR: walking, observing, listening (2 hours)

On the day of the audit, the team meets early in the morning with a focused mind and a clear agenda. After a quick introduction and review of the process, the members of the internal team walk together with the external auditor through their value streams in flow direction from input to output, evaluating people, processes, setup, and system (PPSS). A typical tour of the plant or office takes two hours to review the top 10 processes for 10 minutes each, plus 10 minutes for setup, and 10 minutes to interview employees about their work, one person at each observation point. The total time for the audit is therefore (10 x 10) + 10 + 10 = 120 minutes or 2 hours total. During the tour, each team member takes notes, recording what they have observed and learned from the people they talked to. A dedicated member of the team consolidates all findings on one summary report after the tour.

3. CHECKLISTS: guided self-assessment (2 hours)

After a short break, the team meets in the conference room for a guided self-assessment, moderated by the external auditor or internal team leader. The audit questionnaire is displayed on the screen and the moderator leads the group through the process, question by question, one key at a time. After reading the question and possible answers out loud, the group quickly discusses the different views and agrees on the rating. This process is repeated for each checklist. If members have different views, visual cues and evidence are introduced to reach a conclusion. One person acts as timekeeper to ensure a consistent pace of one minute per checklist to guarantee completion of the audit within two hours. The moderator ensures that a certain level is selected only when all stated criteria are attained; if not, the next lower level must be chosen. It is crucial to select the "normal" condition that corresponds to 80% of all cases and not the favorable exception that accounts for 20% or less. This rule keeps the team honest and prevents exaggerated scores, thus ensuring a repeatable process and reproducible results.

4. ACTION PLAN: translating insights into improvements (2 hours)

Led by the external auditor or internal group leader, the team decides on an ambitious yet realistic advancement rate, taking the target minus baseline, divided by the number of years to accomplish the target. When setting the goal, it is important to stay within the sustainable limit of +0.5 levels per year, representing a world-class improvement rate. With the insights gained from the audit, the team selects the priorities for the next 12 months and the top three keys to improve. Then the roadmaps and action plans are developed to act on those priorities.

Once the planning is complete, the audit report, roadmap and detailed schedules are posted on the communication board. When more transparency is provided to the people affected by the change, they feel less anxious about the future. Audit charts and roadmaps are regularly updated and the impact on operating performance (quality, delivery, and cost) is evaluated every three months at least. This close tracking provides positive feedback on what is being achieved and also highlights areas where the team has fallen short. At the end of each year a formal audit is conducted to report health and maturity level, and published along with the company's operating performance and financial results.

Note: the experts among you may want to correlate the advancements in maturity level with the gains achieved in operating performance—we'd be interested to hear about your experience and share news from our research, please email us at audit@leanmap.com.

Now that we have discussed the *process* surrounding the Lean Audit, we will present the "nuts and bolts" of the Lean Audit scoring system. We will outline those attributes—the "keys"—we use to tabulate the scores and ultimately determine the overall fitness of any manufacturing or office operation.

2. KEYS

There are many types of business assessment tools, and most are specific to a function or sector, making it difficult or even impossible to compare results across departments or industries. The Lean Audit is more general in its application and can therefore be applied more universally. Both, the factory and office audit utilize a set of keys that are critical to the enduring success of any business operation and have thus been incorporated as the main components of the Lean Audit. The following table shows keys that are specific to the Lean Factory Audit (LFA), specific to the Lean Office Audit (LOA), and those shared by both audits.

Audit Keys		Factory	Shared	Office
	Costing and budgeting process and system		✓	
	Efficiency management, resource planning	✓		✓
	Information management and system			✓
	Inventory amount and system	✓		
	Layout, distances, communication, ergonomics	✓		✓
	Leadership and policy deployment		✓	
	Maintenance and uptime management	✓		
	Management, priority setting, decision making		✓	
	Metrics and performance measurement		✓	
	Quality level, process capability, yield	✓		✓
	Readiness, willingness to change, flexibility		✓	
	Renewal through innovation and improvement		✓	
	Roles, responsibilities, and ownership			✓
	Service level to internal, external customers		✓	
	Solving, root-cause elimination, prevention		✓	
	Standards, policies, procedures, instructions		✓	
	Structure, organizing and housekeeping, 5S	✓		✓
	Teamwork, cooperation, coordination		✓	
	Technology, equipment, computers, systems	✓		✓
	Time management, deadlines, commitments	✓		✓
	Training, capability building, skill flexibility		✓	
	Visuals, status signals, visual management		✓	
Number of keys used by the Lean Factory Audit (LFA)		20		-
Number of keys used by the Lean Office Audit (LOA)		-	20	

Figure 2.1 - Table of keys used for the factory and office audit

In this section we describe each key along with the corresponding factors that determine its score in the Lean Audit. Later on, in the Results section, we provide even more detail on the scoring system and how it is used to assess manufacturing and service operations. In the final section, the Certification, we will discuss how attaining a certain maturity level will qualify for a certificate in *Lean Manufacturing* and *Lean Service*.

Now, let's review the keys used for the audit system in alphabetical order.

Costing

About Costing

To set optimal prices and make bottom-line oriented decisions requires a solid understanding of costs. Costing involves collecting and classifying costs that occur while carrying out an activity or accomplishing a purpose. This also includes allocating expenditures to different functions or various stages of a process. Budgeting, which is closely related to costing, is the process of translating quantified resource requirements for capital, people and materials into time-phased goals and milestones. The Lean Audit assesses how well costs are defined, allocated, and controlled. Relevant concepts include the budgeting process, costing system, cost drivers, reviews and controls, accounting of non-performance cost and the cost of poor quality.

Cost Accounting

An activity is an event that incurs cost. A cost object is anything that requires a separate measure of cost. A cost driver is any factor that has a direct cause-and-effect relationship with the resource consumed. A cost unit is an item of production or service for which it is useful to have cost information. Cost accounting is the process of identifying, analyzing, summarizing, recording, and reporting costs. Fixed costs are invariant with respect to changes in output and accrue even if no output is produced; the rent, interest payments, property taxes, and executive salaries must be paid. Variable costs change in proportion to the level of output. Prime or direct costs can be directly assigned to the unit of output, such as direct material costs and direct labor costs. Overhead and indirect costs are not directly attributed to a particular unit of a production or service; examples are supplies, utilities, and supervision. The Lean Audit requires that we understand the common costing and overhead allocation practices.

> "Money is the language of management; you need to show them the numbers." – Philip B. Crosby.

Overhead Application

For most businesses, overhead represents that portion of total cost that cannot be individually traced to a particular product or service unit. It is allocated by a job, process, activity, or key. The Lean Audit uses the allocation method as an indicator of maturity level, which assesses how effectively overhead cost is measured and managed.

Direct Costing

The simplest form of costing is direct costing, where variable costs, such as parts and labor, are directly assigned to products and services. In contrast, fixed costs, such as rent and management salaries, are considered overhead and not assigned to any particular product or service. Direct costing is appropriate for simple operations and small businesses with low overhead, like a doctor's office or a coffee shop.

Absorption Costing

For larger companies that offer a variety of products or services, absorption costing provides a quick and easy way to spread overhead evenly across the different areas. A single absorption rate allocates overhead as a percentage of direct labor hours, work orders, material amount, or machine hours. In this scenario, with all products being treated equally, products with high margins subsidize less profitable products. This makes absorption costing simple but not very accurate for larger or more complex organizations due to the reduced visibility on subsidies.

Activity-Based Costing

Companies with high overhead use activity-based costing (ABC) to establish clear relationships between overhead costs and activities. Managers measure or estimate the overhead amount for each activity, such as engineering or sourcing, and assign the associated costs to products and services based on cost drivers. In such a case, each product incurs design costs once, and then sourcing and selling costs for each batch, and a processing cost for each unit of output. Most technology firms assign engineering hours to product families, which is more meaningful than assigning them as a percentage of direct labor because assembly time of a product is rarely proportional to its development effort.

Job Costing

Companies that provide multiple types of goods or services use job costing, which is also referred to as job order costing. This method is appropriate for costing a custom machine, designing a software program, constructing a building, or manufacturing a small batch of items. It accumulates overhead costs in *cost pools*, and then spreads these costs to jobs according to an allocation key. The key is based on standard rates, which are based on historical information. The allocation is by definition inherently inaccurate, since the underlying costs cannot be directly associated with a job. Consequently, residual amounts in the overhead cost pool are usually charged to the goods or services sold, or to jobs that were open during the accounting period.

Process Costing

Companies that make a homogenous product, such as juice or cement, use process costing to spread overhead cost across various processing departments. For example, 10% might go to department A, 50% to department B, 20% to department C, and 20% to department D, so that 100% of the overhead is allocated. Then, the overhead amount per department is divided by the respective allocation base, such as labor-hours in department A, machine-hours in department B, material-kg in department C, and truckloads in department D. Example: $5,000 overhead allocated to department C, divided by 50,000 kg processed equals $0.1 overhead cost incurred per kg produced.

Budgeting Function

Budgeting is a key management function that includes fiscal planning, accounting, revenue and expense controls. Optimal budgeting requires a thorough understanding of objectives and future programs, a sense of economic conditions and realities, a feel for trends to predict the unpredictable, and specific planning skills. Once the budget is defined and agreed upon, it functions as a guide to those operating in an environment of constant change. The budget should not be viewed as a frozen analysis that is generated once a year and stored as a static document; rather it is a continual process that involves active review and revision to accommodate changes in the operating environment.

Non-Performance Cost

Besides overhead, we need to consider another important cost driver: *non-performance*, which refers to defects, delays, and disconnects. We often calculate costs under the ideal assumption that nothing will go wrong, and we are then surprised by cost overruns. A robust budget must therefore include a certain amount of non-performance cost (NPC) to account for tangible losses caused by shrinkage, rework, repairs, returns, penalties, lost hours, and scrap. Cost of poor quality (COPQ) additionally accounts for non-tangible costs that include lost orders, missed discounts, decrease in goodwill, and lower brand image or value. For example, people are less likely to buy from a company that just had major problems reported in the newspaper.

Signs of Excellence

World-class companies understand their costs and how to control them. Drivers of direct costs are defined for all core activities, and overhead is allocated to projects and processes by actual consumption. Cost centers are treated as businesses within the business, where teams define and control their own budgets within a given framework. Costs are regularly tracked and the financial performance of each team relative to its target is posted and reviewed monthly. Cost increases are either accepted as being part of a new, favorable business case or considered problems and subject to an improvement project to get them back in line with expectations. Non-performance costs and opportunity costs (a cost incurred to achieve something else, i.e. education tuition) are an integral part of long-term planning, while end-to-end margins are fully transparent for each product and service. World-class companies use tables and charts for each value stream to show cost breakdowns by category and driver. This detailed cost information, together with key market data, allows continuous optimization of the cost structure and keeps the pricing model competitive.

Efficiency

About Efficiency

Efficiency refers to the degree resources are used to produce economic value; it is an organization's ability to deliver products or services that meet customer requirements—in terms of functionality, quality, and service level—while consuming minimal resources. The Lean Audit assesses how well time, money, and energy are used for the intended purpose. Efficiency concepts relevant for the Lean Audit include resource conservation, value generation, waste reduction, efficiency controls, overall equipment efficiency and process efficiency measures, flow of material and information, quick setups and rapid changeover techniques, and complexity reduction.

The Importance of Efficiency Improvement

To maintain historical gross domestic product (GDP) growth and rising living standards that advanced economies have been long been accustomed to, efficiency must be dramatically improved. According to a recent McKinsey study, just to offset the effect of an aging population, labor productivity must rise over the next two decades by 34% in the US and even 60% in Germany and Japan. Such improvements in labor productivity and operating efficiency are achieved through the reduction of losses caused by demand spikes, redundancies and duplications, while leveraging available resources to maximize the return on investment and effort. It essentially means accomplishing more with the same resources or the same with fewer resources, or even more with less. Higher efficiency improves operating margins, which, in turn, strengthens competitiveness and leads to more business in the long run.

Measuring Efficiency

Overall process efficiency (OPE) and overall equipment efficiency (OEE) are well-established metrics to track manual and automated processes. Efficiency is calculated by multiplying the rates of availability, speed, and quality. Efficiency can only reach a maximum when all three factors are carefully optimized. For example, requiring operators to work faster will not improve efficiency when they get sick (reducing availability) or tired (reducing speed) or making mistakes (reducing quality). One manager in Asia attempted to increase operating efficiency by demanding that his people *run* between workstations. Two people ran into each other, destroying a large batch of expensive parts that were worth several times the speed gain of a single employee during an entire year. He clearly did not understand the efficiency formula.

Maximizing Efficiency

The optimal process delivers the maximum value from the process inputs, the materials, hours, knowledge, and capital. Sub-optimization occurs when processes compete for the same resources or compromise each other because of misaligned targets and degrade the overall result. A common example is buying parts from a cheaper source overseas in an attempt to improve purchasing efficiency. The decision adds costs for qualifying the new part and supplier, increasing inventory and safety stock to compensate for longer lead times and less reliable deliveries—and for massive losses when a lower quality part fails and stops the entire production line. In the worst-case scenario, which is not rare, the purchasing team earns a bonus for increasing sourcing efficiency while the operation has to absorb the speed and yield losses caused by lower quality parts. Such spot optimizations are one of the biggest efficiency killers. Maximizing efficiency therefore demands a *cross-functional* view to reduce life cycle costs, not individual cost components.

Overall Equipment Efficiency (OEE)

The overall equipment efficiency (OEE) framework provides simple and consolidated formulas to measure performance of individual machines and also the entire production system. The OEE index makes losses transparent; it allows performing diagnostics across the factory to highlight inefficiencies, and it allows comparing production units across different industries. OEE is the backbone of total productive maintenance (TPM) and part of the lean manufacturing toolkit. Confusion exists as to whether OEE is an effectiveness or efficiency measure as both are used in the literature; we will stick to the traditional vision that refers to overall equipment efficiency for this presentation.

Calculating OEE

In essence, OEE is the net time during which the equipment produces an acceptable product (valuable operating time) divided by the time the equipment is expected to run during a day, week, month or year (loading time).

- OEE = valuable operating time / loading time

The OEE model allows isolating losses that degrade the equipment performance:

- A = calendar time = 365 days x 24 hours
- B = loading time = A – planned downtime
- C = operating time = B – breakdowns and setups and adjustments
- D = net operating time = C – minor stoppages and reduced speed
- E = valuable operating time = D – quality losses and reduced yield

Now we can calculate:

- Availability = operating time / loading time = C/B
- Performance = net operating time / operating time = D/C
- Quality = valuable operating time / net operating time = E/D

And calculate overall efficiency:

- OEE = availability x performance x quality
- Availability = (loading time – downtime) / loading time
- Performance = (actual output x optimal cycle time) / operating time
- Quality = (actual output – defects) / actual output

Evolution of OEE and TEEP

To fit a broader perspective, the concept of OEE was extended to accommodate what was important to investors. While OEE quantifies equipment performance relative to its designed capacity during the periods when it is scheduled to run, the total equipment effectiveness performance (TEEP) measures equipment performance based on the amount of time the equipment was present, measured against calendar time, 24 hours a day, 364 days a year.

- TEEP = valuable operating time / calendar time
- TEEP = OEE x (loading time / calendar time)

TEEP shows how well equipment is utilized, making it important to be maximized before capital dollars are spent on building more capacity. TEEP is also referred to as "Business OEE" or "Investment OEE" because it takes the entire calendar year into consideration when the equipment (theoretically at least) can run. Here is a simple example that shows the difference between OEE and TEEP for a commercial aircraft:
- OEE = flying time / loading time
- TEEP = flying time / 24 hours

Applying the OEE Concept to Factory Effectiveness

The key to measuring overall factory effectiveness (OFE) and overall asset effectiveness (OAE) is a solid understanding of the relationships between different parts of the equipment and integrating the information across many independent systems and subsystems. OFE and OAE can be computed by synthesizing the subsystem level metrics, thus capturing their interconnectivity information, which is a complex process and therefore implemented in various industries under different formulations. As there is no standard method defined, we will use a more practical approach and measure OEE at the end of the line or process chain:
- OEE = ((actual output − defects) x theoretical cycle time) / loading time
- OEE = effective output (units) / theoretical output (units)
- OFE = effective factory output (units) / theoretical factory output (units)

This is not a perfect method as the complexity of the OEE measurement arises where single or multiple sub-cells are constrained by an upstream or downstream operation. Assuming full load, we can say that flow is always restricted or limited by a bottleneck operation, just as a chain is only as strong as its weakest link. So we can measure OEE in real time at the bottleneck. Any variations at the bottleneck correlate directly to upstream and downstream process performance, including OEE and OFE.

Difference between Efficiency, Effectiveness and Productivity

When you are productive, are you also efficient or effective or both? Let's clear up the confusion that surrounds these measures.

Efficiency refers to the actual input over the standard input. It measures the amount of time, money, effort, and energy required to obtain a certain result. Efficiency is not linked to output and company goals, while effectiveness takes customer demand into consideration, making it a measure of produced value without any reference to cost.

Effectiveness refers to the degree to which objectives are achieved, calculated by the actual output over the standard output. Handing out 5,000 brochures in one day might be an efficient rate if given out at 10 per minute, but ineffective when only 50 brochures (1%) lead to new business while the target was 500 (10%). When producing 100 units, of which 95 pass specification and only 50 of those can be sold, and the remaining 45 end up in inventory, efficiency is 95% and effectiveness just 50%.

Productivity is defined as the actual output over the actual input, such as the number of units made per employee or direct labor minutes per unit (DLMPU), and influenced by efficiency and effectiveness. Eliyahu Goldratt takes a high-level view and defines productivity as "the extent in which a company generates money" so the goal of improving productivity is therefore not to reduce expenses but to generate as much money as possible.

Operating in a lean environment requires an understanding of all three metrics: *productivity* to track daily work center performance, *efficiency* to improve manual and automated processes, and *effectiveness* to optimize the configuration and business model.

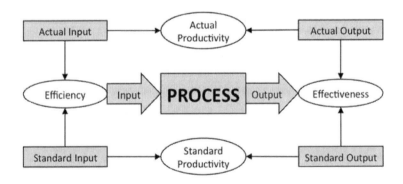

Figure 2.2 - Relationships between efficiency, productivity, and effectiveness

Balancing Productivity with Efficiency

When the quantity aspect of productivity is emphasized by paying a bonus on the amount produced or sold, it drives productivity but hurts profitability when yield decreases from a higher defect rate or the sales mix shifts to lower margin products. This might still be acceptable if the incremental gain outweighs the incurred loss, as in the case of accepting a rush order at lower yield or placing a large sales order at lower margin. On the other side, when punishing people for making mistakes, compliance to quality standards increases but speed of production falls as a result. Only at the right balance between productivity and efficiency, the net result reaches its maximum.

Signs of Excellence

As a clean and organized workplace does not necessarily operate efficiently, we must look below the surface level and understand how things work. In world-class environments, assets are grouped by value streams and organized in lines or cells rather than process villages. Workstations and equipment are right-sized and movable, and easily reconfigurable to meet changing demands. People are cross-trained and able to rotate between jobs, allowing flexible assignment of labor to balance the workload to the demand. Their pay grade is based on capability and degree of flexibility. Continuous flow limits overproduction and inventory build-up between stations, while work items flow naturally from station to station without supervision or management intervention. Activity value-add (AVA) analysis is systematically used to reduce waste in direct labor and overhead. In companies pursuing lean for several years, value-add (total task time to total lead time) of core activities approaches double-digit percentages, while processes below 1% AVA are under scrutiny with the goal to improve efficiency. People are conscious about conserving energy and water, reusing and recycling materials, and they take pride in reducing waste and inefficiencies. Products and processes are developed with a strict focus on minimizing cost and complexity. Efficiency is monitored continuously; trend charts show actual consumption versus reference inputs. In the office, any repetitive work, even common aspects of engineering design are subject to efficiency management. In the factory, setups and changeovers are completed below 10 minutes or within 20% of the physical limit. In world-class environments in the non-process industry, equipment runs between 85% and 90% efficiency (OEE), and people perform at 75% to 80% efficiency (OPE) on manual workstations. These benchmarks vary by industry; repetitive operations are closer to the upper end, batch productions are in the mid-range, and the lower end represents the top efficiency rating for a job shop and project work. The key thing to remember is not to peak on those levels but to exhibit a stable efficiency that approaches a world-class level.

Information

About Information

Information refers to data that is accurate and timely, specific and organized for a purpose, and presented within a context that gives it meaning and relevance, which in turn leads to an increase in understanding or a decrease in uncertainty. Information is a valuable asset because it affects behavior, decisions, and outcomes. Since most office work today involves information processing and decision-making, the Lean Audit assesses the quality of data and effectiveness of information management—which encompasses all the systems and processes for the creation and use of corporate information. Concepts include relevancy and quality of information, accessibility of information, information maintenance, effectiveness of reports, and capability of the document management system to provide relevant information to its users.

> "Information is a source of learning. But unless it is organized, processed, and available to the right people in a format for decision-making, it is a burden and not a benefit." – William Pollard

Information Management

Information management covers the entire life-cycle of electronic files and paper documents. It entails acquiring, organizing, retrieving, securing, and maintaining information from one or more sources and distributing that information to one or more audiences. The goal of information management is to provide relevant and accurate information on demand, when needed, and where needed. Losses occur when information is irrelevant, inaccurate, missing, or excessively precise—the four types of waste in information management.

Translation Waste

Translation waste is the effort spent to change data or formats between different process steps or between different owners. It is caused by (a) the lack of standards that define the right type and format, (b) the lack of capability to generate the right information, or (c) the attempt to change ownership by repackaging existing content and publishing them under different authorship. Good processes and systems are capable of providing the right information the first time, so knowledge workers can spend their time creating new content instead of translating existing content.

Missing Information Waste

Missing information adds a cost for gathering or recovering information, and rectifying the consequences when information is unavailable at the time a decision is made; it's like the cost of "flying blind". For example, accepting a customer order without understanding the costing information can easily lead to wrong pricing and financial losses. Another example is taking blind action in an attempt to fix a problem quickly. Without understanding the cause-and-effect relationship between the problem and the action, it's easy to pick the wrong course of action, which adds frustration, increases expenses, and introduces additional problems that must be resolved.

Transfer Waste

Transferring or handing off information to a department outside the process chain adds time and increases expenses. For example, a manager needs more production capacity to meet market demand. He fills out the required investment form to purchase another workstation for $5000 and sends it to headquarters for approval. During the next six weeks, he sends many emails and makes many follow-up calls attempting to expedite the process; the form is approved, and two weeks later the equipment is finally ready. A gross profit of $40,000 was lost during the eight weeks of constrained capacity, of which 6/8 x $40,000 = $30,000 was due to transfer waste.

Excess Information Waste

Excess information requires additional effort to sort the relevant from the irrelevant. This happens when (a) information is not well organized, (b) requirements are unclear, (c) standards are not defined, and (d) when quantity takes precedence over quality. A manager who requires his team to upload all documents to a shared drive will soon find a messy archive when folder structure, relevancy filters, and quality standards are missing. Companies that operate without effective email policies lose productivity from excess information waste, i.e., due to internal "self-spamming".

Inaccuracy Waste

Another source of inefficiency is when information is inaccurate and must be corrected. Examples of inaccuracy are double booking of an airplane seat, a rush-order that was not properly checked and is full of errors, or a poor measurement process that produces useless data. A common response is to put more inspection and approval procedures in place in an attempt to filter out problems and prevent them from reaching the next step. This approach however adds cost and slows down the overall processes; a better way is to address the source of the inaccuracy waste.

Information Systems

Central information systems, such as enterprise resource planning (ERP), attempt to merge databases, analysis, planning, and reporting tools into a single integrated entity so that accurate real-time data can be drawn by all levels of management—such as contract details, order status, material availability, labor hours consumed, inventory levels, service specifications, customer address, process routing, yield information etc. Information systems that are set up correctly can be a valuable asset, while an ineffective setup adds costs and complexity, and ultimately has the potential to cause more harm than benefit.

Signs of Excellence

A key criterion to achieving excellence is that valid information is available on demand. When you walk through a plant or office, look at process documents and into archives. Are all those papers, procedures, books, binders, files and folders useful? Is the information correct and updated? In world-class environments, the logic by which the information is organized and controlled becomes apparent by just looking at its structure. There is a central place defined to store shared documents and the process for producing, using, and maintaining information is clear and consistent. No document is out of place or out of date, indicating a high level of discipline. The information management system has been designed while taking into account technological, organizational, cultural, and strategic factors to ensure it is utilized enough—and complete enough—to make it a true asset. Service engineers use the *content management system* to retrieve and update service manuals; lecturers use the learning *content management system* to deliver e-learning packages to their students, and front-line sales staff captures call details in the *customer relationship management system*. A good information system meets the demands of compliance regulations, drives operating efficiency by automating administrative processes, and provides new value-added services to managers and customers that enhance the firm's competitiveness. Success criteria include the following: a clear strategic direction for the overall technological landscape, a small number of disparate information systems with no direct competition between them, strong integration and coordination between information systems, only a few systems that require an upgrade or replacement, effective controls that ensure consistency and prevent duplication of data, corporate-wide taxonomy for information types and values, single sign-on methods to access all authorized applications, a single intranet or equivalent platform to access all information and tools, and a consistent look-and-feel across all applications, including standard navigation and page layouts.

Inventory

About Inventory

"Inventory" refers to materials and information held for later use, controlled by inventory management processes and systems that ensure availability at minimal cost of capital. The auditor evaluates inventory structure, method of organization, degree of standardization, limits and controls, classification of items, amount of buffers and safety stocks relative to demand, replenishment triggers and process, sequence of withdrawal, items in-queue versus in-process, degree of separation, obsolescence rate, handling and internal logistics, and how overproduction is addressed. Concepts include days of sales in inventory (DSI), flow versus batch process, pull versus push method, and economical batch sizes (EBS).

Inventory is Waste

Inventory encompasses all items in the supply chain that are waiting to be processed or moved. Physical inventories include raw materials, work-in-process, and finished goods. The role of inventory in the supply chain is to bridge demand and supply. On the balance sheet, inventory is accounted for as an asset, while it is considered waste and a liability from a lean perspective. Inventory is waste because it ties up money that is then unavailable for value-generating activities; it is a liability because its value diminishes over time until items eventually become unsellable.

Inventory Categories

Inventories are categorized by position and purpose. Raw materials are untouched items that are scheduled for later use. Work-in-process items have begun their transformation, and finished goods are completed items that are ready for use or shipment. Raw, in process, and finished are attributes that describe the state of the inventory within the value chain, while buffer, safety, and shipping stocks describe its purpose. Safety stocks protect the provider from supply chain instabilities and variability. These are caused by late delivery, quality problems, customs inspection, equipment breakdowns, and also disruptions from fire, bankruptcy, and natural disasters. Buffer stocks protect the customer from starvation when short-term demand exceeds available capacity. Shipping stocks or cycle stocks are items in proportion to shipping batch sizes and frequencies, such as a container awaiting shipment or data to be entered for the month-end report. The same item can therefore be buffer stock and finished good. In lean systems, distinguishing between the different types and stages of inventory becomes less important since the value chain is typically short, which also reduces physical movements and the effort needed for inventory tracking and control.

Inventory Drivers

Inventory builds up whenever resources are applied to a product or service before it is actually required. Lean thinkers strive to create a balance between availability and efficiency by defining the right amount of inventory to (a) protect the producer from instabilities in the supply chain, (b) ensure availability to the customer, and (c) take advantage of scale economies and load leveling opportunities. Lean inventory management identifies the optimal amount and position of the parts and information required by downstream customers. To prevent stock-outs, it only lowers inventories under stable demand when downstream variability has been reduced and upstream capability has been improved. The process takes into account order forecasts, supplier lead time, carrying costs, price projections, scale economies, inventory valuation, quality rates and return of defective goods, pitch, replenishment cycles, physical storage space, and internal logistics. Effective inventory management requires balancing many competing factors to achieve optimal stock levels.

Raw Materials

Raw materials (R/M) are mainly driven by two factors: instabilities in the supply chain and purchasing incentives to get the lowest price. When items are sourced from a distant or unreliable supplier, it requires safety stocks to offset supply chain risks. When purchasing items in bulk to take advantage of volume discounts, the excess items tend to end up in inventory and are often discarded years later. This is like buying an extra pair of sneakers just because they are on sale. Modern supply chains operate in pull mode, or they use material resource planning (MRP) systems to order economic order quantities (EOQ) that balance sourcing and holding costs.

Process Inventory

Work-in-process (WIP) builds up, when resources are expended on items that cannot yet be used by downstream processes. A certain amount of WIP is necessary to balance delivery cycle times (pitch) and process cycle times between departments, while excess WIP is driven by constraints, asynchronicity, and inflexibility. Overflowing inboxes, stacks of unprocessed parts or documents are signs of poor synchronization in front of a bottleneck, while idling machines or people without work are signs of starvation behind the bottleneck. When WIP is piling up without a noticeable constraint, it indicates that resources are not balanced to demand. This happens when managers attempt to maintain high productivity scores at low demand with inflexible resources, producing more or earlier than required so that the excess items end up in inventory.

Finished Goods

Finished goods (F/G) are stored in shipping lanes or cycle stock inventory locations. Businesses that stock too little inventory cannot take advantage of large orders from customers since they cannot deliver. The conflicting objectives of cost control and service level often pit operations against the commercial department, especially when salespeople are driven by sales commissions. In this scenario, a lack of inventory leads to a reduction in their personal income, making them advocates of keeping plenty of stock. Reducing production time to be near or less than the delivery time customers expect minimizes that conflict. Traditional methods emphasize labor efficiency ratios and labor cost control, while throughput accounting focuses more on the relationship between revenue or income on one hand and controllable operating expenses and changes in inventory on the other. This way, a healthy balance between inventory cost and service level can be achieved.

Push Increases Waste

Traditional manufacturers operate in push mode, producing product according to forecasts and schedules that differ from actual demand. Producing too many, too early, or without an actual requirement is referred to as overproduction. The excess parts then must be transported to the warehouse (waste) and stored as finished goods (waste) with the risk of damage (waste); without demand the inventory declines in value over time (waste), until marketers artificially create demand through discounts (waste) and advertising campaigns (waste), so that products are moved out of the warehouse to the loading docks (waste) for shipment or for disposal when they're obsolete (waste).

Pull Reduces Waste

Lean manufacturers prefer to work in pull mode. Nothing is produced without a confirmed customer demand. Pull systems are classified in the types A, B, C. Type-A is the simplest system and works like a supermarket, where the upstream process reproduces what the downstream process has consumed. Buying a can of beans for example awakens the pull process. As the shelf runs low in cans of beans, a message is sent to the back room to restock. The back room messages the warehouse for overnight delivery to restock. And so it continues down the value stream with messages to grow beans and manufacture cans to meet customer demand. The pull process gets supply and demand in sync. Type-B, the sequential pull system, is based on a FIFO lane and works like a hamburger grill. The order is given to the grill, and once the beef is ready, it is moved through all assembly steps to add the bun, tomatoes, lettuce, and ketchup before it is handed to the customer. Type-C is a mixed system having both type-A and type-B systems. It is ideal to produce commodity items in high volume in parallel to customized items at high-mix and in low-volume, such as making lots of standard hamburgers and few customized dishes in the same kitchen. The pull method eliminates overproduction, as only the required amount is produced in every stage. When processes work in sync with minimum inventories, it makes the production system highly flexible and responsive to changing customer demand.

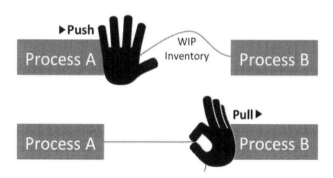

Figure 2.3 - Push versus pull method

Bullwhip Effect

Traditional planning of multistage processes tends to amplify actual demand at the process level. When orders move upstream from customer to supplier, the demand pattern becomes increasingly erratic since demand variability is amplified at each step. This demand amplification, or "bullwhip effect", is driven by the number of work centers, the cumulative lead time, and the human preference of holding additional parts "just in case" (JIC) to be "better safe than sorry". Each work center represents a decision point where order quantities are fixed or adjusted. Hence, the more work-orders, the more decision points and the higher the variability is in the system. The time an item or batch is waiting to be moved or processed increases variability as well. The more time between steps, the greater the chance for demand amplification since the production schedule is based more on guesses than actual demand; accuracy declines and amplification increases with longer forecasting horizons.

Pull Stops Bullwhip

Here is a simplistic example to illustrate the impact of demand amplification. Let's assume that a value chain consists of five process steps and that variability at each step is 15%. Forecasted demand is 100 units. Understanding the variability of +/-15%, the planner wants to be sure to meet the demand and plans 100+15 units to account for variability. This planned demand of 115 units is then given to the upstream process, which in turn amplifies it by 15% as there is a potential variability of 15%. Going five steps upstream, the order has been amplified to over 200 units, double what was forecasted. To minimize the bullwhip effect, lean manufacturers arrange processes in value chains, merging work centers into cells and connecting processes in pull-mode. The resulting gain in speed and transparency drives down variability to a small fraction of what it is in a traditional push environment.

Inventory Reduction

Strategies for right-sizing inventory follow the three phases of the product life-cycle. During prototyping, obsolescence risk is particularly high due to ongoing engineering changes; avoiding a buffer from just-in-case (JIC) mentality is key. During product launch and ramp-up, demand volatility is at its peak, which requires controlled buffers to ensure broad availability. At full maturity, the supply chain is most stable and demand can be forecasted with good accuracy. Integrating suppliers and pursuing just-in-time (JIT) delivery reduces lead times, holding costs, and waste from internal transportation. At the end of the product life-cycle, when demand declines towards phase out, buffers must be reduced and successively eliminated. Systems like JIT, vendor-managed inventory (VMI), and customer-managed inventory (CMI) help to reduce on-hand inventory and increase inventory turns. But here is a word of caution: reducing inventory without improving processes always leads to shortages and frustrated customers. Successful inventory reduction programs therefore account for the capability of downstream processes such as production and distribution, and the variability of upstream processes such as sourcing and feeding.

Inventory Turns

The most common way to measure inventory management performance is in turns, i.e. how quickly materials move through the value chain. Inventory turns are calculated by dividing the annual cost of goods sold (COGS) by the average amount of inventory on hand during the year. Using COGS is more accurate than a calculation using revenue since it is unaffected by promotions, discounts, and market-driven price adjustments. Traditional manufacturing companies turn their inventories four to 12 times per year, keeping an equivalent of one to three months of inventory. Lean manufacturers operating in JIT mode can achieve up to 1,000 turns per year, while keeping just a few hours of parts from domestic suppliers and a few days of parts supplied from overseas, just enough to cover the time-frame between two deliveries. Supermarkets typically turn their inventories 12 times per year and keep goods worth one month of sales on their shelves, retail stores turn theirs six times per year and keep two months of inventory, and hardware stores turn theirs four times per year and keep three months of stock.

Cost of Inventory

To optimize stock levels, we need to weigh the cost of keeping inventory against the cost of stock outs. As a rule of thumb, the monthly financing cost of inventory is 1% of acquisition cost, assuming 12% weighted cost of capital (WACC), the company internal financing rate. In addition to the financing cost, there is the cost for warehouse space, utilities, labor for handling and internal logistics, obsolescence, theft and errors, insurance and overhead. Holding costs typically run 1% of acquisition cost when stored in-process, 2% when stored in a dedicated warehouse, and 3% when stored in an external warehouse, in a climate controlled environment, or managed by a complex system. The total cost of inventory runs easily at 2% to 4%

of its acquisition cost per month when including operating and non-performance costs, such as obsolescence.

Inventory Math

Here are basic formulas and approximations for financial inventory tracking during an accounting period:

- Inventory = raw materials (R/M) + work in process (WIP) + finished goods (F/G)
- Cost of goods available = cost of beginning inventory + purchases + cost of prod
- Cost of goods sold = cost of goods available − cost of ending inventory
- Inventory turns = cost of goods sold / average inventory during past 365 days
- Average inventory = (beginning inventory + ending inventory) / 2
- Days of sales in inventory (DSI) = 365 days per year / inventory turns
- Financing cost of inventory = weighted cost of capital (WACC) x purchase cost
- WACC range = 5% to 20% for most companies, if unknown use 12%
- Holding cost estimate = 1x financing cost for point-of-use storage
- Holding cost estimate = 2x financing cost for internal store or simple system
- Holding cost estimate = 3x financing cost for ext. warehouse or complex system
- Obsolescence cost = value of unsellable items + disposal and handling costs
- Total cost of inventory = financing cost + holding cost + obsolescence cost

Signs of Excellence

World-class manufacturers strive for pulling items just-in-time through the supply chain so they are only made when required by the end customer or the next process step. Inventories are closely monitored and items are stocked in the right quantities to ensure availability. The replenishment process is well defined and strictly controlled. Inventory requirements are based on scientific analysis of timing and risk. Stock keeping units (SKUs) are divided into "runners", "repeaters", and "strangers" (ABC categories by velocity), with an effort to reduce repeaters and strangers and turn them into running parts. Inventory is stored in controlled locations, so that items can be picked at first touch without time wasted searching. Buffer levels, safety stock, batch sizes, order lead times, and delivery frequency are clearly defined. Visuals allow continuous control of common parts without the help of computers and reports. Labels or marks indicate minimum quantities (triggers) and maximum levels (limits), while process inventory (WIP) is only present in supermarkets and flow lines. First-in first-out (FIFO) sequence of withdrawal is fail-safe within lots and naturally achieved. Strict life-cycle and inventory management processes keep the obsolescence rate below 0.1% per year or in the lower quartile of industry average.

Layout

About Layout

Layout refers to the way assets are arranged to support people and machines as they perform work in a safe, efficient way. The audit evaluates the effectiveness of the physical layout and ergonomic aspects of the overall workstation design, as well as the interactions between humans, machines, systems, and the operating environment. The auditor looks at the configuration of spaces, level of transparency, effectiveness of walk-pattern, the time it takes to fetch parts and information, degree of continuous flow, and how people exchange information. Concepts include lean plant and lean office layout, cellular versus functional concepts, distances and transportation waste, workstation ergonomics and motion waste, interactions between people, ease of communication, traffic pattern analysis and flow optimization, level of transparency and conditions for visual management.

Asset Waste

In times of growth, when assets are added with little consideration of workflow and traffic patterns, major inefficiencies enter into the operating system. The three principles of asset wastes are that (a) every wall stops flow, (b) each process that is out-of-sight adds cost for extra motion, coordination, and internal transportation, and (c) all empty spaces fill up over time; we can see this in our drawers, closets, cabinets, basement and in our garage. When an executive selects his office based on size and view (status symbol) rather than proximity to his team, he creates asset waste due to limited face-to-face communications, a lower level of cross-functional cooperation and increased bureaucracy, added costs to rectify problems caused by poor coordination, and bad decisions that are made in isolation.

Waiting Waste

People cannot create value while they are *waiting*. Resources are lost when people wait for material or information to arrive, a service agent to become available, a meeting to start, a request to be approved, a system to boot, or a broken machine to be repaired. Waiting is one of the most common and broadly accepted wastes, and is systematically analyzed only when it annoys a customer or executive.

Motion Waste

Movements, such as walking, reaching, bending, stretching are waste. When a printer is located far away from the desk, it requires sales people to get off their desks and walk to the printer to pick printed orders after every call; quality time is lost in motion instead of calling new customers. In an optimized layout, people are arranged around the shared equipment to pick the prints just by turning the chair or eliminating papers altogether by using electronic forms.

Lean Layouts

Lean operations require an effective arrangement of assets that reduces motion and transportation, and allows people to interact with each other efficiently, without filling papers or reporting their status in the computer system. When a layout is open and transparent, and teams are co-located in the same area, people can communicate frequently, exchange information, align schedules, balance the workload, and address abnormalities in real-time without a computer between them.

Design Approach

The science of plant design and workstation ergonomics is concerned with the fit between man-machine, man-system, machine-machine, and machine-system. It seeks to optimize the interactions between humans, equipment, and the operating environment, and to facilitate quick access to parts, tools, supplies, stores, documents, computers, and washrooms. The four design objectives for a lean layout are: (1) safety and human well-being through the reduction of motion, (2) productivity through the reduction of internal transportation, (3) flow through connection and synchronization of workstations, and (4) visual management through an open layout and a high level of transparency. The choice of layout must take into account the capabilities and limitations of people and machines to suit and support each other. An optimal layout promotes multi-machine handling, multi-process handling, and reduces major motions to micro-motions.

Functional Layouts

Grouping people and machines of similar function together creates process villages such as a press hall, test lab, customer service team, or purchasing department. Functional arrangements are more robust to breakdowns. They share common resources such as machines and experts, and they allow high levels of demarcation, but they also disrupt flow. When walls and doors encapsulate departments, flow stops and work starts to pile up in front of and inside the barricade, and eventually needs to be moved and synchronized between process villages.

Cellular Layouts

Cellular systems take advantage of similarities between parts and services through standardization and common processing. In cellular systems, machines and people are grouped together by value streams, product families, or service categories. Imagine going to a car shop to repair a broken light, exchange oil, and wash the car. In a functional layout, you would need to make three appointments with three distinct departments, which would probably take three times longer than in a cellular layout where only one team takes care of all three functions. Cellular configurations allow people to work in semi-autonomous and multi-skilled teams, so they are able to manufacture complete products or handle complex service requests without issuing a support ticket to another department. In general, cells are more flexible and responsive than traditional mass-production lines and departmentalized service organizations, enabling people to operate multiple processes across multiple functions, such as planning, processing, balancing, and controlling.

Ergonomics and the Waste of Motion

An ergonomic layout minimizes the waste of motion, therefore impacting internal and external productivity. Architects and workstation designers typically focus on improving external productivity by eliminating excessive movements and motions on the mega and micro level, such as walking, bending, stretching, reaching. When parts and procedures, tools and terminals are located at the point-of-use, macro motions are minimal. A true ergonomic design also improves internal productivity by helping employees produce more output with no increase in risk of injury or errors. An example is adjusting a monitor to eye height to reduce micro and nano motions. The four types of motion waste are:

- Mega waste from poor plant layout and excessive walking,

- Macro waste from poor methods or suboptimal processing,
- Micro waste from bending, stretching, and reaching, and
- Nano waste from hand and finger motions; gets and grasps.

As long there are no accidents, motion is usually out of focus, making it an overlooked source of efficiency improvement. There is a direct positive correlation between risk reduction and cycle time reduction, i.e. as risks are reduced (less wasted or risky motions) the cycle time is reduced with direct impact on productivity.

Multi-Machine Handling

Traditionally operating plants split work into functions and arrange machines into process villages. In a lean plant, processes are arranged in cells, allowing operators to work on multiple machines and workstations, not just one. Multi-machine handling requires the separation of human work from machine work, facilitated by intelligent automation or "autonomation" (jidoka) and auto-eject (chaku-chaku), so that operators just load machines and level the load. The same principles apply to the office, physically arranging people, desks, and printers according to the flow of decisions and documents.

Multi-Process Handling

When highly qualified people with flex-skills work in close proximity, they can share tasks and operate multiple processes. In an ideal case, a single operator can complete all process steps of a product or service from start to finish. Multi-process handling requires thorough training to build certified flex skills. It is the prerequisite for load leveling and cellular processing, where the lean layout functions as an enabler. See also "Roles" and "Training" keys.

Layout in Service

Service layout requirements are somewhat different from manufacturing layout requirements, but the same terminology is used. In both instances, we find the fixed-position layout, process layout, and product-based or service-based layout respectively. In *fixed-position* layouts, the customer remains in one place and the service is relocated there, as with landscaping, nursing, and home decorating. In other cases, the equipment can't be moved and therefore dictates a fixed position as is the case for dialysis machines and beauty salons. In *process* layouts, similar machines are grouped together to produce batches of services, such as university classrooms and movie theaters. This is similar to the disconnected line-flow process in manufacturing. If equipment is sequentially arranged according to the steps of the service process, the layout is said to be service-based, as in a driver's license renewal office or in a coffee shop.

Signs of Excellence

A good layout has an obvious logic that makes it easy to navigate, like in a modern airport. Supermarkets and department stores often use purposely-inefficient layouts to confuse their customers and route them through many isles, increasing their shopping time. From an efficiency standpoint, an ideal layout has no dividing walls to promote continuous flow and enable visual management. Without physical barriers, operators maintain a constant visual contact that allows them to synchronize processes and balance the workload. With end-to-end transparency, managers can overlook the area and get a full status overview from one spot, similar to the view from an aircraft control tower. In world-class environments, the layout is planned and optimized based on scientific analysis, rather than just grown and patched over time. Spaghetti diagrams and value stream maps show how high-ranking processes have been re-engineered to shorten distances, reduce handovers, install point-of-use stores, optimize flow, and improve communication efficiency. As a result, people from the same value stream are co-located in the same area, so that items and information can be exchanged within seconds at minimal motion. Workspaces are highly flexible, equipment is mobile, and shared hardware that is used in multiple configurations is mounted on wheels. Work teams take pride in optimizing the physical layout of their workstations and frequently reposition furniture, equipment, tools, and stores to minimize motion waste. Space is consciously used and effectively managed; activity areas are compressed to minimize motion and transportation while empty spaces are blocked off and not available for use.

Leadership

About Leadership and Policy Deployment

Leadership is a process of using social influence to maximize the efforts of others towards achieving of a goal. It involves making strategic decisions, organizing a group of people, and inspiring them to perform. When assessing leadership as an activity, there are timing implications to understand since the leader might chose to trade short-term gains for long-term benefits. There are also soft factors to consider that are hard to measure, such as influence and inspiration. For the purpose of the Lean Audit, we focus on the leadership framework and policy deployment process. Concepts include values, orientation, vision, mission, strategy, actions, prioritization, and feedback.

"Leadership is the capacity to translate vision into reality." – Warren Bennis

Characteristics of Effective Leaders

Effective leaders are able to set and achieve challenging goals, take swift and decisive action in difficult situations under calculated risk, outperform their competition, and persevere in the face of failure. They act with confidence, possess strong communication skills, are willing to embrace change, and are able to influence others. Effective leaders strengthen an organization by creating focus, structure, and discipline in addition to engaging the hearts and minds of the people they lead.

"The only definition of a leader is someone who has followers." – Peter Drucker

Leadership versus Management

True leadership is unrelated to a person's title, attributes, or position on the organizational chart. Many executives are not leaders; rather, they just manage. Leadership is mainly concerned with the purpose of an organization or entity, the goals to pursue, and where to apply resources, while management focuses on how to use resources for the intended purpose. Managers plan, coordinate, monitor, solve, hire and fire; they manage performance, while leaders set the direction and lead people. Leadership stems from social influence and not from authority or power. It requires the engagement of others—who do not need to be direct reports—to achieve the intended outcome.

"Management is doing things right; leadership is doing the right things." – Peter Drucker

Poor Leadership

Weak or ineffective leaders produce four types of waste: (1) *Strategic waste* occurs when decisions satisfy short-term goals or internal needs at the expense of customer value or long-term sustainability. An example is when a company is taken over by a new owner who cuts the product development budget below the sustainable level and redirects the resources to buy a new yacht. (2) *Planning waste* occurs when the chosen path to attain the strategic goal is flawed. Many mergers promise—on the spreadsheet—to deliver scale and synergies, but when the two cultures are incompatible, the turf battles and added complexity often outweigh the benefits. (3) *Execution waste* occurs when the chosen path is right but the execution is flawed. An example of this would be when a leader underestimates the effort, resources, and commitment required to realize the plan. (4) *Focus waste* occurs when priorities are unclear or when everything is important, and nothing is accomplished. When insufficient focus is given to key objectives, energy is dispersed instead of bundled. Demanding perfect quality at lowest cost right now is an effective recipe for failure, and the attempt to maximize all three objectives concurrently leads inevitably to a sub-optimal scenario. Where to apply resources to gain a competitive edge is a strategic choice made by the leader. A well-defined trade-off decision behind each goal, what to give up to pursue something else, is a sign of good leadership.

Long-Range Planning

Long-range planning focuses attention on future issues that will become vitally important to the organization in the next few years. It involves studying societal trends and issues, surveying customers, and being aware of ongoing research and changes in technology. While senior managers lead the activity, all levels of management are involved to achieve an optimal solution and broad acceptance—especially from those managers who must execute the plan. The long-range plan serves as a compass, gives direction and meaning to shorter term planning activities. Think of it like this: the organization is a huge ocean liner, and the captain must turn the ship slowly over a long period of time, adjusting to the new course.

> *"You must have long-range goals to keep you from being frustrated by short-range failures."* – Charles C. Noble

Strategic Planning

Strategic planning refers to defining the long-term objectives of an organization and allocating resources to their accomplishment. A strategy determines the direction in which an organization needs to move to fulfill its mission. A strategic plan serves as a roadmap for carrying out the strategy and achieving long-term results; it bridges the gap between ambitions and current results. To boost performance, people must feel ownership in the strategy. A stronger, more capable and efficient organization can be realized simply by defining how its employees can support the overall strategy. Strategic planning is different from long-term planning. Long-term planning builds on current goals and practices, and proposes modifications for the future. Strategic planning, however, considers changes or anticipated changes in the environment that suggest more radical moves away from current practices. When doing strategic planning, the organization should emphasize team planning. By involving those individuals affected by the plan, the leader builds an organization-wide understanding and commitment to the strategic plan. The five elements of a strategic plan are:

- Mission statement, the "what"
- Strategic analysis, the "why"
- Strategic formulation, the "where"
- Long-term objectives, the "when"
- Operational plans, the "how"

Policy Deployment

Hoshin kanri is the Japanese term for control-of-direction or management-by-compass. Hoshin planning refers to policy deployment, i.e. the strategy involves applying a systematic and disciplined focus on a few breakthrough objectives that create a competitive advantage. The policy deployment process cascades strategic goals down through all levels of an organization and aligns them with its tactics, programs, projects, and daily activities. Hoshin planning systemizes strategic planning while taking into consideration the following: economic projections, corporate objectives, customer preferences, quality requirements, current trends and other insights about the future. It is based on the concept that employees are the experts in their jobs and that the collective thinking power of all employees makes an organization the best in its field. The prerequisites are: (a) cross-functional planning that promotes cooperation along value streams and (b) the willingness of managers to delegate decision-making authority to people closest to the action.

Following Deming

Policy deployment and problem solving processes use the Deming cycle "plan-do-check-act" (PDCA) to develop shared goals, communicate and cascade those goals, involve people in planning, hold participants accountable for their role in the plan, and drive focus down into the organization to meet critical objectives. Because Hoshin planning is a cyclic process, the review of the previous year's performance becomes the basis for the next year's plan. Managers and work teams alike use Hoshin reports to assess their performance; each table includes a header that shows the author and scope of the plan, a description of the situation that gives meaning to the plan, milestones and objectives that define what needs to be achieved and by when; as well as the tactics, priorities, metrics, and tasks that make the plan actionable and the progress measurable.

The X-Matrix

To get people involved and committed, the management process must align the organization with its strategic objectives, resources, and activities. This alignment is part of the policy deployment process, and the degree of alignment is mapped visually in the X-matrix, a tool that links strategic objectives to operational targets, and those targets to functions and processes. Planning horizons vary widely between cultures and companies; one to two-year plans are common in the United States, while Japanese companies prefer to plan 10 and more years into the future. The matrix translates breakthrough objectives into operational targets. Then teams work bottom-up to identify the required resources, skills, and structures to achieve those strategic objectives. Once this information is available, targets and timelines are refined and the process starts once again for the next planning cycle.

Building the X-Matrix

The strategy deployment matrix consists of four components: objectives, strategies, tactics, and measures. Breakthroughs are the long-term objectives derived from the strategic plan, such as: "Attain a 30% return on assets". Those long-term objectives are then translated into strategies and annual targets, such as: "Improve margins from loss to break-even". Tactics are cross-functional priorities that directly support strategy; they are tracked monthly. Here are some examples: optimizing process flow, researching how competitors achieve a two-day delivery, developing a virtual community, or selecting a consulting firm to assist with a new project. Measures are specific programs, projects, and processes that support tactics; they are reviewed weekly to keep them on track. Examples are automating the order confirmation process or implementing a new charter template.

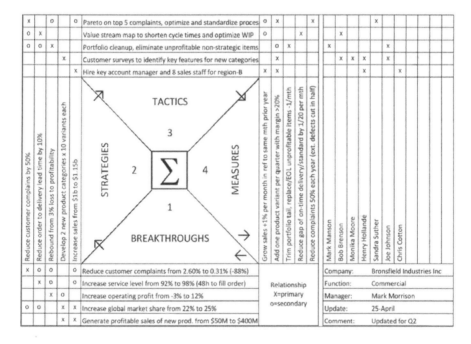

Figure 2.4 - X-matrix for strategy deployment

→ Download the X-matrix template from www.leanmap.com/tools

Signs of Excellence

When there is a history of achieving consistently strong results, and roadmaps are in place to sustain those successes in the future, it's usually a sign of good leadership.

In times of change however, past performance is not a reliable sign of strong leadership. Regardless of whether an organization is in a cruising or crisis mode, if it operates in a stable environment or is going through a merger or turnaround, the signs of good leadership are the same—there is absolute clarity on what the organization stands for, what needs to be achieved and how to get there. Values, vision, and mission are not only written on posters but these concepts are also understood and supported widely. There is a strong sense of purpose; teams and individuals know clearly how they contribute to the overall mission. Objectives are easy to understand and easy to measure. Decision-makers clearly understand what drives price and competitiveness, and they are able to quickly draw cost and profit trees. Organizational structures, markets, customers, delivery models, policies, priorities, and the changes necessary to achieve the future state are all well-defined. Policy deployment maps show specific goals for cost, service, quality, skills, capability, and technology. Teams understand how they compare to world-class performers that do similar work, and each team receives regular feedback on how they are doing relative to expectations. When asked, employees willingly and accurately explain how their organization performed over the past period and how it compares to its competitors in terms of costs, quality, delivery, and customer satisfaction.

Maintenance

About Maintenance

The goal of maintenance is to prevent breakdowns and to increase reliability and equipment life so factories can run at maximum efficiency. The Lean Audit assesses how well equipment is maintained and uptime controlled, and the ability of machines to run at zero unplanned downtime. Concepts include equipment availability, downtime tracking, efficiency ratios, planned versus unplanned stoppages, response process, downtime analysis, machine performance data, maintenance tasks and ownership, as well as maintenance process and system.

> *"If you don't understand how to run an efficient operation, new machinery will just give you new problems of operation and maintenance. The sure way to increase productivity is to better administrate man and machine."* – W. Edwards Deming

Downtimes Stop Deliveries

In many companies, maintenance does not get much attention as long as production runs reasonably well and shipments are on time. However, when a critical machine breaks down, it becomes painfully clear to everyone that a poorly maintained machine can cause a major crisis and affect all key metrics. To protect processes from starvation and customers from stock-outs and missed deliveries, a common remedy is putting costly inventory buffers in place to bridge the time the equipment is under repair. Additional buffers address the symptom (shortages) but not the cause (breakdowns). Lean thinkers are not willing to pay for unplanned downtime and extra inventory; they remove the root-causes of downtime through effective maintenance.

Maintenance Indicator

A simple and practical way to evaluate maintenance performance is by tracking availability of machines or by tracking unplanned stoppages due to equipment issues. When a machine is a pacemaker or bottleneck, each minute of unplanned downtime translates into a loss in the entire process chain or value stream. Capital-intensive industries therefore strive for "triple-zero" maintenance performance: zero unplanned downtime, zero intervention, and zero rework of maintenance activities.

> *"Watch the little things; a small leak will sink a great ship."* – Benjamin Franklin

Utilization versus Availability

For the purpose of the Lean Audit we need to understand the difference between availability and utilization. Operational availability or operable rate is the percentage of time an asset functions properly when needed, whereas utilization or operating rate is the percentage of time an asset is used to process something. If you use your computer one hour per day, its utilization or operating rate is 1/24 = 4%. Over the course of a year, the computer runs a total of 365 hours, of which you spend 4 hours waiting to complete system updates and solve software issues, so the operational availability or operable rate is (365-4)/365 = 99%. Improving availability is top priority, i.e. ensuring that an asset works reliably with near zero unplanned downtime. The second goal is to improve the utilization rate (asset effectiveness) to just the amount required for load leveling purposes, and thus prevent overproduction (waste).

Maintenance Strategies

The primary goal of maintenance is to avoid or mitigate the consequences of equipment failure through corrective, preventive, risk-based or condition-based maintenance strategies. The challenge for developing an effective strategy is to strike the right balance between reliability and cost. This means that we have to determine the cost of downtime and the cost to prevent it.

Corrective Maintenance

Trouble-shooting or corrective maintenance refers to repair after an anomaly has been detected to restore normal operating conditions. It is based on the belief that the cost of downtime plus repair is lower than the investment required for a maintenance program. This reactive approach is only suitable for non-critical faults, such as replacing light bulbs that are burned out.

Preventive Maintenance

Partial or complete overhauls at specified intervals reduce the risk of failure and performance degradation of equipment. Such preventive maintenance preserves and restores equipment reliability by replacing worn components before they actually fail. An example is changing a car's oil every 15,000km and changing the timing-belt every 100,000km. In addition, operators can record equipment deterioration so they know when to replace or repair worn parts before they cause system failure. The ideal preventive maintenance program would prevent any equipment failure before it occurs.

Risk-based Maintenance

Risk assessments involve periodic tests and analysis together with preventive maintenance. The gathered data are viewed in the context of the environmental and operational conditions of the equipment as it functions in the system. The aim is to understand health conditions and breakdown risks to determine the appropriate maintenance program. Any piece of equipment that displays abnormal values must be refurbished or have the necessary parts replaced before breakdowns occur. In this way it is possible to extend the useful life and guarantee high levels of reliability, safety and efficiency. Example from a dentist visit: repairing a damaged tooth during the annual checkup.

Conditional Maintenance

This method enhances scheduled maintenance with sensory information that provides an alert when maintenance is required. Operators of heavy machines and manufacturers of airplane turbines, electricity generators, professional coffee machines, and modern cars use telemetry to send data about acceleration, vibration, sound levels, and in-line gauging to determine the optimal time to replace parts. This strategy drastically reduces maintenance costs, thereby minimizing the occurrence of faults and optimizing the available resources. An example would be when a service representative at a car dealership calls you because he knows (after analyzing the data transmitted from your car) that it's time to have your transmission overhauled.

Autonomous Maintenance

In traditional organizations, operators and technicians have distinct roles with little or no overlap; operators run equipment until it stops and maintenance personnel repair it once it stops. Both parties often blame each other for poor equipment performance and low operating efficiency. Preventive maintenance assigns simple maintenance tasks to operators, while technicians perform scheduled overhauls. The goal of autonomous maintenance is total elimination of the three evils of equipment failure: (a) improper cleaning, (b) improper lubrication, and (c) improper use. Prerequisites are that operators are well trained, maintenance activities are well defined, and ownership is clearly assigned, following the four pillars of autonomous maintenance: (1) daily cleaning and inspecting to identify abnormalities, (2) scheduled lubrication to reduce friction and vibration, (3) adherence to standards to ensure correct operation and eliminate misuse, and (4) completion of checklist tasks such as tightening, adjusting, and replacing worn parts.

Total Productive Maintenance

Lean factories require reliably running equipment to maximize overall equipment efficiency (OEE). Every machine must perform its task when required. To pursue zero downtime, potential breakdowns must be understood, effectively predicted, and addressed before they can occur. Total productive maintenance (TPM) offers a systematic way to prevent unplanned downtime by allowing operators to handle all regular maintenance tasks so that technicians are free to analyze and eliminate failures, implement efficiency improvements and perform equipment upgrades. TPM-thinking is based on three principles:

(1) Total participation at all levels. Operators perform routine maintenance, technicians are responsible for preventive maintenance, and managers optimize the maintenance program to maximize return on investment.

(2) The total life-cycle of equipment determines appropriate practices. Maintenance activities and frequency are dynamic; schedules and checkpoints are continuously adjusted relative to the age and condition of the equipment.

(3) Attaining total productivity by eliminating the main causes of poor equipment performance, the six big losses.

The Six Big Losses

- Failures – downtime from equipment failures and repairs,
- Setups – changeovers and adjustments,
- Halts – minor stops below one minute,
- Slowness – speed losses from processing low-grade material,
- Scrap – non-conforming parts that cannot be repaired, and
- Rework – items processed more than once.

Maintenance Service Levels

The following matrix, used for maintenance services, establishes the relationship between reliability and maintainability, and unscheduled versus scheduled downtimes. The four clusters provide the service requirements for basic availability and high availability, as well as continuous operations and continuous availability. Let's say you run an efficient office and demand a high degree of reliability and maintainability from your office equipment. The printer you want to buy must therefore meet the criteria for "Continuous Availability" as specified in the maintenance service grid on figure 2.5: (a) scheduled overhauls by a service technician do not exceed 8 hours per year, (b) the printer is inoperable for no more than 22 hours per year or 3.6 minutes per day, and (c) the mean time to repair (MTTR) is less than 15 minutes to clear up a paper jam, replace the toner or refill paper. The key point here is that we need to consider not only the purchase price but also the reliability and maintainability (running costs) of the equipment to make optimal capital investment decisions.

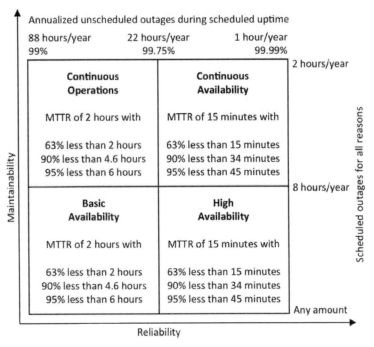

Figure 2.5 - Maintenance service grid

Signs of Excellence

World-class factories strive for zero downtime and track overall equipment efficiency (OEE) as a key performance indicator (KPI) on the factory scorecard. Management regards maintenance as a key factor to their success and has installed the programs and teams necessary to protect valuable assets from hazards and failures. Operators and technicians work together to prevent breakdowns. Maintenance actions are planned, displayed and monitored for progress. Maintenance schedules are posted in each area, and checklists are physically attached to each major machine; activities are well defined and clearly assigned. A response process is in place for major downtime events, specifying (by the minute) what needs to be done, by whom, and how. Availability and mean time between repairs (MTBR) is tracked at least for complex equipment that is prone to failure. Downtime events are systematically analyzed for improvement using root-cause analysis and failure prevention techniques, such as 8D (see "Solving" key). Quick response teams are in place to attend at least 90% of breakdowns within two minutes. In world-class environments outside the process-industry, maintenance service calls account for no more than 5% of technical downtime, while unplanned repairs consume less than 1% of planned operating time.

Management

About Management

Management refers to the organization and coordination of resources to attain defined objectives in the best possible way. It involves organizing, planning, resourcing, measuring, directing, controlling, and correcting. The Lean Audit evaluates performance management, i.e. how effectively processes and behaviors are managed to achieve desired results. Concepts include planning and decision-making processes, effectiveness of actions, priorities and incentives, performance reviews and feedback, and cross-functional interactions.

> *"Management is the art of securing maximum results with a minimum effort so as to secure maximum prosperity and happiness for both the employers and employees and give the public the best possible service." –*
> *John F. Mee*

Key Management Activities

A manager must do eight things well to be successful: (1) develop and clarify the mission, policies, and objectives of the organization, (2) establish organizational structures to delegate authority and share responsibilities, (3) set priorities and revise objectives to align with changing demands, (4) maintain effective communications between employees, suppliers, customers, and community, (5) select, motivate, train, and appraise staff, (6) secure funds and manage budgets, (7) evaluate results and correct deviations, and (8) be accountable to staff, owners, and the greater community.

Performance Management

Performance management constitutes activities that ensure goals are consistently met and deviations are properly addressed. It essentially means influencing processes and behaviors. Performance improvement can be thought of as a cycle, from identifying the opportunity or problem to closing the gap between the actual and desired performance. It involves planning, enabling, and appraisal:

- Planning – developing roadmaps and setting specific goals
- Enabling – coaching and intervention to adjust performance
- Appraisal – formal validation, documentation, and feedback

Planning

A key activity for all managers is planning the work under their direction. This involves outlining the philosophy, policies, objectives, and the techniques to use. Working with each other and with the people who will execute the plans, managers clarify objectives and set goals for each team and process. They develop programs, strategies and schedules, and establish the policies and procedures that guide those who do the work. The process of planning is best understood by following the basic stages of decision-making. This includes diagnosing the problem, finding alternative solutions, projecting the result of each alternative, and selecting the action to take.

Organizing

Once the work of an enterprise grows beyond what a single person can do, organization becomes necessary. Tasks must be defined and assigned to different people, and their efforts must be coordinated. This process leads to the development of departments and divisions, each with a particular mission. Because these social arrangements are composed of people rather than physical assets, to get the work done, the manager must be able to influence people while building the social structures to support them. The process of organizing refers to establishing structures and systems through which activities are arranged, defined, and coordinated.

Resourcing

Resourcing encompasses the deployment and directing of human, financial, technological, and natural resources. It involves providing money, labor, knowledge, access, and tools to a process, product, project, or program. On a broader view, resourcing also includes selecting and training staff and maintaining favorable work conditions.

Directing

Managers provide rules and guidance for teams to follow, issue instructions that embody their decisions, all while integrating the needs of subordinates with the welfare of the company. Good managers try to strike a healthy balance between individual motivation and efficiency. They foster an atmosphere of trust, respect and confidence; they help subordinates perform their duties and achieve their personnel aspirations. At certain times they also must be tough and exercise power to hold others accountable to standards and commitments.

Coordinating

Managers bring different elements of a complex activity or organization together to form an efficient relationship with one another. Such coordination involves analyzing the multidirectional flow of information and harmonizing roles and responsibilities within and across functions, the organization, and the broader community. There are two forms of coordination, the *vertical* coordination with supervisor and staff, and *horizontal* coordination with peers. Due to the growing complexity of contemporary organizations, the increasing demands for public accountability, the many government regulations and policies, increasing competition, and changes in technology, the coordinating role is increasingly more important. Success criteria are: managerial competence, open communication, the ease of information flow, the clarification of mission and objectives, effective meetings, and the full alignment on cross-functional topics.

Reporting

Managers keep employees, shareholders, and the community informed. Reporting involves preparing regular summaries and statistics, and informing staff of current developments. It is also an evaluation process to determine how well objectives are being met with the current strategy and structure, capability and capacity, policies and priorities.

Discipline

To accomplish goals in a focused, structured, and consistent manner requires discipline and the ability to control one's behavior and actions. It involves determination and courage, adherence to policies and procedures, and observance of checks and balances. Discipline is a force that drives people to do what is expected or else there will be consequences in the form of training, coaching, and direct feedback to get back on track, or personnel changes if necessary.

Ownership

Good managers create a sense of ownership on the part of employees over their work area and process. They motivate people to contribute at their highest capacity. In contrast, when control is more important than contribution, people will only do what is required to stay out of trouble. Prisons and sweatshops are run with focus, structure and discipline, but the lack of ownership makes people act like robots, following orders and meeting quota only as long they are tightly controlled.

Signs of Excellence

In well-managed companies, a sense of purpose permeates the atmosphere. People know their jobs and clearly understand the mission; they understand how they contribute to the overall objectives. Individuals and teams take pride and display their achievements; action plans and tracking charts are well maintained and openly displayed. Standards for behavior and performance are defined and posted. Work is planned and expectations are clearly set for all teams and functions. Performance is tracked against targets that are specific, measurable, aligned, realistic, and time-bound (SMART). Ask anyone what a successful day and week is like, and you will get a quick yet firm answer. There is a clear expectation and measurable outcome (deliverable) defined for each process, project, and program. Performance is in control or counter measures have been defined to get back on track. Action plans are up to date and fully transparent. Resources are allocated only to the "3C", i.e. those activities that ensure *Compliance* with required regulations, improve *Customer* value, or increase *Competitiveness*. All other activities have been deprioritized or deleted. Service level agreements (SLA's) regulate the interactions between departments; they are available upon request for any department. Cross-functional teams meet daily to coordinate work and resolve interface issues. Internal disconnects are treated as seriously as external customer complaints. They are openly discussed, quickly addressed, and effectively solved. Managers have brief, one-to-one exchanges with each subordinate daily to address barriers and provide support. Together with all team members, at the end of each week they review results, analyze gaps and trend patterns. They meet at the end of each quarter with each employee to discuss performance and expectations, and everyone receives formal feedback (a performance appraisal) at least twice a year. Those performance reviews are directly linked to the reward system and training program. Group results, team contributions, and individual performance are included in the incentive scheme. Without exception, top performance is rewarded and low performance is corrected in a predictable and timely manner. There is a general consensus within the group that they are continuously making progress. Members of the management team sense that customers and investors are confident the group will deliver on present and future commitments.

Metrics

About Measures and Metrics

Metrics are standards of measurement to evaluate the performance or progress of a plan, process, product, project, or person against known standards of accuracy, completeness, speed, or cost. The Lean Audit assesses the effectiveness of the measurement process and system. Concepts include goal alignment, performance indicators, balanced scorecard, measurement process, and performance reviews.

"Measurement is the first step that leads to control and eventually to improvement. If you can't measure something, you can't understand it. If you can't understand it, you can't control it. If you can't control it, you can't improve it." – H. James Harrington

Measures and Metrics

This module is about measures, metrics, and indicators. A measure or measurement is simply neutral information, a reading from an instrument, such as a scale or compass. A metric is a measure that provides vital information to someone who can influence the measure through direct efforts. An indicator can be a measure or a metric, whereas a key performance indicator (KPI) provides information that is mission-critical for an individual or a team. Revenue is a key indicator in sales and a measure for the controller. For a runner, lap-time is a key performance indicator, heart rate is a metric, and shoe size is a measure.

"Measure what is measurable, and make measurable what is not so." – Galileo Galilei

Metrics for Teams

Here are some examples for metrics and measures from the perspective of a work team. Team metrics are: items processed daily, time to generate a quote, labor minutes consumed per unit, number of processing errors per day, average response time to customer requests, number of calls returned within the same day, accuracy of output, and defects per order. Measures cannot be directly influenced by the work team; they include: stock price of their company, brand image per customer survey, overhead costs, design-driven shrinkage, and so on.

Developing Effective Metrics

Good metrics can define progress and predict outcomes, but no single metric can fully describe the entire situation with all its complexities; we always must look behind and beyond the numbers to judge the entire system with its interconnections. Only when numbers are embedded in the management infrastructure do the measures become metrics that provide a viable means for effective management. Here is an example to illustrate how to judge the effectiveness of a measurement system by looking at the metrics used for performance evaluations and bonus payouts: when a manager is rated "outstanding" for just "making the numbers" on irrelevant or shortsighted objectives, the metric is not really helping the business.

To be effective, a metric must meet 10 criteria:

- Actionable – under direct control of the people responsible for the outcome,
- Relevant – is relevant and important to the customer,
- Proximate – measures performance close to the action in time and location,
- Accurate – is correct in detail and able to measure or predict an outcome,
- Proportional – measurements correspond in size to changes in performance,
- Responsive – responds quickly to any changes in inputs or outputs,
- Causal – measures causes rather than effects on overall performance,
- Simple – data are easy to measure, can be collected without much extra work,
- Meaningful – engages teams and individuals to take action, and
- Valuable – drives focus to external customer needs instead of internal reports.

Use this 10-point checklist to evaluate metrics and measurement systems; attaining ten points indicates a maximum or 100% effectiveness rating.

Metrics Must Be Specific

Metrics must be specific to the product or process they measure. Here is an example of how "throughput" is used in different contexts. Throughput is a measure of productivity over a period, expressed in output per hour, cash-turnover during the accounting period, or number of orders shipped per day. In computing, throughput is a measure of a system's information processing capabilities. In telecom, throughput is a measure of network efficiency expressed as the data transfer rate of non-redundant information. Internet throughput is a measure of a web server's performance expressed as number of data requests handled per time unit. In manufacturing, throughput is the processing speed expressed as units per hour under normal operating conditions.

Balanced Score Card

The balanced scorecard (BSC) focuses the attention of management on the set of metrics that drive the business, such as quality, delivery, cost, and customer satisfaction. The scorecard allows the management team to check status, appraise progress and identify critical issues that require action. It works like a car's dashboard, allowing the driver to determine if an action is required based on a quick scan of the instruments. The balanced scorecard is an invaluable tool in aligning the entire organization to one set of key figures.

"The heart of science is measurement." – Erik Brynjolfsson

Performance and Progress Measurement

Regular measurement promotes frequent feedback and the detection and correction of abnormalities early on to keep performance in line with expectations. Daily reviews include safety and housekeeping level, hits and misses of the prior day, average processing rate per hour, first pass yield, overtime due to rework, and the status of improvement actions. Monthly reviews focus on trend information; for example, they include all ongoing programs and initiatives, overall quality and productivity rates, skill score versus training plan, site performance versus budget, and latest activities on key customer accounts.

Signs of Excellence

In world-class environments, all measures are metrics, driving appropriate responses that support strategy. Being cascaded down to all levels, they are part of daily planning and weekly reviews to ensure activities are aligned and performance is on track. Those metrics are part of the company's scorecard and linked to the reward system. Measurement processes are under constant scrutiny and subject to elimination if the numbers collected and the reports generated do not directly influence decisions. Key performance indicators (KPI) track mission-critical activities per voice of the customer (VOC) and voice of the business (VOB). The mix of short, medium, and long-term indicators allows managers to make more balanced decisions. Here some examples: a plant engineer tracks equipment availability to effectively allocate maintenance hours; a controller tracks the timeliness of accounts closing, the labor hours consumed to produce required reports, the board's satisfaction level with the service provided, and the forecasting accuracy of the system; and the head of product development is certainly interested in time-to-market and success rates of new designs. In world-class companies, there is a scorecard in place for every team to drive performance on a departmental level or by value stream.

Quality

About Quality

Quality is a measure of excellence or a state of being free from defects, deficiencies, and significant variations. It is achieved by strict and consistent commitment to established standards that drive uniformity in a product or processes to satisfy specific customer or user requirements. The Lean Audit assesses the ability to deliver goods and services that are "fit for purpose" and it determines how well quality is designed into products and processes to meet market expectations. Concepts include process variability, sigma level, quality management approach, quality organization, quality system, quality controls, mistake proofing, process capability, yield and defect rate, and quality-driven costs.

Quality by Industry

The definition of quality varies by industry. Academia refers to quality as an effective knowledge transfer to students to prepare them for the future. Customers expect from a quality airline a high standard of safety and on-time performance. In the automotive realm, most customers associate quality with a car's reliability but also with its recognition as a status symbol. Quality criteria in consumer goods are ease-of-use, good looks, and reasonable cost. Guests visiting a quality restaurant expect fresh food and attentive service in a comfortable environment. In health care, quality refers to correct diagnosis, minimum waiting time, and effective treatment. The quality of a military organization relates to rapid deployment and effective intervention. Quality industrial machines are reliable, accurate, and easy to operate. A quality insurance policy provides broad coverage at reasonable cost with effective customer support when required. Quality in transportation and logistics means quick and accurate delivery.

Common Definitions

Quality is delivered when both explicit and implied needs are fully met. The ability to accurately define and consistently satisfy customer needs related to design, performance, price, safety, delivery and other criteria places a firm ahead of its competitors in the market. Some notable quality definitions include: the totality of features and characteristics of a product or service that bears on its ability to meet a stated or implied need (ISO, 1994), fitness for use (Juran, 1988), and conformance to requirements (Crosby, 1979). Since quality is a very broad topic that means different things to different people, Harvard professor David Garvin has defined five views on quality: the transcendent, product based, customer based, provider based, and value based.

Customer View

Quality is fitness for use, meeting the expectations of customers and consumers. As preferences vary widely, so the customer-based view of quality leads to the choice between a niche strategy and a market aggregation approach that tries to identify those product attributes that meet the needs of the largest number of consumers. For example, there are millions of simple plastic pens sold each year for $0.25 each and there are also diamond-decorated writing instruments going for $2,500 and more, and both are considered high quality within their specific customer segment.

Provider View

Quality is conformance to specifications. Conformance however does not necessarily ensure quality from a consumer's perspective, as many junk products with a "QC-passed" sticker break upon first use. A way to bring specifications and expectations into alignment is to use the quality function deployment (QFD) process; a matrix that diagrammatically maps customer needs to product and service specifications.

"Good is not good, where better is expected." – Thomas Fuller

Product View

Quality can be viewed as quantifiable and measurable characteristics or attributes. For example, reliability can be measured and the engineer can design a product or process that meets those measures. Although this approach determines quality objectively, it is not necessarily relevant to the customer and can even be misleading.

Consider the megapixel-hype surrounding digital cameras. Lacking a comprehensive understanding of the entire spectrum of digital camera features, many shoppers fixate on the high-profile measure of "resolution", and in so doing wrongly judge the overall quality of a camera by considering only the resolution of its sensor (i.e., megapixel = quality). This drives the manufacturers to squeezing more pixels into smaller sensors, which in turn increases noise levels and decreases picture quality.

Value View

Quality can be viewed as the best combination of price and performance to get the most user-defined quality attributes at an acceptable price. For example, a leading manufacturer sells quality trucks at premium prices, stating lowest operating costs in dollars per mile, which is a value-based view on quality. Another example would be purchasing batteries based on the amount of power they deliver per dollar rather than by the lowest purchase price.

Transcendental View

Quality can be viewed as something we can recognize but not define. The transcendental view emphasizes the intuitive and spiritual above the empirical and material and judges quality based on *sensation* rather than *specification*. It's like Plato's description of the ideal or Aristotle's concept of form. An example of how transcendental messages are used in marketing is BMW's slogan of "The Ultimate Driving Machine", which implies quality through superior performance.

Errors and Mistakes

Errors and mistakes are different from each other since they originate from distinct sources. A mistake refers to *incorrectly applied* knowledge, while an error results from *insufficient* knowledge. Humans make mistakes and errors, while machines only produce errors. In essence, errors occur and mistakes are made. Some errors however can even occur when individuals have the required knowledge, such as forgetting to do something when distracted by something else.

Ten Human Errors

Most defects result from the ten human errors, as defined by Shigeo Shingo: (1) forgetfulness, (2) misunderstandings, (3) errors in identification, (4) errors made by amateurs, (5) overconfidence errors, (6) inadvertent errors, (7) errors due to slowness, (8) errors due to lack of standards, (9) surprise error, and (10) intentional errors or manipulation. If an error or mistake is not found and corrected quickly, it will produce a defect.

Mistakes Create Defects

Human beings are not perfect. Mistakes are inevitable. It is unrealistic to expect people to completely understand instructions and be fully concentrated every minute of the day. A defect results from allowing a mistake to reach the customer or the next process. The goal of mistake-proofing (poka-yoke) is to prevent the ten sources of defects: (1) omitted processing, (2) processing error, (3) item incorrectly setup, (4) missing item, (5) wrong item, (6) processing the wrong item, (7) adjustment error, (8) miss-operation, (9) equipment setup incorrectly, (10) tools and jigs improperly prepared.

Defect

A defect is a failure to conform to customer requirements, whether or not those requirements have been articulated or specified. More broadly, any type of undesired result is a defect. In the realm of software coding, a mistake in the source code is an error, an error found by a tester is a defect, a defect accepted by the development team is a bug, and a final build that does not meet the stated requirements is a failure.

Defect Rate

Defects per million opportunities (DPMO) is the average number of defects per output divided by the number of opportunities to produce a defect, normalized to one million. Each component of an assembly and each step in a process represent an opportunity for a failure. Mass production is measuring defect rate in DPMO, while science and service is using parts per million (ppm) to measure variability.

Yield Rate

First pass yield (FPY) is a key metric on the balanced scorecard and a factor of the efficiency calculation (OEE, OPE). Yield provides vital information on process capability and the degree of waste from defects and rework. FPY is calculated by the amount of work that meets specification first time (single touch, no rework), divided by the total amount processed. For example, if 100 units enter a process, 99 are finished to specification, 2 are reworked, and 1 is scrapped, then FPY = (99-2) / 100 = 0.97 = 97% and the overall process yield is 99%.

"If you don't have time to do it right you must have time to do it over." –
John Wooden

Variability Waste

The lower-case Greek letter sigma (σ) is used as a symbol for a standard deviation, a measure of variability that denotes the average distance between a score in a distribution and the average (mean) of the distribution. As a distribution increases, spreading farther from its mean, the standard deviation of the distribution and the likelihood of failures increases. Resources expended to rectify failures and to correct deviations from the expected result is variability waste.

Six Sigma

The safety margin of a process is expressed in sigma levels. One sigma stands for one standard deviation, the typical variation that meets roughly two thirds of the population. A distance of six standard deviations between the average of a distribution and the closest specification limit is referred to as six sigma or 6s. It is considered the "gold standard" for most processes because the odds are very low that a stable process will produce a defect. Six sigma is synonymous with a process capability Cpk = 2.00, allowing no more than 3.4 defects per million opportunities (DPMO) at a first-pass yield (FPY) of 99.9997%.

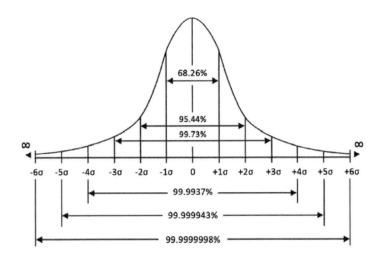

Figure 2.6 - Sigma quality level

Six Sigma Program

Six sigma as a process improvement program brings together guidelines and tools for statistical analysis, variability reduction, process control, problem solving, and project management. It is effective where variability strongly affects outcomes, such as continuous processing and mass production. The concept of six sigma compliments lean, perfecting processes after wastes have been removed. Reducing variability follows the five steps of the DMAIC process: *Define* the problem, *Measure* current performance level, *Analyze* data and identify causes, *Improve* performance by eliminating the causes, and *Control* the process to stabilize performance.

Process Waste

When everyone is busy doing something and no major mistakes surface, managers usually assume that everything is running well. Performing work in a complex or suboptimal way however causes processing waste as a result of poor design, poor training, or poor management—even without any apparent defect or rework. For maximum process quality, work must be performed in an optimal way every time, over the shortest possible distance, and by using the fastest and most capable method. A high level of repeatability and reproducibility results when teams identify best practices and translate them into standard operating procedures (SOPs), train team members on those standards, and follow them with discipline. Read more about this in the "Standards" section.

> *"Almost all quality improvement comes via simplification of design, layout, processes, and procedures."* – Tom Peters

Error Waste

Resources required for duplicating work that is rendered useless by a mistake or error is *rework*. When the amount of rework becomes excessively high or the impact of an error is extreme, the typical response is more inspection to ensure conformance. Such symptom treatment is short lived when process capability is not permanently improved; errors bounce back as soon as the crisis passes or attention lags. The money spent on additional inspection and rework is considered error waste.

Conformance Cost

The cost of conformance (COC) is the money spent to avoid failures. This includes the cost of quality assurance (QA) activities such as training and process documentation, and the cost of quality control (QC) activities that include testing and inspection. The COC represents an organization's investment in the quality of its products.

Non-Conformance Cost

The cost of non-conformance (CONC) or non-performance cost (NPC) is the money spent because of failures. These costs are divided into internal and external failure categories: *internal* or in-process failure costs for scrap, rework, investigation, and downgrading, and *external* or post-delivery costs to account for handling complaints, repairs, recalls, refunds, replacements. Generally speaking, there is a correlation between the amount of money spent on conformance and the cost implications of non-conformance.

Poor Quality Cost

The cost of poor quality (COPQ), or poor quality cost (PQC), represents the sum of all costs that would disappear if the system, process, and product were perfect. It includes both, direct costs that can be accounted for and indirect costs that must be modeled: (1) direct controllable costs for prevention and appraisal, i.e. training, analysis, design reviews, testing, inspection, sampling, and audits, (2) direct resultant costs for internal and external errors from scrap, rework, repairs, design changes, safety stock, downgrading, customer returns, penalties, complaint processing, field service, warranty obligations, (3) direct costs for equipment used for inspection and to measure quality relevant parameters, (4) indirect customer incurred cost for loss of productivity, downtime, stock outs, defective item returns, repairs post-warranty, backup and safety stock to cover failure periods, and (5) indirect customer dissatisfaction costs shared by word of mouth and loss of reputation cost due to the perception of the firm. If data are unavailable, we use the following table to estimate COPQ based on first pass yield, defect-rate, or process capability index.

Sigma	Yield	Defects	Cpk	DPMO	COPQ
1	32%	68%	0.33	691,462	45%
2	63%	37%	0.67	308,538	30%
3	93%	7%	1.00	66,807	20%
4	99.4%	0.6%	1.33	6,210	15%
5	99.98%	0.02%	1.67	233	10%
6	99.9997%	0.0003%	2.00	3.4	5%

Quality and Profits

As defects and variability are built into processes, the cost of poor quality is mainly hidden and not accounted for. For any hidden cost, the improvement potential is large. Per Philip Crosby, you can easily spend 15-30% of your sales dollars on non-conformance. Joseph Juran said that in most companies the cost of poor quality runs at 20-30% of sales. Here is an example of a fairly "normal" company where net profit is 5% of sales and the cost of poor quality runs at 20% of sales, assuming 3-sigma process capability end-to-end. Raising the quality level from 3 to 4 sigma would reduce COPQ from 20% to 15% and double (double!) net profits from 5% to 10% of sales.

First Time Yield

First time yield (FTY), the most common way to calculate process yield, is the probability of a defect-free output from a process. This metric does not take into account weather a unit was reworked in process and only considers the criteria at the end of the process. FTY is unit sensitive and calculated simply by the number of good units produced divided by the number of total units going into the process. The FTY therefore will not detect the "hidden factory" where all the rework is being done. It typically indicates that a process is performing better than it really is, by burying the rework and spreading the cost of defects across the numbers of units successfully completed. This practice protects under-performing products and processes by diluting the measure (defect rate) with those that are doing better. Consequently, the calculation of FTY is not very helpful to identify and correct process problems; first pass and throughput yield are much better indicators for that purpose.

First Pass Yield and Throughput Yield

First pass yield (FPY) and throughput yield (TPY) are essentially the same; they are defined as the number of units coming out of a process divided by the number of units going into that process over a specified period of time. FPY and TPY are defect-sensitive; they are based on the number of defects found instead of the yield on produced units. Only good units that were touched once without any scrap or rework are counted, making the FPY and TPY a true measure of quality.

Rolled Throughput Yield

Rolled throughput yield is the probability of passing all in-process criteria for each step in a process, as well as all end-process criteria. Like TPY, RTY is defect-sensitive and based on the number of defects found at each process step. Mathematically, RTY is the result of multiplying together the FTYs or TPYs from all process steps along the value chain. When a process step produces a defect, the yield for that step will be less than 100%. Even if the defective output is successfully reworked, the throughput yield for this step remains unchanged. The next paragraph explains the relationship between FTY and RTY.

Yield Calculation Examples (FTY, FPY, RTY)

Here are a few practical examples of yield calculation. A process consists of two steps with 95% yield and 5% rework at each step. We start with 100 units and assume that all defective units can be successfully reworked so that 100 units are shipped to the customer. First time yield FTY = 100/100 = 100%, indicating a good process as no defects reached the customer. The problem is that FTY does not capture the effect of the 5% defects at each process step, so 10% of the outputs were reworked, requiring labor and machine hours equivalent to the production of 110 defect-free units, which will show up as cost of poor quality (COPQ) on the cost variance account. For both steps, the first pass yield FPY = 95/100 = 95%, only counting units that were touched once at each step. The rolled throughput yield RTY = 0.95 x 0.95 = 90%, indicating a marginal process that wastes 10% resources for the rework done by the two "hidden factories". Here is another yield calculation example: a five-step process with 80% yield and 20% rework at each step results in 0.8 x 0.8 x 0.8 x 0.8 x 0.8 = 0.33 = 33% RTY, while 67% items must be touched multiple times for rework, repair, return, reissue, reschedule, and double handling. In conclusion, only FPY and RTY highlight where improvement effort is needed most.

Process Capability Definition

Process capability is the ability of the process to meet specifications. The nominal value is the target for the process design. The tolerance is an allowance above or below the nominal value. The process capability ratio (Cp) is the tolerance width divided by 6 standard deviations. The process capability index (Cpk) takes centering into account and measures the potential for defects relative to the upper and lower specification limit, whichever is closest. The Cpk ratio is the width between the nominal value and the closest tolerance limit divided by 3 standard deviations.

Process Capability Example

A process takes on average 26.2 minutes at a typical variation or standard deviation of 1.35 minutes. The target is 25 minutes with an upper specification limit of 30 minutes and a lower specification limit of 20 minutes. The goal is to attain a 3-sigma quality level. Can the process deliver such a performance? We first calculate the process capability ratio Cp, the delta between the upper and lower specification divided by 6 standard deviations: Cp = (30 – 20) / (6 x 1.35) = 1.23. A value greater than 1.00 indicates that variability meets the 3-sigma quality criterion. Now we calculate the process capability index, Cpk, as the distance between process average and the nearest specification limit divided by 3 standard deviations: Cpk = minimum of (26.2 – 20) / (3 x 1.35) = 1.53 and (30 – 26.2) / (3 x 1.35) = 0.94. We find that the process does not meet the 3-sigma or Cpk = 1.00 target value, due to a shift in mean that results in Cpk = 0.94, while variability is under control, since Cp = 1.23 and therefore above the 1.00-target.

Process Capability Maturity Model

Many processes in design and development, service management, and business administration lack hard data to quantify process capability. In such cases we use a qualitative approach and evaluate process capability according to the 5-point maturity model:

1. *Unstable*: chaotic, reactive, undocumented, fire-fighting, individual heroics
2. *Repeatable*: process defined, but inconsistent results or low discipline
3. *Defined*: process standardized with evidence of continuous improvement
4. *Managed*: quantitatively managed using control chart and capability index
5. *Optimizing*: perfecting performance through innovation, systematic updates

The 7 Quality Tools

Defined by Kaoru Ishikawa, the seven basic tools of quality that every professional should be able to apply are: (1) Cause-and-effect diagram to identify possible causes of a problem and to sort them into useful categories. (2) Check sheet, a structured form for collecting and analyzing data. (3) Control chart to display process performance over time. (4) Histogram to display frequency distributions, how often each value occurs in a set of data. (5) Pareto chart to display the most significant factors on a bar graph, used for prioritization. (6) Scatter plot to graph pairs of numerical data, one variable on each axis, to reveal a relationship. (7) Stratification, a technique to separate data gathered from a variety of sources so that patterns can be seen; alternatively use a flowchart or run chart.

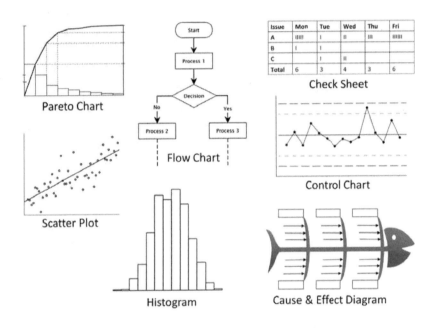

Figure 2.7 - The 7 Quality Control Tools

ISO-9000 and QS-9000

The International Organization for Standardization defined the minimum acceptable business practices as the ISO 9000 standard. It has become a required certification for many suppliers in an attempt to improve quality. ISO 9000 consists of a set of minimum standards for contract review, design control, quality management, inspection, and training. ISO 9000 is the general standard, 9001 applies to producers that also design and service their products, 9002 to manufacturers without design function, and 9003 for service companies. The problem with the ISO certification is that it focuses more on the administrative part of the processes and does not provide strong guidance on how to improve quality by taking waste and variability out from the system. To judge quality, we must look beyond the ISO criteria and assess how well processes meet the explicit and implied needs of the customer(s).

Signs of Excellence

Quality is a strategic pillar and not just empty words on a mission statement. It is defined based on market needs when voice-of-the-customer (VOC) requirements have been systematically translated into critical-to-quality (CTQ) parameters, serving as inputs to a quality function deployment (QFD) process. When QFD matrices are posted or available on demand, it is a sign that teams are seeking a thorough understanding of "Quality". In quality-driven companies, procedures are frequently updated as requirements change; they have entirely displaced or at least complement the often-stagnant ISO manuals. There is a strong process orientation; quality control plans (QCP) and statistical process control (SPC) charts are posted in all key areas. Sampling techniques have been replaced by continuous controls. Error-proofing (poka-yoke) and built-in quality (jidoka) effectively prevent problems in critical areas, so that downtime records indicate only minor stoppages. The concepts of quality level (Sigma), capability index (Cpk), defect opportunities (DPMO) or defect rate (ppm), cost of conformance (COC) and cost of poor quality (COPQ) are well understood and data are readily available for at least two of them. Quality metrics focus on defects rather than yield, making managers unsatisfied with a 99% yield as this indicates 1% or 10,000ppm defects. Common cause and special cause variations are clear to supervisors and team leaders. Process performance analysis (PPA), analysis of variance (ANOVA), and failure mode and effect analysis (FMEA) are actively used to eliminate the causes of variations and defects. Internal process capability (Cpk) is correlated with external customer satisfaction to ensure the right criteria (CTQ's) are being measured. And finally, people in quality-driven companies enjoy talking about how they have gained a competitive advantage from superior quality.

Readiness

About Readiness

Readiness refers to the state of preparedness needed to face and implement change. It involves having a vision and resources in place, engaging people, and creating the motivation to act. Readiness is strongly influenced by the thoroughness of planning, adequacy of training, and availability of support services. The Lean Audit assesses how prepared an organization is to adapt to (a) advances in technology, (b) a shift in customer preferences, and (c) changes in the competitive landscape. It scores awareness and openness towards change, attachment to the status quo, the sense of urgency, the capacity to lead change, scope and approach, and change culture.

"They must often change, who would be constant in happiness or wisdom."
– Confucius

Progress Demands Change

An organization is always in motion, moving from one state to another, continuously responding to internal and external forces caused by a strategic shift, new regulatory policy, an emerging competitor, disruptive technology, or an internal improvement program. Progress in any field requires continuous change and adaptation. Key factors to succeed are attitudes, conditions, and resources: (1) *Attitudes* – the vision of a different future and the commitment to achieve it, the conviction and will. (2) *Conditions* – the structures, rules, and systems necessary to mandate, manage, and support the change. (3) *Resources* – the human, physical, and financial resources needed to support or facilitate the change.

"Action springs not from thought, but from a readiness for responsibility." –
G. M. Trevelyan

Conditions for Change

Change is inevitable but efforts often fail when the reason for change is based on rational thought and business logic alone while ignoring human behavior. The required change must appeal to the head and touch the heart, so people are ready to take charge and direct resources and intellectual energy to what moves the organization forward. If these forces are ignored, they generate confusion, friction, frustration, and misguided energy. Resistance builds when people are not interested and not supported. Frustration results when they are capable and willing, but not supported by their superiors when trying to remove obstacles. Learning is the outcome when unskilled people are motivated, properly supported, and willing to learn whatever is required within their frame of capability. And finally, when skill, will, and leadership are in place, successful change is possible.

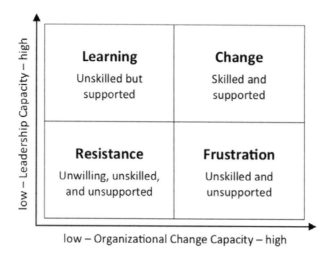

Figure 2.8 - Change capacity matrix

Readiness Tree

Readiness for change is a function of capability and commitment. Commitment gets people involved and emotionally attached to the team and task. Commitment and involvement require conviction and motivation. Conviction is the intellectual understanding of the need for change and will is the emotional response to a need. Capability is a measure of the ability of a person to change based on the conditions that enable or disable the person to perform and the skills of that person. If people are not willing or unable to change, the efforts to implement change will fall short of expectations, regardless of how well they are supported. Good leaders not only create the need but also build the required capability and commitment that make their people ready for the change.

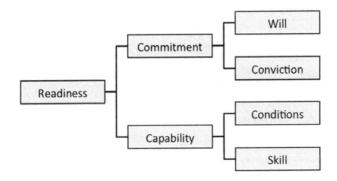

Figure 2.9 - Readiness tree

Criticality & Complexity

The greater the complexity or criticality of the required change, the more important it is to understand the degree of readiness and possible resistance that requires intervention. Change is considered to be critical or complex when it meets one or more of the following criteria: (1) involves more than ten people, (2) requires new knowledge, (3) introduces new variables, (4) is based on untried processes, (5) is technically challenging or outside current performance levels, (6) requires alignment between different hierarchy levels, (7) involves powerful external stakeholders, (8) is cross-functional or cross-divisional or cross-site, (9) is likely to trigger resistance, or (10) involves a radical shift in the known way of working. If all ten points are answered in the affirmative, then 100% push-back must be expected as worst case.

Understanding the Culture

Assessing readiness is not as easy as assessing the completeness of a report or the cleanliness of an office; it requires a feel for people and culture. Culture is simply the behavior that is expected, reinforced, supported, and valued over a long period of time, and behavior comprises of thought, emotion, and action—of which action is the only aspect that is under direct control of the person and directly observable during an audit. Since words are actions, it is very insightful to talk with people about their work, their ideas and ideals. Do they have everything they need? What would they change if they could? When confronted with change, is their first reaction searching for a solution or an obstacle? Responses are important cues when assessing readiness and openness to change.

"If you always do what you always did, you'll always get what always got."
— Henry Ford

Paradigms – Progress Stoppers and Enablers

Doing something new or different can be challenging; finding a justification for not moving forward removes any guilt and responsibility for the outcome – and there are plenty of them. Here is a list of my favorites—eighty paradigms that keep us within our comfort zones when confronted with change:

We are too busy • It's not my job • It's not possible • We are different • We tried this before • It's not in the budget • It's not our problem • Let's think about it • It's tradition here • It doesn't suit me • They will not like it • I found an exception • Let's collect more data • It only works in theory • The union will scream • It doesn't feel right • My computer crashed • It's not for us • I am not supposed to • It won't work here • We will never manage • It costs too much • You can't have it all • It's not the right time • We heard that before • Let's wait with that • We are different • We have other priorities • We still make money • We'll be screwed • I haven't read that memo • It does not fit to our culture • Let's create a committee • We're not ready for that • It's not our problem • I wasn't trained for this • Let's get back to reality • We could lose money • That only works in theory • We have always done it like that • It's against company policy • It could increase overhead • It's not the way we do things here • Our business is too small for that • We don't know where to start • It's never been tried before • There is no procedure for that • Good idea but not practical • It doesn't say so in the manual • We don't have the money • They will fight back • Management does not believe in it • Something always gets in the way • We are not responsible for that • We don't have enough people • It's too difficult • Management isn't ready for this • It will make our equipment obsolete • We can't expect this from our people • Nobody is doing it, why should we • The investors won't like it • I am not getting any younger • Some things you just can't change • The customers won't like it • We don't have the knowledge • We need a master plan first • It's a politically sensitive issue • The numbers don't reconcile • Our competitors do the same • We will be called back at the end • I know someone who tried it before • We have never done this before • We don't have enough time • We don't have the discipline • We don't have the authority • This should be analyzed first • The customer isn't ready for that • We should have waited with this • How about putting it on paper first • That should be handled by a higher level •••

"All progress takes place outside our comfort zone." – Michael John Bobak

Let's turn things around and look at paradigms that are motivating and enabling. Note that the list is much shorter than the previous:

Let's do it • The sky is the limit • We'll find a way • There is a solution to everything • No problem • Yes, we can • I will do it • We will succeed in the end • That's a great idea • Nothing can stop us • Success breeds success • We will be first • It will be tough but worth it • Now or never • I can see the light • There is no way back • The time is right • Let's go for it • We'll make it fit • There is no other option, no plan-B • I found what works • There are no problems, only temporary setbacks • We are the culture • It can be done • We'll make it a reality •••

"Nothing can stop the man with the right mental attitude from achieving his goal; nothing on earth can help the man with the wrong mental attitude." – Thomas Jefferson

Readiness Factors

There are ten factors that enable successful change: (1) a *Vision* that is clearly defined and broadly communicated so that managers are able to derive operational objectives and resource requirements from it; (2) the *Desire* to achieve the vision, the willingness to change the current approach, and the resolve to overcome challenges, follow-through and complete the transition; (3) a compelling *Need* for change through pain or gain, while everyone understands the benefits of achieving the future state as well as the consequences of failing to implement it; (4) a solid business case that defines how the change generates an *Economical Benefit*, showing the funding as well as potential risks; (5) *Ownership* is established via sponsorship and leadership, which are well defined and broadly shared; accountability is clearly assigned and leaders keep their teams focused on strategic goals while sponsors ensure full alignment with senior management; (6) *Governance* is in place to exercise authority, ensuring that corporate interests are served and objectives are achieved; (7) people held *Accountable* to specific assignments and appropriate responsibilities, measurable contributions against expectations are recognized, and decision-making focuses on people and processes most impacted by the change; (8) the *Execution* approach is appropriate for the task and players know their roles; it is clear to everyone how the change will be implemented, monitored, and how alignment will be achieved; (9) *Capability* is sufficient to execute all required tasks, assess gaps, prioritize and chose appropriate trade-offs, and make decisions under tight timelines, and (10) changes can be fully *Absorbed* by the organization to successfully operate in the new way.

> *"Progress is impossible without change, and those who cannot change their minds, cannot change anything." – George Bernhard Shaw*

Signs of Excellence

The entire organization has embraced change as an engine of their success. A clear vision is established and communicated to everyone. Strong and capable leadership is in place, key stakeholders have agreed on direction and goals, appropriate resources are allocated, and expectations for behaviors are established. Managers lead by example and demonstrate their support, while senior management is not only sponsoring the change, but also removing organizational barriers and steering the transition. People most affected by the change are actively involved in designing the future state; their capability and motivation is sufficient to overcome identified obstacles. Key decision-makers and people in power ensure that political forces will not derail efforts or redirect resources. Continuous change is supported by the organizational culture and existing structures and behaviors will not stop new ideas, innovations and improvements from being implemented. Systems are in place to document progress and report results. Feedback is timely, everyone knows how well they meet expectations, priorities are reinforced and milestones celebrated.

> *"Intelligence is the ability to adapt to change." – Stephen Hawking*

Renewal

About Renewal

Perpetual renewal is a prerequisite for sustaining success in the marketplace; it allows an organization to maintain continuity in a discontinuous operating environment. The Lean Audit evaluates an organization's ability to renew itself, to continually create more effective strategies, structures, products and services based on the premise that different is not necessarily better, but better is always different. Concepts for evaluating renewal include improvements, innovations, and interventions.

> *"A corporation is a living organism; it has to continue to shed its skin. Methods have to change. Focus has to change. Values have to change. And the sum total of those changes is called transformation." – Andrew Grove*

In Motion

An organization moves continually from one state to another as a result of internal and external forces. Some transitions occur quickly, triggered by a merger, new concept, new regulation, new technology, or any shift within the industry. Other changes occur more slowly and often remain unnoticed until their effects cannot be denied anymore, such as the erosion of competitiveness due to a failure to adjust to new market conditions. There are also changes driven from within an organization to satisfy an internal need, such as introducing a new product, installing a new computer system, integrating an acquisition's personnel, or moving a facility. For the purpose of the audit, we evaluate the gradual improvements (kaizen) as well as the step-changes (kaikaku) introduced to sustain the business long term.

Gradual Improvement

Kaizen is the Japanese term for a gradual or evolutionary change to ever-higher standards. This bottom-up approach involves everyone from operator to executive to achieve small but continual improvements i.e. 5%-20% for each change event. The main focus of kaizen activities is solving problems in a particular area, such as improving the ergonomics of a workstation or improving a replenishment process to prevent material shortage.

> *"Continuous improvement is not about the things you do well – that's work. Continuous improvement is about removing the things that get in the way of your work, the headaches and the things that slow you down. That's what continuous improvement is all about."* – Bruce Hamilton

Radical Improvement

Kaikaku is the Japanese term for radical redesign with the goal of overhauling the entire system. This *discontinuous* approach is used when continuous improvements no longer deliver adequate results in relation to the effort spent. It is also used when step-change is required, such as cutting defect rate or lead-time in half. Senior management commonly initiates step-changes when deploying a new strategy, building new knowhow, developing a new methodology, or implementing new technology. A cross between both methodologies is a kaizen blitz or breakthrough kaizen, which implies a radical improvement during an intense workweek in a limited area, such as a cell or department. We speak of a *breakthrough* when performance is doubled (e.g. +200% efficiency) or non-performance cut in half (e.g. –50% defects).

> *"Improvement usually means doing something that we have never done before."* – Shigeo Shingo

Innovation

In essence, innovation is the practical application of knowledge to improve efficiency, coordination and control, deriving greater value from available resources. An innovative idea fuels renewal when it is new or different, replicable at an economical cost, and satisfies an existing or created customer need. In a social context, innovation helps creating new methods for alliance creation, cross-functional teamwork, joint venturing, flexible work hours, and creation of buyers' purchasing power. Innovations are divided into two broad categories, the (1) evolutionary or continuous innovation through incremental advances in methodology or technology – kaizen, and the (2) revolutionary or discontinuous innovation that is new or disruptive in nature – kaikaku. Innovation is synonymous with risk-taking, while continuous improvement is not, or is to a much lesser degree.

> *"Nature does constant value stream mapping, it's called evolution."* –
> Carrie Latet

Threats to Renewal

Renewal is threatened when product modifications, operational improvements and cost cutting measures take overwhelming priority over innovation at the core business strategy level. Superficial innovations, such as adding a new product variant (different shape or color), might create some success in the short-term, but they fail in the long-term when adding more complexity to the system than value to the customer. The real challenge for most businesses today is not growth, but perpetual renewal to ensure the organization continually prospers, year after year and decade after decade, despite the massive and ever-increasing turbulence in the external environment.

Strategic Renewal

To succeed in the long-term, companies must develop the capacity to anticipate and adjust to the fundamental changes in their operating environment; this allows them to dynamically reinvent their core business models and strategies as circumstances require and as new threats and opportunities emerge. The conventional thinking that innovation automatically leads to wealth and growth is not valid anymore; rather, only true innovation (not variants) leads to strategic renewal and perpetual growth. By developing this understanding, companies can fully appreciate the role that innovation plays in shaping their destinies.

Renewal Factors

Renewal relies on five elements: a vision, skills, incentives, resources, and an actionable plan. Without a vision, there is confusion. Without skills, there is anxiety. Without incentives, motivation is low and change is slow. Without resources, there is frustration. Without a plan, there is a false start and energy is lost in many course corrections. For successful renewal, make sure that all five elements are in place.

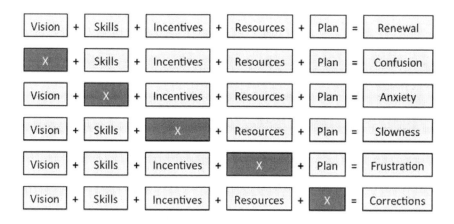

Figure 2.10 - Key factors for successful renewal

Signs of Excellence

Because companies generally do not openly post their strategic plans in the hallway, we look for other renewal cues during the audit. The first impression counts. If the setup looks antiquated, the equipment is outdated, and the methods of working are old-fashioned, those are clear signs that the organization is stalled. In such companies, the planning horizon is usually short and improvements are often focused on cost reductions to offset eroding margins and trouble-shooting customer complaints. In contrast, the planning horizon of world-class companies span many years, driving programs that improve competitiveness through systematic innovation and improvement. Policy is effectively deployed and specific goals are defined for each function, such as a 0.5% productivity gain per month. Clear decisions cease non-value adding activities and terminate lower priority projects to free up resources for continuous renewal. All employees from the senior executive to the cleaning personnel are involved in continuous improvement activities. They are empowered to make changes within their area of responsibility and frame of authority; they have firm tasks assigned in projects, and they implement at least ten improvement ideas per year per head. They are proud to explain what they have changed over the past months and how those changes affected the key metrics in their area. Quality circles, suggestion schemes, and continuous improvement programs are all in place, making it easy for anyone to submit ideas and initiate changes. In leading companies, customers and vendors are an integral part of the value stream, sharing the same metrics and systems. At a world-class level, organizations operate at the pulse of the market using modern concepts and methods. They regularly surprise customers by bringing new innovations to market rather than reissuing variants of existing products and services. A robust bottom line, clear decisions on what to grow and what to eliminate, and a favorable trend in most (if not all) key indicators are clear signs of ongoing, successful renewal.

"Learning and innovation go hand in hand. The arrogance of success is to think that what you did yesterday will be sufficient for tomorrow." –
William Pollard

Roles

About Roles and Responsibilities

Roles are jobs or positions that have a specific set of expectations attached to them. A responsibility is an obligation to satisfactorily perform a task, which has a consequent penalty for failure. A clear definition of roles and responsibilities is a prerequisite to effectively manage people and processes. People understand where they fit into the organization, what their management structure is, the jobs and tasks they are assigned to do, and which results they are accountable for. This also prevents disputes and misunderstandings over authority. The Lean Audit assesses how roles and responsibilities are assigned, how competency and authority levels are balanced, and how ownership and accountability for results are defined.

Organizational Structures

Structure is the basis of any organization. It can be described as a system of inter-related jobs and the corresponding level of authority to carry them out. It involves the explicit and implicit institutional rules and policies that define decision-making authority, and how roles and responsibilities are delegated, controlled and coordinated. An organizational structure can be viewed as a living organism with arms and legs representing the various functions attached to the body of physical and intellectual resources, with the body controlled by a mission and objectives sent from the head. Each part has a specific function, while all parts are required to work together to advance and prosper. There are four primary elements involved in designing an organizational structure:

- *Job Specifications*: definition of tasks, what an individual is responsible for
- *Departmentalization*: grouping jobs and responsibilities for better coordination
- *Span of Control*: roles per unit that require coordination by a manager
- *Authority Levels*: the right to make decisions without having to obtain approval

The resulting organizational structure will vary according to these four elements. An organization with decentralized authority and very heterogeneous departments will appear very different from one with a centralized authority, delivering a very homogeneous product or service.

Locus of Control

Centralized organizations put key authority and decision-making power into the hands of a few individuals. In decentralized structures the authority is distributed among many managers. As various roles become more diverse or spread over several geographical locations, a decentralized structure tends to be more effective where authority is delegated to those people closest to the market activity. Centralization refers to authority, whereas centrality refers to the proximity of the organization to its stated mandate and objectives. Even an organization with a decentralized structure—with each unit being responsible for its own programs, staffing, and budget—can still stay very close to the main mission and objectives, as set by the headquarter.

Line and Staff

Another important point in terms of structure is the concept of line and staff functions. Line functions are those involved in creating and delivering a product or service. Staff functions are those that support line functions with advice, analysis, planning, accounting, internal logistics, and administrative activities. In summary, line functions contribute directly to the attainment of the organization's objectives, and staff functions contribute indirectly to them.

Chain of Command

By delegating authority, an organization automatically establishes a chain of command, a formal channel that specifies the levels of authority, responsibility and communication relationships from top to bottom. Thus authority flows from director to manager, from expert to assistant, from senior to junior, and from supervisor to operator. Being aware of the organizational structure and chain of command is a key requisite to getting things done.

Responsibility Assignment Matrix

A common tool for defining the roles, responsibilities, and authority levels is the RASCI matrix. It maps functional roles to processes and deliverables, and defines who is responsible, accountable, supportive, consulted, and informed: *Responsible* are those who do the work and report to the person accountable, *Accountable* are those who own the result and hold accountable those who are responsible, *Supportive* are those who provide assistance to those responsible, *Consulted* are those whose opinions are sought before decisions are made, and *Informed* are those who receive the information after decisions have been made or results have been achieved; they have no influence over the process or result. Defining RASCI parameters is a prerequisite to building an effective organizational structure.

Signs of Excellence

People know their jobs and what roles they play in the organization. In world-class companies, roles and responsibilities (R&R) are developed for each team and individual to ensure full alignment with strategy and structure. Those roles and responsibilities are continuously evolving; job profiles and authority levels are reviewed and updated at least once a year to meet changing needs. Skill matrixes and RASCI-matrices are posted in conspicuous locations for each team and department to leave no room for misunderstandings. As part of the human capital development (HCD) system, RASCI-matrices are linked with job profiles, training programs, and cross-skilling processes. The ultimate goal is to develop a flex-organization where everyone is qualified on all core processes within their area, and the capabilities of all team members are tracked on departmental skill matrices. Skill flexibility and a high degree of standardization allow people to move freely between stations, balancing workload without being reassigned by their supervisor. Additional signs of excellence are when work is organized around *processes* instead of *people*, and when core skills have been duplicated so that a fully qualified deputy covers each key position on the organizational chart.

Service

About Service

A service is a type of economic activity that is intangible, cannot be stored, and does not result in ownership. A service is consumed at the point of sale. Services are one of the two key components of economics, the other being goods. Examples of services include the transfer of goods, such as shipping product or delivering mail, and the application of knowledge by a teacher, doctor, or consultant. Service level is a measure of responsiveness to meet customer requirements, making it a key performance indicator for essentially all businesses. The Lean Audit assesses delivery performance to internal and external customers, capability of the service process, expectations versus needs, customer service and satisfaction levels, service quality references, service level agreements, and net promoter score.

> *"There is only one boss, the customer, and he can fire everybody in the company from the chairman on down, simply by spending his money somewhere else." – Sam Walton*

Service Definitions

With respect to supply chain management, *service level* is the probability of not hitting a stock-out, a key figure that can be used to compute the optimal amount of buffer stock. Intuitively, the service level represents a trade-off between the cost of inventory and the cost of stock-outs from missed sales, lost opportunities, and upset customers. In call centers there is a similar trade-off between operating efficiency and customer service, i.e. a perpetual balance between number of staff and customer waiting time.

Service Metrics

The way service level is calculated varies largely by industry and function. The common characteristic is that it measures the degree of meeting service goals. Examples are calls answered versus calls received, percentage of orders served per period, percentage of customers that do not experience a delay or stock out, percentage of requests satisfactorily answered first time by a helpdesk, percentage of equipment breakdowns rectified within one hour. Note that service level can only be measured when the service promise has been defined.

The Consequences of Poor Service

Outstanding customer service has become an imperative for superior performance, if not for the long-term survival of a business. Surveys from Accenture and Jupiter Research have shown that existing and prospective customers will deflect to competitors if companies deliver poor service or do not keep their service promise: 46% of respondents quit doing business with a supplier in the past year due to poor service and 62% said that they are less likely to buy from a store that failed to resolve a service problem. Continuous service level improvements are a prerequisite to remaining competitive. Here is a quick self-check: if your standard lead times and service cycle times haven't shortened over the past two years, you run the risk of losing business to competitors.

Six Sigma Service

Six Sigma methods, commonly applied to reduce variability in mass-production venues, are receiving more and more recognition by service providers motivated to improve customer experience and operating efficiency. The key for a successful application is to let the customers define acceptable service levels and variability, which is then used to compute the amount of resources required to meet it. A second criterion is that processes are defined as operating standards, as well as service level agreements (SLA) and staff incentives are in place to ensure compliance with the agreement and consistency in delivery.

Net Promoter Score

Net promoter score (NPS) is a management technique that evaluates the degree of customer loyalty to a brand or company. It is an alternative to traditional customer surveys that typically focus more on the customer satisfaction with a particular product or transaction. This limited focus tends to skew the results since they are susceptible to the mood of the customer and environmental factors, such as commercials and social media. Measuring customer loyalty is an effective way to determine the likelihood that the customer will buy again, talk up the company and resist market pressure to deflect to a competitor. The net promoter score is based on one simple, direct question: "How likely are you to recommend our company to your friends and colleagues?" Scores are plotted on a 10-point scale that defines the following metrics: (a) promoters with a score of 9-10 are considered loyal enthusiasts, (b) detractors with a score of 0-6 represent unhappy customers, and (c) scores of 7-8 points are excluded. The NPS is then calculated by subtracting the percentage of detractors from the percentage of promoters, NPS = Promoter% – Detractor%. A good practice is to follow the direct question with an open-ended request for elaboration, soliciting the reasons for the rating or what actions can be taken to improve it. Responses provide vital information for front line people to adjust their behavior and inputs for managers to improve processes. Asking process customers during a Lean Audit how satisfied they are with internal processes gives the auditor a sense of service level and internal net promoter score.

Customer Define Requirements

Many organizations measure service performance based on financial indicators alone, such as dollars shipped. They form their own opinions about what is important to their customers with the risk of managing and improving the wrong aspects. This way, resources can be allocated to projects and departments that don't really improve customer service. Even when processes are working perfectly and the measured performance is good, customers still may not be satisfied, especially when they judge service quality using different criteria than what the provider uses. High-performing organizations always strive to reach a balance between performance, processes and perception. For the Lean Audit we look at service process performance and customer feedback.

Service Level Agreements

With the increasing complexity of service offerings, a clear definition of service specifications is necessary to build capable teams and processes that serve customer needs. A service level agreement (SLA) is a contract between two or more parties that specifies the nature, quality, and scope of the service to be provided. It covers key parameters, delivery process, communication protocol, performance levels or limits, the escalation path and the consequences of failing to meet the service promise. It's a contract between seller and buyer, provider and user, server and guest, doctor and patient, controller and director, and any supplier and its customer.

Customer Satisfaction

Traditional service level agreements cover tangibles and intangible aspects, such as communication, reliability, competence and accessibility. But there can still be a lot of reasons for the customer to be unhappy, despite all numbers being met. The opposite is possible as well: the customer remains satisfied—despite the provider's failure to meet the specified service levels—because of the responsiveness and helpfulness of the provider's staff. Capable auditors interview process customers, asking open-ended questions about responsiveness and service quality, which allows them to assess service level relative to specifications and customer perception.

100% Service Level

Since a balance exists between service cost and quality, many managers believe that total customer satisfaction is impossible to achieve; therefore, they hesitate to give service guarantees. On the other hand, customers prefer guarantees rather than a promise. If a provider fails to meet certain service criteria, the failure is compensated by a discount, penalty, coupon, extra effort, or anything else that both parties agree to. The compensation is often informal and based on the balance between performance, process, and perception. The ultimate objective is always total service quality based on customer needs.

Ten Dimensions of Service Quality

In their book "Winning the Service Game", Benjamin Schneider and David E. Bowen defined ten different dimensions which determine a customer's perception of service quality: (1) *Reliability* – consistency of performance and dependability, (2) *Responsiveness* – the willingness or readiness of employees to provide service, (3) *Competence* – possessing the required skills and knowledge to provide service, (4) *Access* – approachability and ease of contact, (5) *Courtesy* – politeness, respect, consideration and friendliness of contact personnel, (6) *Communication* – listening to customers and keeping them informed in a language they understand, (7) *Credibility* – trustworthiness, believability and honesty, (8) *Security* – freedom from danger, risk or doubt, (9) *Understanding* – making an effort to understand the customer's needs, (10) *Tangibles* – physical evidence of the service. This ten-point framework is proven to be effective when conducting focus groups and service interviews during the Lean Audit process.

Expectations and Needs

To design optimal service processes, it is important to understand the differences between expectations and needs. Apart from the hard directives provided by the service process and service contract, good service performance must always consider the hidden needs as well, the feelings and unstated needs of the customer. If a provider dissatisfies its customers by failing to meet their expectations, it is still possible to recover by responding swiftly and effectively to the failure. But if a provider dissatisfies customers by not meeting their basic needs, they will be lost.

Service by ISO

Many companies have set up a quality system following the ISO 9000 principles and standards. Their goal is to improve service processes and boost service quality. Those systems assess how well processes are organized in conformance with internal standards as a measure of quality. We need to remember that an ISO certified process only ensures *compliance*; it does not guarantee *quality*. For example, a company can make cars without wheels and still get ISO-certified, despite making a totally useless product. The ISO certificate is one-dimensional in that it only proves an organization met a certain standard at a certain point in time. It does not prove that the quality requirements of the customer are met, which adds another very important dimension. The Lean Audit takes it a step further: in addition to meeting a standard at a certain point in time, for the Lean Audit we consider customer satisfaction and the presence of continuous service improvement.

Service Level Example

A machine in a factory signals an abnormality. The operator stops the process, informs the maintenance department and waits for a technician to fix the problem. The agreed response time is 5 minutes between the request and the point in time that a technician attends to the problem. After waiting for over an hour, the operator notifies the shift manager and the priority is escalated on the request. A technician arrives 10 minutes later, 80 minutes after the initial call, and quickly resets the equipment. The technician records 100% service level in the maintenance log as the machine is fully operational again. For the operator as the process customer it was a frustrating experience since the service level received was just 5/80 = 6% when measured against the maintenance-SLA of 5 minutes. In conclusion, the customer's assessment of the service must be the reference to judge the service provided, never the provider's records.

Signs of Excellence

The presence of happy customers is the most reliable indicator of service excellence, as their satisfaction index is highly correlated with service quality. The absence of complaints on the other hand indicates conformance with requirements, but not necessarily happy customers. In world-class environments, schedules are firmly defined and rarely missed; commitments are consistently met with few exceptions, making delivery performance nearly perfect. Service level agreements are in place between any two entities, making expectations explicit and performance measurable. Deadlines are firmly set, communicated and measured, and the ownership of every aspect of managing commitments is defined. Processes are able to deliver consistent service quality, and systems are in place to track service performance and give an alert when deviations and exceptions are present. The team is skilled in service management and able to proactively eliminate most issues, while effective response processes ensure that remaining deviations are quickly corrected before they cause major interruptions. When asking internal and external customers about delivery expectations, they indicate they are confident that services and deliveries will be on time, every time.

Solving

About Solving

Problem solving is the process of correcting a deviation from a standard or target, or closing the gap between the initial state and the desired state. The auditor assesses the effectiveness of the problem solving process and system, and how well problems are addressed and solved. Concepts include abnormality detection, problem solving skills and process, the speed of intervention, problem solving effectiveness and re-occurrence rate.

> "We can't solve problems with the same thinking that created them." – Albert Einstein

What is a Problem?

A problem is a deviation from a standard or target that cannot be fully explained or controlled. Without a standard and target, there is no problem, and conversely, we need a reference point to recognize deviations and defects. After a problem is recognized, a formal process guides people through all essential steps to contain, analyze, and solve the problem, and ideally to prevent it from reoccurring. Most common tools for problem solving are plant-do-check-act (PDCA), the eight disciplines (8D), the five why's (5W), and fishbone diagrams.

What is a Solution?

A solution is the treatment of a problem in a way that successfully meets the standard or target. This may involve the elimination of its root causes entirely or it may involve treating the effects of the problem, all of which is dependent upon the ambition, capability, and capacity of the problem solver.

Three Problem Sources

Problems are created by a gap, opportunity, and hope. A gap between the initial state and the target state represents a problem to solve. An opportunity for improvement is a problem since the awareness of new possibilities brings up a problem to solve. Recognizing imperfection and the belief in a better future creates hope, and such hope challenges us to aim for a better future, which creates a problem to overcome. In essence, the Lean Audit intentionally creates problems (by identifying gaps and opportunities) that make an organization advance as those problems are being solved.

Problem Solving Approaches

The term problem solving is used in many disciplines, including psychology and computer science, and often with different perspectives and different terminologies. Solving problems usually involves dealing with pragmatics and semantics, causes and logic, as well as the different interpretations of the problem. The ability to understand current conditions and determine which approach to use is key to effective problem solving. The two basic approaches are (a) treating the symptom and (b) eliminating the cause. For simplicity, we call them patch and cure, of which each has three basic forms.

The Patch

Patching focuses on the effects of a problem by treatment, tolerance, or redirection. *Treating* an injury by applying a Band-Aid does not remove the cause of the injury but it stops the bleeding. Intervening with quick fixes or first aid treatments is often necessary to prevent bigger problems before the more lengthy diagnostics and elimination or reduction process can begin. *Tolerance* is a way to deal with the effects of the problem by putting up with it. The effects are taken for granted and measures are taken to endure them, such as putting a bucket under a leaking roof. Redirection deflects the problem by reframing it as not a problem. The following exemplifies redirection: occasionally catching a cold keeps our immune system active.

The Cure

The cure removes or reduces the problem by prevention, elimination, or reduction. *Preventing* a problem from occurring or recurring is the ideal but also the most difficult approach, as it requires predictive foresight. What we see today will become a problem if we do not act now. Examples are: a diagnosed illness, performance degradation, overfishing or deforestation. *Eliminating* a problem involves removing the cause by following a structured process, such as the eight disciplines (8D). *Reducing* a problem is a valid option when the problem cannot be entirely eliminated. For example, the amount of trash we produce can be reduced through recycling.

5 Why

The *5 why* technique—asking "why?" at least five times—is used to peel away symptom layers to expose the cause of the problem. Here are two examples:

- Why do customers return a product? Most returns are due to dents. Why are there dents? Items are inspected before shipping, thus they must be damaged in transport. Why are they damaged in transport? Because they are not packed correctly. Why are they not being packed correctly? Because the team does not know how, and they do not have any packaging specifications available. Why not? Because the product release process does not include packaging specifications. The 5W-process reveals that a flaw in the product release process resulted in customers returning product.

- Why does the car not start? The battery is dead. Why is the battery dead? It's not charged. Why not? The alternator does not work. Why not? The belt is broken. Why is it broken? The belt has never been replaced. Why not? Because the car was not maintained according to the required service schedule. The 5W-process reveals that a flaw in the maintenance process is resulting in the car not starting.

The Fishbone Diagram

The cause and effect (C&E) or fishbone or Ishikawa diagram is a graphical method for identifying the relationship between a problem and potential causes. It resembles the skeleton of a fish, with the problem stated on the fish's head and main bones labeled with major cause categories. In manufacturing, it is common to use the M-categories Man, Machine, Method, Material, Metrics, Milieu, Mindset or Mindpower, Management, Money, and Moon or Miscellaneous. In the service sector it is common to use the P-categories Price, Planet, Programs, Projects, Promotion, People, Process, Place, Products, Policies, and Procedures. Under each category or fishbone, potential causes are listed. Here is an example: the potential cause "process not defined" should be listed under the category "Method" or "Procedure", and the potential cause "procedure not followed" falls under the category "Man" or "People".

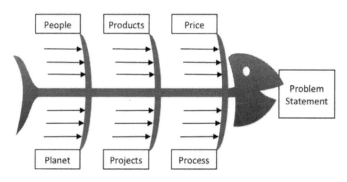

Figure 2.11 - Fishbone diagram for service

Problem Solving Strategies

There are several common strategies to solve problems: (a) *Abstraction* – solving the problem in a model before applying it to the real system, (b) *Analogy* – applying a solution that solves an analogous problem, (c) *Brainstorming* – generating many ideas and developing them until an optimum solution is found, (d) *Divide and conquer* – breaking down a large or complex problem into smaller, solvable problems, (e) *Hypothesis testing* – assuming a possible explanation to the problem and trying to prove or disprove the assumption, (f) *Lateral thinking* – approaching solutions indirectly and creatively, (g) *Means-ends analysis* – choosing an action at each step to move closer to the goal, (h) *Morphological analysis* – assessing the output and interactions of an entire system, (i) *Proof* – trying to prove that the problem cannot be solved; where the proof fails is the starting point for solving it, (j) *Reduction* – transforming the problem into another problem for which solutions exist, (k) *Research* – employing existing ideas or adapting existing solutions to similar problems, (l) *Root-cause analysis* – identifying the cause of a problem, (m) *Trial-and-error* – testing possible solutions until the right one is found. For the audit, we need to find out whether or not there is at least one approach consistently used to address problems.

Popular Methods

Most of the clients we have worked with over the past years use some kind of problem solving methods (figures are rounded): 80% use plan-do-check-act (PDCA), 30% the six sigma process define-measure-analyze-improve-control (DMAIC), 30% use failure-mode and effect analysis (FMEA), and 20% follow the eight disciplines of problem-solving (8D). More than half of them use more than one method.

PDCA

The Deming cycle plan-do-check-act (PDCA) is an iterative four-step method used for problem solving, process control, project management, and continuous improvement: (1) *Plan* – establish objectives and processes necessary to deliver expected output, (2) *Do* – implement the plan, execute the project or process, and collect data, (3) *Check* – study actual results and compare them to standards or expectations, (4) *Act* – standardize the improved condition or start another improvement cycle. PDCA is a simple, effective tool for smaller issues that can be resolved quickly, while complex problems and large projects are better addressed using DMAIC or DMADV.

DMAIC and DMADV

The Six Sigma approach of process control and problem solving is based on the notion that if the causes of a problem can be removed or controlled, the problem can be solved or reduced. The DMAIC and DMADV are part of the Six Sigma toolkit and used to implement projects and improve processes. The five steps of the DMAIC process improvement cycle are: (1) *Define* – determine process characteristics that are critical to customer satisfaction and identify gaps, (2) *Measure* – quantify the current performance level, (3) *Analyze* – collect data and perform process analysis, (4) *Improve* – modify or redesign existing methods to meet new performance objectives, (5) *Control* – monitor the process to ensure that high performance levels are maintained. In DMADV, the last two steps refer to *Design* and *Validation*, rather than Improve and Control as used in DMAIC.

FMEA

Failure mode and effect analysis (FMEA) and its derivative methodologies are designed to (a) identify potential failure modes for a product or process, (b) assess risks associated with those failure modes, (c) rank issues in terms of importance, and (d) identify and carry out corrective actions to address most serious concerns. FMEA as part of a problem-solving process requires the identification of functions and failures, causes and effects, controls and counter-measures. It involves evaluating the risks associated with the identified issues and allows prioritizing corrective actions based on assessed risks. The formula for calculating the risk priority number RPN = S x O x D = *Severity* of the failure x likelihood of *Occurrence* x likelihood of prior *Detection*. Each factor is ranked 1-10, resulting in a RPN between 1 and 1000 where a score of 1-10 indicates low risk (green flag), 11-100 some risk that requires escalation and mitigation or de-escalation for acceptance (yellow flag), and a score of 101-1000 that indicates high risk that requires action (red flag).

8D

The eight disciplines (8D) of problem solving were originated by Ford in the automotive industry and are now widely used in many sectors. The process includes the following eight steps: (D1) establish team, (D2) describe problem, (D3) contain problem, (D4) identify root cause, (D5) chose corrective action, (D6) implement corrective action, (D7) prevent re-occurrence, and (D8) recognize contributors. The eight disciplines is a very powerful tool to address systemic problems.

GROW

The GROW model is a popular and broadly used tool for goal setting and coaching. It focuses on solving the problems that stand in the way of personal achievement and productivity in four steps: (G) *Goal* – defining the end point or desired state, (R) *Reality* – defining the starting point or current state, (O) *Obstacles* and *Options* – identifying barriers and choices, (W) *Will* and *Way* forward – planning and committing, taking action.

Mental Barriers

Barriers between a problem and the solution are not only related to capability and capacity, but also to five mental constructs that impede our ability to address problems effectively: (1) *Confirmation bias* refers to collecting selectively specific data that favors a preconceived notion, while ignoring others to prove a point or established belief: "beating the data until it confesses". (2) *Mindset block* by choosing methods that worked in the past while ignoring other possibilities: "when all you know is a hammer, every problem looks like a nail". (3) *Functional fixedness* from having the primary function of an object in mind hinders our ability to see how it could serve another purpose: "it's made for this, so I can't use it for that". (4) *Unnecessary constraints* by putting boundaries around a task which makes it difficult to see anything but the chosen path and limitation, narrowing thoughts rather than thinking outside the box "it's my way or the highway". (5) *Irrelevant information* includes unrelated or unimportant information that only causes confusion and extra effort to separate the relevant from the irrelevant.

Signs of Excellence

In world-class organizations, the entire workforce is trained in problem solving and everyone regularly uses those methods to objectively analyze problems and systematically eliminate root-causes. Considered an essential skill, problem solving is part of introductory training and added to the skill matrix of each team. A minimum of 10% of employees are certified problem solvers and capable of leading solution teams, while managers and experts are qualified in the extended toolkit that covers PDCA, 5-why, C&E, FMEA, DMAIC, GROW, and 8D. To trigger problems as a way to continuously improve operations, leading companies encourage their people to (a) stop any process anytime for any abnormality to prevent larger problems and (b) formally address at least one problem or inefficiency per employee per week. First pass yield (FPY) and zero defects passed on (jidoka) are guiding principles, and all major defects and delays must be formally addressed. Problem solving is delegated to the people closest to the process and problem-prevention is defined as a management priority. Non-performance cost (NPC) and cost of poor quality (COPQ) are part of the executive scorecard and closely watched. As a result, most problems are permanently solved, reducing the recurrence rate to a single digit percentage.

Standards

About Standards

Standards capture current best practices, define the right way of working and establish a baseline for improvement. The Lean Audit assesses to which degree processes follow standards and the effectiveness of procedures to produce predictable outcomes. Concepts include accessibility of standards, content and controls, usefulness to guide people, update frequency, and link between standards and improvement process.

> *"If you can't describe what you are doing as a process, then you don't know what you are doing." – W. Edwards Deming*

Definition of a Standard

A standard is a widely accepted, agreed upon, or established means of determining what something should be. Generally, it is a written definition, limit or rule, approved and monitored for compliance by an authoritative agency or recognized body as a minimum acceptable benchmark. The General Agreement on Tariff and Trade (GATT) defines a standard as a "Technical specification contained in a document that lays characteristics of a product such as levels of quality, performance, safety, or dimensions. Standards may include or deal exclusively with terminology, symbols, testing and methods, packaging, or labeling requirements as they apply to a product."

Classifications of Standards

Standards are classified in the following main categories: (a) government or statutory agency standards and specifications enforced by law, (b) written limits or rules approved and monitored for compliance by an authority or professional as a minimum acceptable benchmark, (c) material standard for a substance whose properties are known accurately enough to use it as a physical reference in measuring the same properties of another substance, (d) performance standard as a principle or norm established by an agreement or authority used as a model to measure the performance of another practice, (e) proprietary standards developed by a firm or organization and placed in the public domain to encourage their widespread use and adoption, and (f) voluntary standards established by consultation and consensus and available for use by any person, organization, or industry. The auditor is mainly concerned with rules and references, described in the categories (a) to (d), while the Lean Audit system by itself is based on a standard that belongs to the categories (e) and (f).

Standard Work

Documenting a best practice as a work standard establishes the basis for continuous improvement. As the standard is improved, the new standard sets the baseline for further improvement as a never-ending cycle to raise the level of safety, quality, and speed. Standard work is an instruction that is based on customer requirements and aimed to make processes consistent and efficient. Examples of standard work are when a worker follows assembly procedures to prevent mistakes, a cook follows the recipe to put the right amount of chili in the soup, a soccer team follows the training routine to improve strength and coordination, a user follows the instruction sheet to correctly fill out the tax return, or when a machine operates according to a preprogrammed logic. All those recipes, rules, and routines are considered standard work.

Standards Free People to Serve

Bill Marriott describes that consistent systems and procedures are the main engines for the company's success and at the heart of "Marriott's Way". He says "At the most basic level, systems help bring order to the natural messiness of human enterprise. Give 100 people the same task—without providing ground rules—and you'll end up with at least a dozen, if not 100, different results. Try that same experiment with a few thousand people, and you end up with chaos. Efficient systems and clear rules help everyone to deliver a consistent product and service." The key point here is that procedures don't create good service—thinking people do! At world-class companies, the idea is to standardize and delegate as many tasks as possible so managers have enough time and energy left to focus on the unusual situations, exceptions, and opportunities.

Standards Enable Improvement

A standard describes the agreed upon way to perform work that is equivalent to best practice, provided that the standard is kept up to date. Once established, any standard becomes subject to scrutiny and kaizen activities aimed to reduce strain, waste, and variability. The two essential rules for managing standards are that they are (1) not static and never perfect and (2) to be followed and improved. Deming dedicated the fourth step of his PDCA improvement cycle, the "Act"-phase, to standardization as any improvement starts and ends with a standard. Toyota teaches that every employee has two jobs: (a) work according to the standard and (b) improve the standard.

> *"Where there is no standard, there can be no improvement." – Masaaki Imai*

5W+1H

A complete standard defines what, who, when, where, why, and how (5W+1H) to do the work. It covers process ownership, required resources, processing steps, quality checks, deliverables, startup inventory, cycle time, setup time, move time, workstation layout, and point-of-use storage. The standard describes how to perform work within the given time and resource constraints in such a way that the lowest skilled, qualified worker will understand it and meet quality and efficiency targets. The process must be fully transparent and not ambiguous in any way. The standard defines what is needed to start up work without delay, how to process, how to check the outcome against requirements, how to replenish parts and supplies, how to position them for optimal flow, how to retrieve items and where to move them. The same principles apply to standards in an assembly plant, accounting department, surgery theater, call center, toll station, and welding shop.

Standard Work Chart

The standard work chart or card (SWC) is a visual tool designed for operators to view all critical work elements on one single page. The chart or card describes floor layout, process stocks, material flow, and operator movements. It also indicates cycle time for each operation, sequence, and required process inventory to balance cycles between steps, to ensure smooth operation and minimal idling for maximum efficiency.

Process Capacity Sheet

The process capacity sheet (PCS) is used to calculate true capacity at a given mix of products or tasks to identify and eliminate bottlenecks. Each process step defines machine cycle time, manual task time, move time, lead time, changeover time, number of setups, total completion time, and total capacity in units per hour or shift.

Standard Operating Procedure

A procedure describes a fixed sequence of activities or course of action with a definite start and end point that must be followed in the same order to correctly perform a task. Repetitive procedures are called routines. When the procedure is confirmed as a best practice or standard, we refer to it as standard operating procedure (SOP), commonly used to describe administrative processes through step-by-step instructions on how to process information, make decisions, or use a system.

Leader Standard Work

Supervisors and managers use standard diaries and checklists as part of their leader standard work (LSW) to ensure discipline and completion of managerial and administrative tasks on time. LSW reduces the chance that anything is avoided or forgotten; notably uncomfortable activities like daily follow-up calls must be listed.

Standard Work Table

The standard work table (SWT) or standard work combination table describes the interactions between operators and machines, the combination of manual task time, walk time, machine processing time, and total time consumed per operator in a processing sequence. The standard work combination table allows recalculating the work content of operators as customer demand or takt time changes. Here is an example: walk to office 2 min, boot computer 1 min, log into system 1 min, wait for system to process report 5 min, walk and get report from printer 3 min, walk and post report on board 2 min, mark exceptions 4 min, walk back to office 2 min, write exception report and send to team 10 min.

Standards Drive Behavior

Structures and standards define the work of an assembly worker, commercial pilot, auto mechanic, surgeon, service associate, front-line teller, lawyer, and insurance broker. Each has its own functional set of requirements and expectations, roles, freedoms, dress codes, and reporting formalities. Structures and standards provide guidance and direction as to what employees should do and how they should do it in the most effective way. Management is actually impossible without structure and standards as they provide the reference points for employees to work and deliver against. Waste and productivity loss occurs when managers fail to create the set of rules and standards that guide behaviors, which is called structure waste.

Poor Standards Cause Waste

Weak or missing standards cause waste from misalignment, bypassing, unpredictability, variability, and tampering. *Misalignment waste* occurs when rules and regulations do not support desired results. Paying a bonus for incremental sales of low margin products while profitability is considered a top priority is an example of misalignment waste from eroding margins. *Bypass waste* refers to additional resources required to go around established procedures and maintain two parallel systems, the published and the practiced way. Here is a scenario where a planner can only purchase material once the customer order has been confirmed. In good intention to meet the request for shorter delivery time, he expedites the process by going around the system; he inflates an existing order so he can start purchasing materials right away. The problem is when the expected order does not materialize, the extra amount purchased ends up in inventory as bypass waste. *Reliability waste* is the extra effort required for correcting unpredictable process outcomes due to initially unknown causes. When work is delegated to someone who has not been properly trained or a system is launched without proper testing; the losses from cost overruns and delays are caused by reliability waste. *Variability waste* occurs when people and machines perform work in different ways or they deviate from the established best practice. With the introduction of visual standards and checklists, the failure rate of routine work can be dramatically reduced. *Tampering waste* is the effort required for compensating unexpected consequences from an arbitrary process change. Adding an inspection point in an attempt to control an incapable process will never ensure conformance; the additional efforts to rectify defects that slip through are tampering waste.

Signs of Excellence

Highly standardized operations run like clockwork, they "click", while chaotic flow and confused people are the result of a lower degree of standardization. In well-run companies, everyday processes and tasks are formally defined to ensure consistency and efficiency. At least 80% of each team's common and critical tasks are based on standards that describe how to schedule and balance work, process materials and information, measure and control results, manage projects and programs, set priorities and solve problems. In mature companies, capacity resource planning (CRP), costing and pricing are based on standard times. Those standards are well established, strictly enforced, and also under continual scrutiny. A policy of "fix or follow" reduces the likelihood of workarounds and encourages people to continuously improve standards, keeping them consistent with current best practices. Stagnant standards are regularly collected and systematically reviewed with the goal of improving work practices to gain 6% efficiency per annum. Innovative ideas are quickly translated into new standards to drive continuous renewal. The degree to which the enterprise information systems control work is a good indicator of standardization as those systems rely on time and routing standards. In less technical environments, the key indicator is how many work practices actually follow written procedures.

Structure

Structure and 5S

Structure is the foundation of a safe, efficient workplace. The Lean Audit assesses organizational level based on the 5S concept that a place is defined for each item and all items are kept at their defined places. The auditor looks at the general appearance and cleanliness of the workplace, organizational standards, training and 5S knowledge, abnormality tagging, checklists, housekeeping process, discipline to standards, feedback frequency, degree of deployment and system coverage.

5S Basics

5S is an organizational methodology that originated in Japan to drive structure and discipline while increasing operational efficiency through better housekeeping. It provides the framework for effective workplace organization, and it is the foundation of all major improvement programs. It guides people to structure their work areas and sustain the order by following the five steps: (1S) Seiri – Sort and remove what is not required, (2S) Seiton – Set items in order and define the optimal place for everything, (3S) Seiso – Sweep clean and repair to shine, (4S) Seiketsu – Standardize activities and ownership, (5S) Shitsuke – Sustain order through self-discipline, using checklists, feedback, actions.

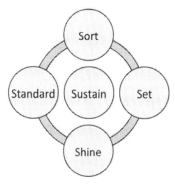

Figure 2.12 - Model of a 5S process

Auditing 5S

To improve and sustain order, we must be able to measure the level of 5S in a simple, reliable way, and we must provide regular feedback. Counting how many items are properly kept versus the total amount would not be practical, considering the sheer amount of parts, supplies, fixtures, furniture, tools, documents, and computer files; it would take hours or even days. Most 5S assessment tools are based on simple checklists with broad definitions and general criteria. It makes the audit quick and easy, but the repeatability and reproducibility of the assessment is low and the variability of results between auditors is high. For a reliable result, the audit must cover multiple dimensions, including cleanliness, knowledge, feedback, actions, standards, and discipline.

Organization for Factory and Office

Even though 5S is a well-established concept for workplace organization, it is surprising how few companies actually practice it. Many managers wrongly believe that 5S is a concept just for factories and not applicable to the office. One manager recently said that 5S is not a priority for his region, but cost and safety is. He did not understand that 5S is the prerequisite for safety and efficiency (lower cost); this is like telling a surgeon that washing his hands before an operation is just a waste of time. The fact is that all well-run companies have robust structures in place to effectively use their resources—and 5S is the foundation of such structure. The following paragraphs explain each step of the 5S process that applies not only to the *factory and warehouse*, but also to any *office and computer*.

1S – Sorting and Sifting (Seiri)

Eliminate all unnecessary parts, tools, equipment, and documents. Review all areas, open doors and cabinets, and question everything! Keep only essential items and eliminate what is not required for work. Determine usefulness per actual demand; everything else is stored away or discarded. If you are unsure about something, like whether you will need to use this document or that old winter coat again, write an "expiration date" on it and discard it when kept untouched till then.

2S – Set in Order, Stabilize and Simplify (Seiton)

Define a place for everything and put everything in its place. Items should be arranged to allow easy access, and stored close to the point-of-use so they can be reached with minimal motion. The use of spaghetti charts and flow analysis tools help to define the optimal storage location.

3S – Sweep Clean, Shine and Sanitize (Seiso)

Clean the workplace, return parts and tools, and perform overdue maintenance tasks, lubricate equipment, replace broken lights, paint walls, fix lose cables, and bring everything to perfect working conditions. Seiso is not an occasional cleaning event; it is daily practice and discipline.

4S – Standardize (Seiketsu)

Standardize the way to work, use demarcations, instructions, procedures, labels, photos, and shadow-boards to define where items should be stored and how work should be performed. The location for each item must be clearly marked and labeled. A high degree of standardization allows operators to consistently produce the same good results. When all employees clearly understand their responsibilities regarding the first three steps—the sort-set-shine—then the standard can be easily defined.

5S – Sustain, Self-discipline (Shitsuke)

The final step is about training people, implementing checklists, measuring conditions against standards and giving feedback. As a basic rule, 5S should be verified daily (by checklist) and formally assessed weekly (by audit) to keep discipline high and housekeeping level consistently above 90%. Disciplined follow-up ensures adherence to standards and triggers new improvements.

Digital 5S

The same principles that are used to structure physical workplaces also apply to the virtual world. The "Digital 5S" method is used to organize information stored in computers. In the first step, essential information is separated from incorrect and incomplete files (1S). Once sorting is completed, files are moved to their optimal locations (2S) and folders are organized to allow easy access to the most frequently used information (3S). File and folder names are standardized (4S), following a defined logic so information can be easily found and quickly retrieved. Lastly, information management procedures are defined and people trained to make data-keeping an integral part of daily activities, sustaining the new order (5S). Here is the benchmark for digital 5S: in world-class data systems, any qualified user can retrieve any specific file from the past 12 months within 10 seconds or less.

How Long to Attain 5S?

Even chaotic and disorganized workplaces can be improved by one level each month, sorting things out during the first month and defining optimal places for all remaining items during month two. Month three is about deep cleaning, repairing leaks, replacing burned out lights, attaching lose cables, lubricating moving parts, removing rust and covering exposed areas with protective paint, with the goal of bringing equipment and infrastructure into perfect working condition. Month four is about attaching labels, marking floors and shelves, writing procedures and checklists, followed by sustaining the new order through training and regular feedback from month five on. Smaller workstations or storage places can be organized much faster and reach full 5S within one month.

5S Benefits

Workplace organization improves operating efficiency, quality, safety, motivation, and company image. *Efficiency* – when tools and information are easily accessible, it avoids wasting time searching. *Quality* – workstations that are organized and maintained produce fewer defects. *Safety* – clear structure minimizes risks of accidents. *Motivation* – people usually enjoy working in an organized place more than being surrounded by chaos, and they are prouder of their work. *Image* – a clean and organized place is highly presentable, making customer and supplier visits welcome promotional events.

5S Efficiency

A frequently asked question is: *How much money can be saved with 5S?* As a rule of thumb, each level improves efficiency by 5%, or 25% efficiency gain is achievable between chaos and control, when going from level zero to five. Waste analysis provides the means to calculate the monetary benefits. To perform such waste analysis, it is most effective to observe people doing assigned jobs. The total minutes spent for searching, waiting, walking, and reworking are waste type-II. Any reduction in this avoidable waste translates into an efficiency gain, either through an increase of throughput with the same resources or lower resource consumption to perform the same work.

Room	Patient	Doctor	Lab		X-Ray	
			Tests	Done	In	Out
1	A. Jackson	S.M.	2	✓	✓	✓
2	T. Smith	W.E.	-	-	✓	
3	M. Cooper	F.B.	-	-		
4	F. Woodfield	K.T.	1	✓		
5	R. Gonzales	L.P.	4			
6	T. Harris	S.M.	-	-		

Figure 2.13 - 5S principles applied to patient processing board

Signs of Excellence

A safe and efficient workplace looks clean and organized at first glance; the first impression is a reliable sign. Buildings, floors, and bathrooms are clean; infrastructure and equipment is well maintained and in perfect working condition. Each cell, line, floor, cabinet, desk, machine, store, office, folder, and database has an assigned owner. For all items there is a place defined, and items are kept at their designated location; it's rare to find an item out of place. Abnormal conditions are apparent to everyone; even a visitor can easily recognize when something is missing or misplaced. Disciplined housekeeping is culture and an integral part of daily activities; the process is well defined and strictly followed. People proudly show off their workplace, open drawers and cabinets and are eager to explain the organizational logic and system. It is expected that everyone address at least one deviation per day to keeping organizational level consistently high. All employees are able to teach 5S principles and perform 5S audits, and tagging events are regularly used to identify the usefulness of items and highlight status. The organizational system is fully deployed and covers all areas without exception. The housekeeping level is measured at least weekly in each area and results are posted for everyone to see. Scores are tracked on control charts, used for feedback and to correct conditions and behaviors.

Teamwork

About Teamwork

Teamwork refers to people working together toward a common goal, sharing ideas, transferring knowledge, and balancing the workload among members. Teamwork is an outcome when activities require more capacity or capability than a single person can provide, or when synergies among team members create more benefits than the sum of individual contributions. People working in teams with a clear purpose and good chemistry not only improve business results, but they improve engagement and job satisfaction; everybody wins.

"The strength of the team is each individual member. The strength of each member is the team." – Phil Jackson

The Definition of Team

A team is a group of people with a full set of complementary skills that are required to complete a process or project. Four characteristics define a real team: (1) team members operate with a high degree of interdependence, (2) they share authority and responsibility to allow self-management, (3) they are accountable for their collective performance, and (4) they work toward a common goal and shared rewards. A group becomes a team when a strong sense of mutual commitment creates synergy, thus generating performance greater than the sum of the performance of its individual members.

"Talent wins games, but teamwork and intelligence wins championships." – Michael Jordan

Close Team and Committee

A close team is a group of individuals who perform tasks on related or connected processes in close proximity for most of their workday. Examples are agents in the service center, planners in the materials department, attorneys in the legal office, operators in the work cell, engineers on a project, and nurses at their station. Close teams share and swap work, substitute and cover for one another, face similar challenges, and benefit from the insights and expertise of each other. But not all teams are close teams. Management teams often function like committees where members do not work on similar tasks or in close proximity to each other.

Effective Teamwork

Successful teamwork largely depends on the ability of individuals to work effectively with other people who have different perspectives, attitudes, and backgrounds. The basis of good teamwork is a shared desire to excel as a group and not just work as individuals. Effective teamwork does not mean avoiding conflict; it means drawing out all viewpoints and ideas, being committed to informed discussion and analysis, active listening, the ability to give constructive feedback, openness to changing one's mind, and the management of conflict. In fact, if team members are getting along peacefully, it may indicate there is a lack of critical thinking or constructive conflict to break down the barriers that block the path to higher performance and next level of maturity.

> *"Great things in business are never done by one person. They're done by a team of people." – Steve Jobs*

Team Meetings

High performance teams meet daily, physically or virtually, to align on plans and solve issues. The pure act of coming together for a short meeting (lasting a few minutes) once per day will, over time, compel individuals to become active members through cognitive dissonance. The team meeting has the purpose of providing "the big picture", communicating and sharing new information, focusing discussions around key performance indicators, creating ownership and accountability, instilling a sense of urgency and discipline, providing a platform for problem solving, and satisfying the need for belonging and contribution.

Collaboration

Collaboration is a structured, recursive process where two or more people work together toward a common goal. It is typically an intellectual, creative endeavor that makes people want to work together to share knowledge, learn and build consensus. Packed in a few words, competition makes us faster and collaboration makes us better. Collaboration does not require leadership and can sometimes generate even better results through decentralization and egalitarianism; the belief that all people are equal and deserve equal rights and opportunities.

"Those who have learned to collaborate and improvise most effectively have prevailed." – Charles Darwin

Cooperation

Teamwork also requires cooperation for the sake of a common goal that the entire team is working toward, such as a sales quota or implementing an improvement project. Teamwork requires that all members contribute their fair share of the workload to accomplish team goals in a timely and satisfactory manner. The willingness to cooperate stems from the relationships between team members or between the employees and the employer. Teamwork cannot exist without this relational component, even if the extent of the relationship is minimal. Teamwork does not occur if each person does his own thing separately from his or her work relationships.

Team Leadership

Teams do not necessarily divvy up the work equally among all members. Instead, each person contributes their part. Within a teamwork environment, this may also involve the establishment of team leaders who help to ensure that the work is coordinated and completed in a timely manner. Teamwork can involve working together under the leadership of one person who has been chosen as leader or is naturally recognized as such by the team members.

Team Rules

All teams require clear ground rules to function. Those rules define how decisions are made, who is responsible for what, who reports to whom, how differences are expressed and resolved, and when and how unsolvable issues are escalated to the next level of management. Tasks and roles must be clearly defined and assigned. Who is responsible for what? Which tasks are shared, by and with whom? Who needs to attend which meetings? When defining team rules and goals, it is important to involve everyone in the process, agreeing on priorities, deadlines, and work plan. Balancing the needs of the group with team member schedules, workloads, and responsibilities improves the level of buy-in. Providing ongoing feedback keeps the team focused and on track, while the team leader holds everyone accountable for their deliverables.

Poor Teamwork

Under-performing teams show signs of decreased productivity, conflicts among group members, tension at team meetings, an increase in complaints, confusion about roles and assignments, a tendency to return to old patterns or attitudes, a lack of trust, and lopsided participation where some dominate and others withdraw.

High Performance Teams

Most people today work in teams or groups. Managers therefore must be skilled in managing individuals and building high-performing teams where people accomplish goals and support one another. This requires the right people in the right positions, doing the right things. Team members must possess the required skills to perform their jobs. When there are skills gaps, the entire team suffers. When people have the right mix of skills, the team thrives. Good leaders know their people's values and interests and the special needs of each member. A clear mission is established for the group with specific goals and objectives that are in line with the organization's goals and strategy. Getting broad participation in goal setting helps people understand how their work contributes to the overall success of the team. People are encouraged to share their ideas and work together, while the team and individuals are rewarded according to their level of contribution to the achievement of the organization's goals. Teamwork must be one of the criteria on annual performance reviews to encourage and recognize employees who collaborate readily with others. Finally, there must be time for informal discussions as well as celebrations and fun, to learn from one another and build relationships.

Signs of Excellence

People consider it rewarding to be a member on a collaborative team because everyone can learn and contribute at their highest potential. High-performing teams share fourteen characteristics: (1) people have a deep trust in each other and in the team's purpose; they feel free to express their feelings and ideas, (2) The entire team is working toward a shared vision and the same goals while collaboratively managing timelines and resources, (3) Everyone has the tools, information, and resources they need to get the job done, while leaders keep priorities in focus and intercede as necessary to remove organizational obstacles, (4) Team members are clear on how to work together and how to accomplish tasks; accountability for results is established, (5) Everyone understands both team and individual performance goals and knows what is expected of them, (6) Team members actively diffuse tension and friction in a collaborative and cooperative atmosphere, (7) When the team engages in extensive discussions, everyone gets a chance to contribute, including introverts and visitors, (8) Disagreement is viewed as critical thinking, conflicts are managed, and criticism is constructive and solution-oriented, (9) The team makes decisions when there is natural agreement; when agreement is elusive, a decision is made by the team lead or executive sponsor, after which little second-guessing occurs, (10) Each team member carries his or her own weight and respects the team processes and other members, (11) The leadership style shifts as appropriate to drive results, while no individual is more important than the team, (12) Members regularly receive feedback and are recognized for their contribution, (13) Incentives are designed to maximize overall performance rather than individual contribution, and finally, (14) there is time allocated to fun and learning, for team building activities, celebrations, and deep discussions that build trust and knowledge.

Technology

About Technology

Technology refers to the applied knowledge and use of methods, machines, systems, modifications and arrangements to achieve a specific goal or to perform a specific function. For the Lean Audit, we evaluate the purposeful application of knowledge in the design, production, and utilization of goods and services, as well as the organization of human activities. Concepts are: benchmarking of site technology, technical capabilities, engineering prowess, degree of automation and autonomation, computer-integrated workflow, maturity of applied technology, work allocation and monitoring processes, and paper consumption in administration.

Benchmarking Technology

Benchmarking technology refers to a measurement of an organization's technical capabilities and capacities compared to a standard, performance of its peers or performance of its competitors. Benchmarking provides a reference point to determine improvement opportunities and needs. It also provides an understanding of how better competitors achieve higher performance levels and the critical information needed to develop more effective policies, products, processes, and programs.

Technology Drivers

Main drivers of technology are changes in the technological environment and the need for rationalization. Both factors impact how a company does business; it may have to dramatically change its strategy as a result of new regulations or innovations or take the opportunity to rationalize its operation through the application of new technology. Consider how the entertainment industry must adapt to the increasing bandwidth of our telecom infrastructure that allows streaming music and videos on demand.

Technology Enables Rationalization

Rationalization refers to applying scientific management principles to increase efficiency or as a cost cutting measure. It often involves selling off or closing down parts of the business and reorganizing a company's structure to focus more on its core competencies. The two most common approaches are asset and footprint rationalization. Asset rationalization focuses on the physical assets to achieve the required returns on the sums invested. Footprint rationalization refers to right-sizing facilities through streamlining and consolidation and removing redundant or inefficient parts from the network.

> *"Rationalization is the organization of life through a division and coordination of activities on the basis of exact study of men's relations with each other, with their tools and their environment, for the purpose of achieving greater efficiency and productivity."* – Julien Freund

Disruptive Technology

New technology is an equal opportunity change agent, disrupting the status quo on one hand, while creating a competitive advantage on the other hand. Market forces use disruptive technology to tip the balance in favor of one outcome and thus gain an advantage over competitors. Once new technology has been proven, costs fall as installed capacity grows; experience shortens learning curves, and operating efficiencies increase. Consider the impact that e-readers, like the Kindle, had on the book printing industry.

Technology Readiness Level

Evaluations in software, biomedical, aerospace, construction, and manufacturing are often based on their technology readiness level (TRL) and scored on a 9-point scale. Levels 1-4 relate to new technologies at the application assessment phase; levels 5-9 relate to existing technologies at the application definition phase. The National Aeronautics and Space Administration (NASA), European Space Agency (ESA), Department of Energy (DOE) and many others use TRL principles when making decisions concerning the development and transitioning of technology. The specific levels from level one to nine are: (TLR1) Research, basic principles observed and reported, (TLR2) Concept published and application formulated, (TLR3) Experimentation and proof of concept delivered, (TLR4) Component validation completed in a laboratory environment, (TLR5) Component validated in a relevant environment, (TLR6) Prototype developed and functions demonstrated in a relevant environment, (TLR7) System and prototype demonstrated in an operational environment, (TLR8) Actual system qualified through test and demonstration, (TLR9) System has been proven through successful operation with acceptable performance. The TRL concept helps developing effective technology roadmaps and deployment plans.

Workflow Automation

Technology improves operating efficiency through allocation and coordination of activities between people. Workflow automation strives to provide the right person with the right information about what needs to be done and in which order. It automates clerical tasks, such as documenting and filing, and also expert tasks such as analyzing and planning. Key technologies are machine-to-machine networks (M2M) and the Internet of things (IoT).

Automation and Autonomation

The main reason for using technology in business is to automate and autonomate. When tasks are taken over by machines it is considered automation; autonomation (jidoka) or intelligent automation refers to the ability of a machine to detect abnormal conditions and immediately stop to prevent more or larger defects. Intelligent automation ensures good results at each process by continuously monitoring quality-critical parameters, minimizing the impact of defective material, wrong or missing data, inappropriate methods, excess variations, human mistakes, and machine errors. It allows separating people and equipment for more efficient work. When machines and systems work autonomously, people are free to concentrate on value-adding activities instead of watching processes to prevent errors. Jidoka is realized in four levels: (1) measuring process parameters and alerting in case of abnormalities, (2) stopping the process until the fault is removed, (3) auto-correcting fault conditions, and (4) self-learning from mistakes at its highest level. To realize just-in-time delivery, it is essential to produce at close-to-zero defects, or else defects will disrupt the production process and orderly flow of work.

Technology Asset Waste

Asset waste occurs when resources are tied up in equipment and when software is not optimally used. Here are two common examples of technology-driven asset waste: (a) implementing a large enterprise information management system that offers thousands of features of which only a few are actually required, adding complexity and cost, or (b) buying a high-speed machine or automating a process to save a few hours labor time, adding more cost in depreciation and maintenance than it saves operating it. Making value-driven judgments when considering new technology is a prerequisite to benefiting from that technology.

"The first rule of any technology used in a business is that automation applied to an efficient operation will magnify the efficiency. The second is that automation applied to an inefficient operation will magnify the inefficiency." – Bill Gates

Signs of Excellence

The firm has gained a competitive advantage from employing advanced technology; strong technical capabilities deliver true innovations that customers delight and competitors try to replicate. Benchmarking is regularly performed, raising awareness of new developments by assessing current capabilities against industry best practices. Managers gain a solid understanding of the most effective configurations to meet market expectations. In world-class companies, computers control pacemaker processes, schedule resources, and monitor the flow of goods and information. Status from order to delivery is fully transparent at all times. Paperless systems make workflow fast and efficient; physical archives store only legal papers, while all other records are in electronic format. Technology that was recently installed has improved productivity and lowered the cost base after considering the total cost for operation, depreciation, and maintenance. Critical processes are equipped with a full jidoka interface, allowing the system to work autonomously without human effort to monitor for quality.

Time

About Time Management

Time or workload management refers to the effective use of the available time to accomplish a task or job. With conscious use of time, productivity increases as more time is allocated to important tasks, and work is accomplished faster with less time wasted by waiting and idling. The Lean Audit assesses how well activities are planned, and time is used and controlled. Concepts include planning and pacing, resource allocation, status and progress tracking, absenteeism and on-time performance.

Most Valuable Resource

Time is not a renewable resource; once it is gone, it is gone forever. We cannot really manage time because every day has the same number of hours, minutes, and seconds, but we can decide what we do during that time. The audit therefore asses how effectively time is used, tasks are assigned and workload is managed, goals and priorities are set, resources are allocated, progress is monitored, and who takes responsibly for the outcome. Without time standards and discipline, time—our most valuable resource—is wasted.

> *"Time waste differs from material waste in that there can be no salvage. The easiest of all wastes and the hardest to correct is the waste of time, because wasted time does not litter the floor like wasted material." –*
> *Henry Ford*

Time Management Systems

Many people believe that smart systems or software will manage their time for them. This is actually impossible because a machine will only hold or act on the information that users put in. It is the user's responsibility to ensure that all tasks are carried out. All task and time management systems do the same thing—they allow us to create and organize tasks. The risk of using such tools is that we spend more time managing lists than making decisions and executing them. Below are the requirements of effective task and workload management.

Effective Planning

Effectively planning time is based on four principles: (1) anything that gets in the way of achieving goals is a waste of time, (2) a solid understanding of capability and capacity is required to prevent underestimating workloads and over-committing results, the enemies of effective time planning, (3) when the workload grows beyond what one person or group can do, delegation becomes a prerequisite to avoid overload, and (4) setting clear priorities by writing down what needs to be accomplished in descending order of importance and allocating resources to activities that yield the highest returns.

Spending your Time

Make a test and write down how you spent your time over the past work week. Working with many executive teams, we found that over 50% of a manager's time is spent on processing information, of which 80% does not lead to a decision or new insight. This means that 50% x 80% = 40% of their time is wasted sorting out irrelevant emails, questioning poorly compiled reports, or trying to make sense of incomplete data. This represents a 60% improvement opportunity by organizing (see "Structure" key) and standardizing relevant information (see "Standards" key), freeing up time that can now be spent on innovation and improvement (see "Renewal" key).

> *"Work expands so as to fill the time available for its completion."*
> *– C. Northcote Parkinson*

Workload Management

For the purpose of our audit, we assess how workload is defined and scheduled, how tasks are prioritized, how much of the work is completed right the first time, how time traps like idling and waiting are avoided, how work is delegated, how discipline is instilled, and how slippage and procrastination are prevented for on-time completion.

Task Prioritization

At work there will be interruptions, meetings, and possibly some urgent situations that require swift action. To remain focused on critical tasks, it is imperative to first list all the tasks and then rank them by importance. Every task falls into one of four categories, according to the 4D-framwork "Do-Delegate-Decide-Delete":

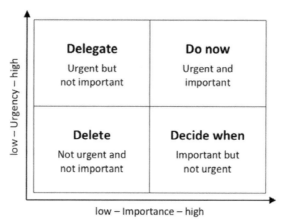

Figure 2.14 - Task prioritization matrix (4D)

Setting Priorities

Decisions that are urgent and important require immediate attention because they impact life values. Completing an important presentation that starts in a few minutes and responding to an emergency call from your spouse are both urgent and important. Actions that have no sense of immediacy might be important but they are not urgent, such as learning a new skill or planning for retirement. Actions that do not relate to your key values might be urgent, but they are not important and are subject to deletion or delegation, such as picking up the telephone from an unknown caller or responding to an email to confirm attendance.

Pareto 80/20

A popular method to allocate time according to priorities is *Pareto's Law* or 80/20-rule. By arranging all items in order of priority, as a rule of thumb, the top 20% if items generate 80% of the benefits. This also means that items on the bottom of the list generate the most waste, which is now subject to decision, delegation or deletion.

Right First Time

Many managers we surveyed said they spend most of their time firefighting and rectifying problems that stem from poor planning, bad decisions, insufficient skills, and flawed execution. Each error and mistake (see "Quality" key) requires time and cost to deal with the consequences. The additional resources consumed by rescheduling, expediting, short cutting, and processing rush orders are referred to as scheduling waste.

Stopping Procrastination

Workload management is at its worst when people procrastinate because they do not want to do the job or they don't know how—it's a function of skill and will. Fear of failure, lack of adequate information, or bad habits are common causes of procrastination. For example, the "student syndrome" that refers to waiting for the last minute to do a job or "analysis paralysis" from overanalyzing a problem to be 100% sure before taking any action.

Planning Time

Good time management means good workload management, which relies on good planning. And a robust planning process demands solid knowledge about capability, capacity, and timing. The planner needs to understand cycle times, takt and pitch, before setting lead-times and scheduling work.

Cycle Time and Takt Time

In German, takt stands for rhythm or drumbeat, the required pace of the system to meet customer demand. Takt is the available work time divided by customer demand. Cycle time is the time from when an activity starts until it is completed. Cycles must be equal or shorter than takt to meet demand. Below are some examples.

Takt for Coffee, Pizza, Camera

A coffee shop serves 300 customers during peak hour or 5 customers per minute, so baristas serve one coffee every 60/5 = 12 seconds to keep up with demand. A tunnel oven runs 8 hours per day to bake 500 pizzas at a takt of one per minute. When camera enthusiasts upgrade their equipment every year, the camera manufacturer must keep the time for research, development, and launch below one year to introduce new models in sync with customer expectations.

Service Center Example

A service center receives 18 calls a minute, of which 12 are answered and 6 are dropped due to long waiting times. Service level is 12/18 = 67%, leaving 6/12 = 33% of customers unhappy. The team of 20 customer service representatives is able to answer 12 calls per minute or one call every 60/12 = 5 seconds. Each employee answers a call every 20x5 = 100 seconds or 1.7 minutes, the service cycle time. To meet demand, a call needs to be picked up every 60/18 = 3.3 seconds. Demand exceeds current capacity by 18/12 = 150%, which means that crew size needs to be increased by 5/3.3 = 152%, from 20 to 30 operators, or the process must be improved to reduce call cycle time by 1 - (3.3/5) = 34%.

Pitch

Pitch is relevant when several units of work are combined before they are getting moved to the next process step; it is the time needed to complete one packing unit. For office processes, pitch is more relevant than takt because it usually requires completing multiple tasks or multiple units before the job is moved to the next department. The formula for pitch is takt-time multiplied by move-quantity, whereas takt time is the available time divided by demanded quantity.

Pitch Examples

When a subway station is served every minute to move the load (demand) of all waiting passengers, the trains operate in a one-minute pitch. When a party of 20 guests consumes one glass of wine every 30 minutes, then takt time is 30/20 = 1.5 minutes. Assuming a bottle fills 5 glasses, the pitch is (30/20) x 5 = 7.5 minutes, so that the server must bring a new bottle every 7.5 minutes to satisfy the thirst of the group. When a group of clerks issues 20 checks per hour and hand them over twice per day to the finance department as a pack of 80 checks, the group operates at a 4-hour pitch. And when a factory produces 100 vacuum cleaners per hour of which 300 fit into one container, it requires a truck to arrive at a 6-hour pitch to pick-up 2 containers per load.

Signs of Excellence

In world-class environments, time is considered a valuable resource and managed with the same rigor as costs and budgets. Schedules are well defined and commitments are consistently met; there is no time wasted due to poor planning, and everyone feels their time is always effectively used. Pace is in sync with demand and workload is well balanced, keeping idle time short, long days rare, and overtime is only used to handle unexpected peaks in demand. Processes are continuously tracked and information is available on demand. Each team maintains their own master calendar to make plans and events transparent, and allow team members to access each other's schedules. Managers and experts are able to spend at least one quarter of their work time in "flow state", working in uninterrupted concentration on strategic and creative topics. People are generally motivated and punctual; they start and complete work on time, which keeps absenteeism in the lower quartile and on-time performance in the upper quartile of industry leading rates.

Training

About Training

Training refers to an organized activity aimed at imparting knowledge to improve performance or to develop a skill. As part of the human capital management (HCM) process, the audit evaluates how well people are being trained and prepared for their future roles in the organization. It scores the robustness of skill assessment, quality of appraisals, effectiveness of coaching and feedback, how training is initiated and delivered, breadth of the training program, quality of the certification process, and how well career development is executed.

Capability and Capacity Building

Capability refers to anything an organization does well that drives meaningful business results, while capacity building is the process by which individuals and organizations increase their abilities to perform core functions, solve problems, define and achieve objectives, and deal with their development needs in a broad context and sustainable manner. It is the planned development of knowledge and skills through acquisition, incentives, technology, and training. The main reasons for an organization to build specific skills and capabilities are because (a) they are a fundamental part of the company's culture, (b) customer demands, (c) to match or exceed a competitor's capabilities, (d) react to short-term external events such as economic downturn, and (e) long-term global trends such as shifting markets.

Training Priority?

The audit assesses how companies create and manage training and skill-development programs and how effective those programs are in maintaining or improving their priority capabilities. Per a McKinsey survey about capacity building in March 2010, nearly 60% of respondents say that building organizational capabilities such as lean operations or project or talent management is a top-three priority for their companies. Yet only a third of those companies actually focus their training programs on building the capabilities that add the most value to the business performance of the company.

Capability Building Challenges

The biggest challenges for companies in building institutional capabilities are organizational resistance to change, a lack of resources, a lack of vision or unclear objectives, the inconsistent application of methods and processes, insufficient funding, a lack of credible metrics, no accountability for execution, a lack of senior management support, and ineffective training approaches. When assessing training effectiveness, it is important to be aware of those barriers.

Training Effectiveness

The type of training provided must be meaningful to produce any value after leaving the classroom. It is pointless to train large numbers of people in narrow technical skills (such as statistical methods) if they are not going to use them after the training is delivered. We learn tools and techniques best as we use them. A business supports training as it draws immediate value from it. For example, instead of teaching PDCA problem solving in a classroom, it's better to learn it by solving an actual bottleneck, process breakdown, or customer complaint.

Human Capital Development

The systematic development of competencies that produce economic value is referred to as human capital development (HCD). Such competencies include knowledge, skills, experience, and personal traits that are demonstrated through a person's behavior. Most companies spend a lot of time and money to select and hire the right people, but very little effort in developing their talent. Companies that pursue human capital development shift the responsibility for developing people from HR to line management, as functional managers can better judge which specific competencies are required in their area to meet requirements.

Competency Levels

The following six levels have been proven effective for assessing skills and setting training targets for individuals and teams: (0) unskilled and skill not required, (1) skill is required but unskilled, (2) training has started, (3) trained and able to perform all tasks but quality needs to be checked, (4) qualified and able to work independently at the required level of speed and quality, and (5) expert, able to train and certify others. Those assessment standards create the foundation for developing effective skill matrices.

Signs of Excellence

Skills and competences meet strategic requirements and are on a par with the best in the field or industry. A structured training program is in place to build relevant skills and capabilities. The development plan is specific and targeted, measurable, aligned to strategy, realistic to achieve, and timely (SMART). All employees are qualified in their respective jobs; most are cross-skilled and able to work in different areas. Qualification boards and skill matrices are maintained in all departments to measure competences against the best within their field or industry. At least 4% of paid work time or 8 workdays per year are reserved for training so employees are able to attend three or more relevant training workshops each year. Professionals, such as engineers and controllers are certified at the master level, regularly conducting workshops, and some of them are recognized authorities and published experts in their respective field. Managers spend at least one hour per week with their direct reports in one-to-one coaching sessions and have time slots reserved in their agendas to make training and feedback a daily practice. Skill building and cross training processes are fully institutionalized. In world-class companies, all core skills have been doubled and deputies are in place to ensure continuance when someone is absent; there is always someone qualified to fill in. The large majority of people have embraced the goal of building a flex organization that requires everyone to be cross-skilled and able to perform all core tasks within their team and 50% of tasks for up and downstream processes.

Visuals

About Visuals

Visuals relay information to and between people so they can perform work without the help of papers and computers. Lean companies use visuals to improve speed and efficiency by involving operators in the decision-making process. The Lean Audit assesses to which degree the operation is managed visually, the types of visuals in use, the degree of transparency, visual processes control, and visual inventory management.

> *"A business should be run like an aquarium, where everybody can see what's going on—what's going in, what's moving around, what's coming out. That's the only way to make sure people understand what you're doing, and why, and have some input into deciding where you are going. Then, when the unexpected happens, they know how to react and react quickly." – Jack Stack*

Visual Management

Visual management refers to the placement of all tools, parts, processes, and indicators *in view*, so the status of the system can be understood at a glance. Visual devices relay information through signals instead of reports, using cards, marks, magnets, lights, bins, or containers. Visual management is faster, cheaper, and more effective than any other system by indicating normal and abnormal conditions without the use of time-consuming reports or complex computer systems. In essence, visuals allow you to lead with what you can see.

Classes of Visuals

Visual devices are the heart of lean management systems. They are classified by the extent the message is likely to be obeyed and the consequences of failure to follow the visual instruction. The four levels are visuals, signals, controls and guarantees. (1) *Visuals* – signs, labels, floor markings, shadow boards, instructions. (2) *Signals* – status indicators, alarm lights, control charts, performance boards. (3) *Controls* – guidance devices, kanban cards, inventory limits. (4) *Guarantees* – electronic door, auto-stop, error prevention, and other autonomation features.

Andon Signal

Andon, derived from a Japanese term for paper lantern, is a simple signaling device that provides visual feedback about the operating conditions of a line, machine, or workstation. It shows when assistance is needed and helps operators, technicians, and managers quickly identify and resolve issues. The signal is either activated manually by a worker pressing a button or automatically set by the equipment itself. A common color scheme is green for normal operating conditions, yellow for changeover or call for adjustment, and red for alarm and line down situations. By giving operators the authority to stop the process and call for assistance, the andon promotes employee involvement, effective communication, and quick response to issues.

Results from Visuals

During the 1970's oil crisis, the Dutch government urged citizens to save energy. As a result, households where the electric meter was installed in the hallway for everyone to see decreased electricity consumption by one third, while those households with the meter installed in the basement had very little change in consumption. Similar to the Dutch results, we have found a high correlation between the degree of transparency and improvement rates. When information is openly displayed, even without any instruction or explanation, people tend to make quicker and better decisions that favorably impact results—the power of visual management.

"People's minds are changed through observations" – Will Rogers

Performance Boards

A performance board displays all essential information in one place. Team members can view how metrics move from their direct efforts, making the board a center of pride and accomplishment. To be effective, the performance board must be placed in a central area, ideally in line of sight to ensure team members stay focused. The board must be maintained daily, ideally at the beginning of the shift to communicate targets and at the end of the shift to record what has been achieved, discuss hits and misses, and initiate corrective actions. It is critical that those meetings are religiously held to instill discipline and keep performance on track. The board must at least cover three elements (1) Work plan and targets, (2) Performance metrics, (3) Daily problem solving.

Daily Problem Solving Board

Visual performance indicators are only effective when coupled with a system to correct deviations from the standard or target. *What happens if there is nothing to correct?* Then the target is not ambitious enough and should be raised to trigger new ideas in the spirit of continuous improvement. A good rule of thumb is 95/5 and 80/20, setting the bar high enough that at least 5%, but no more than 20%, need attention. The daily problem solving system is one of the most effective management tools available. Here is a proven-simple example, using a large board with four columns to record problems (or symptoms), identify solutions (or next steps), assign ownership, and schedule due dates:

Problem	Solution	Owner	Start	Due
Screws missing, happened already five times this year	Quick fix: buy and refill. Solution: develop replenishment procedure.	Joe Mark	May-09 May-09	May 10 May 15
Delivery delayed by 2 days, operators overloaded	Quick fix: expedite order. Solution: hire people to match workload.	Susanne Anthony	May-09 May-09	May 12 June 14
Customer rejected project proposal	Identify cause of failed proposal. New proposal to meet expectations.	Ken Mary	April-23 April-23	April 30 May 15

Figure 2.15: Team board for visual problem solving.

In almost all cases, low-tech solutions (like boards) that team members can maintain by themselves are more effective than computerized systems because it's too easy to blame inaction on a software bug or lack of IT resources, rather than tackling the problems head on.

Signs of Excellence

When visiting a visually managed workplace, information unfolds as you are passing through. Status information relevant to each area is fully transparent at all times. Locations are clearly demarcated and signs make it easy to navigate so that even an unguided visitor does not get lost. Activity areas are structured and neat. For every item, there is a place defined—*fixed locations* for common items used daily or at predictable demand, and *flexible locations* for special items that are used rarely or with unpredictable demand. Simple checklists, control charts, and status signals allow anyone to quickly understand what goes right and what does not, what priority is now and what is planned next. Even a visitor can easily grasp the situation. Performance boards are installed in each area, making success-critical information fully transparent. Performance reporting is organized from the ground up; metrics are easy to interpret and easy to maintain by each team and without a computer. In world-class environments, resource allocation and workload balancing is visual, status information is displayed in real-time, process performance and workflow is controlled visually. The auditor can observe ten types of visual devices during the audit: (1) signs and labels provide basic structure to maintain order, (2) floor markings guide the traffic of people and vehicles, (3) empty containers, as part of a multi-bin system, trigger replenishment of frequently used items, (4) cards signal demand and authorize upstream process to allocate resources and reproduce, (5) lights indicate status and alert in case of abnormalities, (6) flow-lines ensure the proper sequence of work, (7) red tags mark defects, (8) shadow boards encourage people to return tools to their designated place after use, (9) magnets on boards visualize loading, resource allocation, and amounts of inventory, (10) checklists and control charts provide visual feedback on process performance. World-class companies make full use of all types of visual management tools.

3. AUDIT

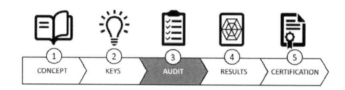

About the Audit System

The following pages represent the heart of the Lean Audit, containing the questionnaires for both the Lean Factory Audit (LFA) and the Lean Office Audit (LOA). These questionnaires are organized in three parts:

1. *Enterprise questionnaire:* checklists posed in both, the LFA and LOA
2. *Factory questionnaire:* checklists specific to manufacturing operations
3. *Office questionnaire:* checklists specific to office and service operations

Regardless if we look at a factory or an office operation, both are converting inputs to desired outputs through the appropriate application of resources, such as material, labor, and information. This value-adding process involves converting

- Raw materials into finished goods in the case of a factory, and
- Consumers into satisfied customers for a service business.

The Enterprise questionnaire is therefore the foundation of the audit system, covering the keys that are common to both the *Lean Factory Audit* and the *Lean Office Audit*. These 12 enterprise keys must be completed first, before answering the remaining 8 keys that are specific to a factory or office operation.

The following image illustrates the Lean Audit scope and checklist assignment, as well as the certification process, which qualifies product and service companies at the Bronze, Silver, and Gold level for Lean Operations. For more details, see chapter five "Certification".

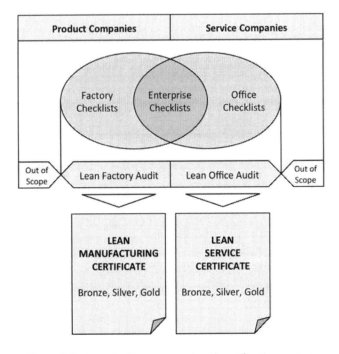

Figure 3.1 - Lean Audit assessment and certification system

Lean Factory Audit – when to use it

The Lean Factory Audit (LFA) is designed for product companies, such as manufacturers and service companies with high product content. It assesses the process of converting raw materials into finished goods based on the 20 Keys to World-Class Manufacturing (WCM). The factory audit is applicable to all five operating environments:

- Project (flexible flow), such as construction and product development;
- Job (jumbled flow), such as a tooling or a car repair shop;
- Batch (disconnected line flow), such as bread baking and shoe production;
- Repetitive (connected line flow), such as automotive assembly, and
- Continuous (continuous flow), such as a brewery or refinery.

As a rule of thumb, use the LFA for all businesses that process physical goods – adding value to items that can be touched, moved, and stored.

Lean Office Audit – when to use it

The Lean Office Audit (LOA) is designed for service companies operating in an office environment. It assesses the process of converting consumers into satisfied customers based on the 20 Keys to World-Class Service (WCS). The five types of services include:

- Business services such as consulting, banking and financial services;
- Trade services such as retailing, maintenance and repair;
- Personal services such as restaurants and healthcare;
- Public services such as government and education;
- Infrastructure services such as transportation and communication.

As a rule of thumb, use the LOA for all businesses that process information – adding value through analysis, design, advice, or control.

Scoring Method

A *key score* is calculated for each individual key by taking the average of all the checklists under that key; the overall *audit score* is then calculated for the entire company by calculating the average of all the key-scores. Here is a key scoring example that uses the "Costing" key:

Suppose points are assigned for each checklist under the "Costing" key as follows:
- 4 points achieved for the "Costing/Budget" checklist
- 2 points achieved for the "Costing/Control" checklist
- 3 points achieved for the "Costing/Defects" checklist
- 2 points achieved for the "Costing/Review" checklist

This gives a total of 11 points for these four Costing keys. Therefore, the key score for "Costing" is determined as follows:

$$11 \text{ points} / 4 \text{ checklists} = 2.75$$

Once the individual key scores are tabulated for all 20 keys, the audit score for the company is then be determined by taking the average of these 20 numbers. The results are reported on the radar chart, and this average of all 20 keys is the measure of "maturity".

Factory Audit Scoring Example:

Points are tabulated for the factory audit by considering both Enterprise and Factory keys:

- 38 points achieved for the common 12 Enterprise keys
- 30 points achieved for the specific 8 Factory keys

This gives a total of 68 points for all 20 keys; therefore, the factory maturity score of 3.40 is determined as follows:

68 points / 20 keys = 3.40

Office Audit Scoring Example:

Points are tabulated for the office audit by considering both Enterprise and Office keys:

- 38 points achieved for the common 12 Enterprise keys
- 25 points achieved for the specific 8 Office keys

This gives a total of 63 points for all 20 keys; therefore, the office maturity score of 3.15 is determined as follows:

63 points / 20 keys = 3.15

Points are recorded after each question, and the average is calculated for each key. This process is repeated checklist by checklist, key by key, until the audit is complete and the final score is calculated. Now let's get started with the first part of the Lean Audit, the Enterprise Questionnaire.

Enterprise Questionnaire

The Enterprise questionnaire contains the 12 common keys of the 20 keys required for a Lean Factory Audit or Lean Office Audit. This marks the starting point of the Lean Audit; the first key to assess is "Costing".

COSTING

Costing checklists assess the effectiveness of the budgeting process and costing system.

COSTING/E/Budgets

How are budgets defined? How well do managers and supervisors understand the cost structure?

(1) No solid budgets or low awareness; only few people can explain basic costs, such as hourly rates by cost center

(2) Budgets decided top-down; line managers understand cost structure and work with teams to resolve variances

(3) Budgets negotiated between management layers; team members clearly understand cost drivers and allocations

(4) Budgets designed bottom-up by each team, reviewed by line manager and approved by senior management

(5) Teams fully in control of resources and budgets; define base, step, variable costs, its drivers and allocations

COSTING/E/Control

How are costs controlled? How advanced is the costing system?

(1) Focus on head count and output quantity; managers consider indirect labor and overhead as fixed costs

(2) Major cost categories tracked against budget; overhead applied as factor of direct labor or output quantity

(3) Direct labor hours tracked by cost center; overhead allocated using fixed percentages by multiple cost drivers

(4) Labor and overhead applied to processes and projects by actual consumption; even managers assign their time

(5) System provides details on life-cycle costs, allowing leaders to balance short-term with long-term decisions

COSTING/E/Defects

How is non-quality accounted for? Consider non-performance cost (NPC) and cost of poor quality (COPQ).

(1) Defects and delays not accounted for
(2) Simple accounting of overtime and failures
(3) Resources allocated in the budget for overtime, failures, lost hours and accepted rework
(4) NPC tracked in financial system; reports show cost of defects, in-station rework, returns, and lost hours
(5) COPQ simulated by system, considering future impact of failures, missed opportunities, and lost orders

COSTING/E/Review

How often are actual costs reviewed against budget and standards? Only consider reviews with formal actions.

(1) Annually or semi-annually
(2) Quarterly
(3) Monthly
(4) Weekly
(5) Daily or real-time

Costing score = (sum of points) / 4 = ☐

LEADERSHIP

Leadership checklists assess the effectiveness of strategic planning and execution.

LEADERSHIP/E/Decisions

Who is leading the audited area? Over the past year, who made most decisions and how were those carried out?

(1) No clear leader, weak or unstable leadership; important decisions pending and poor coordination between levels
(2) Leader sets direction and teams follow without asking many questions; issues with coordination or cooperation

(3) Teams provide critical information for the leader to review and decide; but data and coordination not very strong
(4) Decision after critical discussion between leader and team; cooperation and effective coordination between levels
(5) Empowered teams define own goals and control their own resources; leader works mainly as strategist and coach

LEADERSHIP/E/Deployment

How well is strategy defined and executed? How effective is the policy deployment process?

(1) Senior management decides on goals, but leaves workforce with little understanding on how to achieve them
(2) Goals defined and communicated to all levels, but not all priorities are aligned and initiatives properly funded
(3) Priorities and goals well defined and cascaded to all levels; everyone knows what is important, what to do next
(4) Policy deployment completed; X-matrix links targets, tactics, teams, technology, projects and rewards to strategy
(5) Policy deployment well entrenched, X-matrix for next 5+ years drive all organizational objectives and incentives

LEADERSHIP/E/Feedback

How often do leaders get feedback on their performance? Consider executives and managers.

(1) Leaders do not receive regular feedback, other than clarifying questions and status updates from their staff
(2) Leaders hold regular feedback meetings to discuss what they do well and what they can personally improve on
(3) Leaders openly share their personal goals and development plans to get feedback and support from their teams
(4) Leaders receive quarterly feedback from their staff and full 360-degree performance review at least once per year
(5) Leaders update their development plans with all stakeholders involved; review progress with a coach or mentor

LEADERSHIP/E/Focus

What do leaders focus on? Where do they spend their time? Consider executives and managers.

(1) Most time spent on daily issues and reporting (90%), only little time left for planning and improvements (10%)

(2) Daily activities consume most time (70%), while some time reserved for strategy and forward planning (30%)

(3) Time to respond to daily requests and report past results (50%), equal time spent on planning the future (50%)

(4) Less time spent on daily management (30%), while most hours allocated to improvements and future (70%)

(5) Little time required for issues and reporting (10%), most time spent forward looking, future opportunities (90%)

LEADERSHIP/E/Orientation

What is the planning horizon? Only consider published plans with clear goals, schedules, and ownership defined.

(1) Daily urgencies and expedites dominate; longer term plans not very robust or priorities frequently changing

(2) Short-term orientation with focus on daily issues and deliverables, weekly schedules and monthly results

(3) Medium-term orientation with focus on key strategic projects, quarterly performance and annual budgets

(4) Willingness to trade short-term gains for long-term benefits; strategic plan is robust but not always followed

(5) Long-term strategy with tactical plan kept flexible, allowing team to be proactive towards issues, opportunities

LEADERSHIP/E/Priorities

How are priorities defined? Consider decisions by leaders responsible for budgets, resources, and results.

(1) Priorities change frequently; people are used to adjusting their daily schedules according to latest urgencies

(2) Priorities set top-down by senior management, imposed rather than agreed to, reason for change often unclear

(3) Priorities discussed and aligned; senior managers control resources, teams are responsible for implementation

(4) Priorities set and managed by teams; senior manager approves resources and provides steering assistance

(5) Priorities set by teams in alignment with strategy do not require approval; senior managers only provide guidance

LEADERSHIP/E/Structure

How well are values, vision, mission, strategy, and actions defined and aligned? Ask several people and compare notes. Values: what to stand for, principles and believes. Vision: what to achieve. Mission: why and for whom. Strategy: goals, roadmaps, success factors. Actions: steps, timelines, ownership.

(1) Lack of vision, strategy unclear or changes frequently; people have different views on priorities and future

(2) Top-down ambitions by senior management; weak alignment process causes disconnects and resource shortages

(3) Vision, mission, strategy, goals are defined and aligned, but lack of solid roadmaps cause suboptimal execution

(4) Everyone understands vision and mission; robust framework and detailed roadmaps, goals cascaded to each level

(5) Goal setting is automatic and performance dialog part of culture; full alignment between all teams and org layers

Leadership score = (sum of points) / 7 = ☐

MANAGEMENT

Management checklists assess the effectiveness of daily planning and decision-making.

MANAGEMENT/E/Actions

How effectively do managers take action?

(1) Managers are too busy to recognize problems early, mainly coordinating responses to delays and breakdowns

(2) Managers recognize issues and conflicts but have little time left to address them; many action plans show delays

(3) Managers take actions but consequences not firmly set for missing expectations, causing gaps, persistent issues

(4) Managers address all issues within a few days, actions and consequences well defined; all major issues resolved

(5) Managers address 90% issues on the same day; discipline and responsiveness of entire staff is consistently high

MANAGEMENT/E/Decisions

How do senior managers prioritize and decide? Consider managers responsible for budget, resources, results.

(1) Managers do all they can to make the numbers; busy expediting and coordinating responses to daily urgencies

(2) Decisions mainly based on financial reports, strong sales and cost focus, short-term orientation, quarter to year

(3) First discussions around building better capabilities with focus on quality and agility, medium-term orientation

(4) Most discussions focus on optimizing core business processes, trading short-term gains against long-term benefits

(5) Most discussions focus on optimizing the business model, plans span 10+ years, consider contribution to society

MANAGEMENT/E/Feedback

How do managers deliver formal feedback? How effective are performance reviews?

(1) No formal feedback or evaluations not documented

(2) Formal review process with focus on reporting; reviews are often done late or considered a formality

(3) Reviews documented and managers take the time to write comments on what each member should improve on

(4) Robust review process with focus on people development, firm goals and plans, updated at least twice per year

(5) Quarterly one-to-one performance review for everyone; evaluations linked to reward system and training plan

MANAGEMENT/E/Incentives

How well are incentives designed and aligned with strategy?

(1) Incentives missing, misused, based on unclear criteria, taken for granted, or seen as an entitlement

(2) Incentives misaligned, drive inappropriate response, cannot be directly influenced, or considered unfair by many

(3) Incentives linked to business plan, but functional focus drives spot-improvements, unhealthy balance long-term

(4) Incentives linked to strategy, balancing short and long-term needs, but limited influence or not available for all

(5) Incentives aligned, balanced, relevant; based on group results, team contribution, and individual performance

MANAGEMENT/E/Interaction

How often do managers reach out to connect with direct reports? Ask people how often they receive support.

(1) Managers rarely get in touch with their direct reports; team members typically go to their leads for decisions

(2) Managers follow up with their direct reports several times per month to check status or when there is a problem

(3) Managers connect with their teams several times per week to collect status information and provide direction

(4) Managers connect daily with their team to update each other; the exchange happens as one group or individually

(5) Managers use short interval leadership; connect with each team member individually each day to provide support

MANAGEMENT/E/Interfaces

How well are interfaces managed? How well do managers address cross-functional performance and issues?

(1) No regular feedback between departments; managers blame each other for poor results and missed targets

(2) Internal breakdowns discussed, but informal process and lack of standards and metrics; most issues repeat

(3) Internal service level tracked and major issues addressed, but weak standards and slow actions cause glitches

(4) Service level agreements (SLA) between teams, regularly tracked and improved, goals met with few exceptions

(5) Satisfaction index consistently top, internal issues treated as seriously as external ones, proactive towards risks

Management score = (sum of points) / 6 = ☐

METRICS

Metrics checklists assess the effectiveness of the measurement process and system.

METRICS/E/Alignment

How well are metrics defined and goals aligned?

(1) Metrics missing or measures without meaning; only few people can explain how they can support company goals

(2) Some numerical goals defined and spot performance tracked by department; but not tied into the business plan

(3) Metrics and goals defined, but measurement process not yet stable or teams cannot directly influence numbers

(4) Solid performance indicators and goals for each function, properly aligned and in control of responsible managers

(5) Balanced scorecard fully deployed, linked to strategy and reward system; mission and metrics are fully clear to all

METRICS/E/Effectiveness

How effective is the measurement system? How many numbers collected actually drive actions or decisions?

(1) Most decisions based on opinions and best guesses; only few are based on validated data

(2) Information collected but not timely or not in proper format to support decision-making; few data drive actions

(3) Data used to support decisions, but metrics not robust or definitions change; confusion how to influence numbers

(4) Robust metrics and statistics trigger decisions, but not all reports are effective, more data collected than required

(5) Metrics are highly effective; data policy in place, all data collected must drive decisions or else they are eliminated

METRICS/E/Indicators

How is functional and cross-functional performance measured? What types of indicators are used?

(1) Performance not regularly measured, robust indicators missing, or performance reports not readily available

(2) Simple reports based on easy-to-measure indicators, often not business-critical, tracking hours instead impact

(3) System tracks mainly short-term indicators that are critical to the business, such as cost, quality, and delivery

(4) Scorecard tracks short and medium-term performance, including efficiency in labor minutes per output unit

(5) Balanced scorecard tracks short to long-term performance, including capability index and customer satisfaction

METRICS/E/Parameters

Which indicators are regularly reviewed and effectively controlled? Check boards and reports.

(1) Simple, easy to measure indicators, such as sales and output quantity

(2) Quantity, quality, delivery or service level, and basic financial indicators, such as sales and cost

(3) Quantity, quality, delivery, cost by category, and operating efficiency in output per resource hour

(4) Quantity, quality, delivery, cost details by process, operating efficiency, and process capability such as Cpk

(5) Quantity, quality, delivery, cost by activity, efficiency, process capability, skill index, and internal service level

METRICS/E/Review

How often is cross-functional performance reviewed? Only consider reviews by core team with formal protocol.

(1) Performance reviewed when there is a problem, but no regular performance review meetings scheduled

(2) Monthly review of requirements and issues; focus is on troubleshooting problems and updating schedules

(3) Weekly review of requirements, resources, results (3R) against goals and standards; plans updated after meeting

(4) Daily review of hits and misses and weekly 3R relative to plan and standards, using performance control charts

(5) Performance continuously monitored, status transparent at all times; any deviation over 5% triggers formal action

Metrics score = (sum of points) / 5 = ☐

READINESS

Readiness checklists assess enablers and key success factors for implementing change.

READINESS/E/Attitude

What is the general attitude towards change? What do most employees say when confronted with change?

(1) I always have done it this way, I never did it that way, or I see no reason to change

(2) I think that change is needed but elsewhere in the organization; the others should change or do something

(3) I see the need for change but I am not sure where to start, let me know what to do; we should do something

(4) I can see what we need to fix and I am getting actively involved to change what we have today

(5) I actively search for opportunities, take charge and execute change because I see it as the engine of our success

READINESS/E/Employees

What is the general behavior of front-line employees? Consider hourly employees such as clerks and operators.

(1) Prefer the way it is, some oppose or even hinder change efforts, or voice sarcastic comments in meetings

(2) Interested to learn but not self-starting, assist managers in developing new methods and standards

(3) Guided by a manager, improved several procedures in past 12 months and trained others in those standards

(4) Self-starting and cross-skilled, can handle all primary tasks in their area and develop related training manuals

(5) Lead improvement teams and conduct workshops; inform and guide visitors when supervisor unavailable

READINESS/E/Leadership

How capable are leaders to initiate and implement change? Consider executives responsible for strategy, budget.

(1) Many years in the same position, rely on what they know, prefer the way it is, not experienced leading change

(2) Initiate programs and allocate resources, but unable to provide much support or prefer hands-off approach

(3) Provide structure, resources, and professional input; lead steering committees but often decision bottlenecks

(4) Effective change agents, highly skilled in engaging people, designing roadmaps, resolving conflicts, lead programs

(5) Recognized authorities in transforming organizations, known for pushing boundaries, speak at major conferences

READINESS/E/Managers

How do departmental managers approach change?

(1) Prefer the way it is; see no need to change, or fear or resist change

(2) Realize the need for change, but slow in taking action or not sure where to start

(3) Initiate change projects and quickly approve resources, but prefer hands-off approach, delegate implementation

(4) See leading change as part of their job, design program and roadmaps, and have firm tasks assigned in projects

(5) Spend more time leading change programs than on controlling resources and reporting results

READINESS/E/Phase

Where do most people stand? Assess their current position relative to the readiness curve.

(1) Resistance; I know something is changing; I do not like it and want to stop it, because I believe that this is trouble

(2) Awareness; I know what is coming; I will do what is asked of me but I am not fully convinced that this is helpful

(3) Engagement; I trust that the direction is right and support the change, but have not yet seen a benefit for me

(4) Commitment; I drive the change because I believe that it makes sense, is good for the company and good for me

(5) Culture; I initiate new change, even if it is difficult at first, because I believe that it is the engine of success

READINESS/E/Professionals

How capable are professionals in process analysis and system design? Consider managers, engineers, controllers.

(1) Experimental approach based on trial and error; know what works by experience but cannot always explain why

(2) Structured approach to scientific work; fact-based decision-making based on averages, percentages and trends

(3) Analytical approach to defining scientific questions; create design and simulation tools based on statistical data

(4) Scientific abstraction, definition of scientifically testable hypothesis, design of experiments, forecasting models

(5) Broad knowledge acquisition, models for estimation and interference, experts regularly publish research results

READINESS/E/Resources

How many resources have been committed to a continuous improvement? Consider projects and programs.

(1) Requirements unclear or resources not committed; there is hope to execute improvements parallel to daily jobs

(2) Improvement program has been started with clear ambitions in mind but lacks critical resources for its execution
(3) Funds and people allocated to accomplish specific tasks; but not part of a permanent improvement structure
(4) Budgets and full-time resources assigned to build capability as part of a continuous improvement program
(5) Program is part of strategy; senior managers involved beyond steering, remove barriers, solve structural issues

READINESS/E/Skills

How skilled are people in lean and process management? Consider managers, engineers, planners, accountants.

(1) Superficial knowledge; lean is a buzzword, used as a synonym for cost reduction or tightly controlled resources
(2) Gained insights from media, peers, or training programs; but cannot differentiate value from incidental work
(3) Analyze hits and misses in the context of the three losses (3L) waste, strain, variability or (3M) muda, muri, mura
(4) Apply theory of constraints (TOC) and the four lean principles flow, takt, pull, leveling to eliminate bottlenecks
(5) Regularly use value stream maps (VSM) to break through performance barriers, at least once per process per year

Readiness score = (sum of points) / 8 = ☐

RENEWAL

Renewal checklists assess the level of improvement and innovation to remain competitive.

RENEWAL/E/Approach

What approach is used to improve performance? How robust is the process? PDCA refers to plan-do-check-act.

(1) Large projects initiated from the top, such as new machine or IT system; no formal improvement process in place

(2) Internal suggestions are primary source of improvements; random activities, not tied to program or business plan

(3) Simple improvement process, such as PDCA problem solving templates; goals are defined but actions often slow

(4) Improvement program is well defined and part of strategy; cross-functional process with disciplined follow-up

(5) Improvement is systematic and continual; improvement teams part of organizational matrix, supported from top

RENEWAL/E/Improvement

How is performance improved? What did the core team do over the past 12 months?

(1) Team was busy with day-to-day work; no time left to think about improvements; processes unchanged for years

(2) Team started optimizing processes, organizing people, rearranging equipment, installing boards, shelves, tables

(3) Team improved workflow and updated procedures, significantly reducing efforts and errors by double-digit%

(4) Team doubled (200%) efficiency or velocity of at least one core process by totally redesigning method or flow

(5) Team achieved breakthrough, transformed at least one value stream or one core process across multiple sites

RENEWAL/E/Involvement

How strong is the relationship with customers and vendors? How often does the team meet with third parties to jointly design new products and services, redesign shared processes, and implement efficiency improvements?

(1) Customer complaints and difficult vendor relationships; activities limited to buying, expediting, trouble shooting

(2) Team is open to suggestions but not actively seeking input from third parties; improvements driven from within

(3) Some vendors and customers invited, several joint meetings in past year helped optimizing process, interfaces

(4) Strong bond to customers and vendors; sharing resources that work on joint projects to improve shared metrics

(5) Anticipating and consistently exceeding customer needs; shared strategy and systems with customers, vendors

RENEWAL/E/Resources

How many resources have been dedicated to continuous improvement? How many employees are involved?

(1) Resources assigned ad-hoc to fix processes, correct quality issues, and act on customer complaints

(2) Some people spent time on improvement projects, but resources for continuous improvement not budgeted

(3) 10% employees involved in improvement projects, led by a dedicated project or program manager full time

(4) 50% employees have tasks in improvement projects or were part of improvement teams in past 12 months

(5) 90% employees have tasks in improvement projects; take an active role in the never-ending improvement process

RENEWAL/E/Suggestions

How many improvement suggestions have been implemented in the past 12 months per employee?

(1) Employee suggestions not formally managed; improvements mainly handled by managers and specialists

(2) Basic suggestion scheme, some ideas submitted but less than 1 implemented per employee per year

(3) 1 suggestion implemented per employee per year; feedback is formal and successes are celebrated

(4) 5 suggestions implemented per employee per year; everyone feels empowered to act on opportunities

(5) 10 suggestions implemented per employee per year; most people are capable to lead improvement teams

RENEWAL/E/Trend

How effectively is performance improved? What is the trend of key indicators in control of the team over the past 12 months? Consider changes relative to the environment; +5% gain in a +5% market equals zero improvement.

(1) No improvement, key indicators show unfavorable trend, such as declining revenue or shrinking margins

(2) Yoyo, up and down, despite improvement efforts, trend remains flat; performance not stable or not predictable

(3) Flat and stable, improvements offset unfavorable effects; performance in key areas is predictable and in control

(4) Positive trend for most key indicators; improvement efforts show favorable impact with some minor deviations

(5) All key indicators show favorable trend; improvement efforts deliver solid gains that outperform the market

Renewal score = (sum of points) / 6 = ☐

SERVICE

Service checklists assess delivery performance and service level to internal and external customers.

SERVICE/E/Commitments

How well are commitments met? OTC tracks on-time performance against committed dates.

(1) Regularly missed without accountability; people try to justify reasons for misses; 2.5-sigma delivery or 84% OTC

(2) Frequently missed; some people feel responsible and establish a sense of urgency; 3-sigma delivery or 93% OTC

(3) Commitments usually met with extra effort, overtime, expedites, or workarounds; 3.5-sigma delivery or 98% OTC

(4) Most commitments met without extra effort by following established procedures; 4-sigma delivery or 99% OTC

(5) Performance culture; track record of consistently meeting commitments; 4.5-sigma delivery or 99.9% OTC

SERVICE/E/Delivery

How satisfied are customers with service and delivery? Consider both, internal and external customers.

(1) Poor service level from unpredictable processes; customers frustrated about late delivery, some cancellations

(2) Low service level from unreliable processes; customers complain about excessive lead time but accept to wait

(3) Average service level, inconsistent process times; some delays and disconnects, 90% deliveries meet requests

(4) Good service level, consistent speed and reliable delivery; few complaints, 95% deliveries meet requested dates

(5) Excellent service level, meets high standards; over 99% deliveries meet requested dates, virtually no complaints

SERVICE/E/Queue

How many items are waiting in queue for the next step? Consider untouched parts, unread emails, pending tasks.

(1) Overflowing inboxes and storage spaces, stacks of unprocessed parts and papers pile up; processes out of control

(2) Pending work between departments, many jobs take longer than expected, making people work hard to keep up

(3) Most jobs on time, pending work used to balance load between workdays; few jobs intentionally held as buffers

(4) Work planned and completed daily per strict procedure; all planned tasks must be completed before going home

(5) Virtually no pending items due to continuous flow; work in queue limited to what is required per routing or plan

SERVICE/E/Relationship

Which statement describes the relationship to internal and external customers?

(1) Difficult and cold, characterized by low tolerance and many complaints; emotional bank account is empty

(2) Basic understanding of customer needs and supplier capabilities; teams work together to solve problems

(3) Service level agreements (SLA) in place with all key customers; teams help each other beyond problem solving

(4) Regular exchange between internal and external teams to define value stream maps (VSM) and agreements (SLA)

(5) Teams act as partners, sharing strategies and ownership; high level of trust and strong bonds between people

SERVICE/E/Scheduling

How well is work scheduled and balanced?

(1) Work characterized by stop and go; managers are busy with trouble-shooting, rescheduling, expediting

(2) Work not uniform or not well planned, requires overtime and buffers to compensate for variations and delays

(3) Workload and resource requirements defined by week or month, but unforeseen issues cause some rescheduling

(4) Work schedules leveled by day or week; capacity resource planning process (CRP) is stable and rescheduling rare

(5) Work schedules defined by shift of day, leveled continuously or each hour by reassigning flexible resources

Service score = (sum of points) / 5 = ☐

SOLVING

Solving checklists assess the effectiveness of the problem solving process and system.

SOLVING/E/Alert

How are abnormalities identified and alerts set? Check for flags, lights, tickets, tags, marks, magnets etc.

(1) Most problems remain unnoticed until crisis strikes

(2) Only experts and managers can identify abnormalities before growing to major problems

(3) Some alerts displayed for everyone to see, but inconsistent process or limited to few key processes

(4) Alerts consistently set for core business processes but unclear if someone responded or not

(5) Three-level signals used to indicate problem solving status: set, responded, solved

SOLVING/E/Authority

What happens when a problem is detected? Who is authorized to stop a major process or large customer order?

(1) Authority to stop by senior manager; teams continue working to achieve the plan, unless they are told to stop

(2) Authority by line manager; team members set alert and maintain process by using creative ways around problems

(3) Authority by team leader; team members are encouraged to stop for any issue they cannot solve by themselves

(4) Authority delegated to team members when leader not present; stop protocol well defined and strictly followed

(5) Authority fully delegated; team members stop anytime for any abnormality and initiate formal corrective actions

SOLVING/E/Effectiveness

How effectively are problems solved and root-causes eliminated? Over the past 12 months, how many problems were newly encountered (never seen before) and how many problems reoccurred (seen before, known issues)? Disregard problems that have been officially accepted or considered unsolvable within given constraints.

(1) Chronic problems, symptom-treatment and workarounds; 10% new and 90% repeat

(2) Problems patched, quick fixes with focus on containment; 25% new and 75% repeat

(3) Systematic problem solving but not always effective; 50% new and 50% repeat

(4) Root causes properly addressed and re-occurrence rate significantly reduced; 75% new and 25% repeat

(5) Problems rarely reoccur, most solved at prevention level; over 90% new and less than 10% repeat

SOLVING/E/Frequency

How many problems are formally solved? Count PDCA or 8D forms completed per employee per year.

(1) Problems are addressed as they come up; no formal problem solving process defined

(2) Problem solving process defined but less than 1 problem formally solved per employee per year

(3) 1 problem formally solved per employee per year

(4) 5 problems formally solved per employee per year

(5) 10 problems formally solved per employee per year

SOLVING/E/Process

What is the common way to address internal issues? How many steps of the 8D process are typically completed?

(1) Quick fixes and workarounds; reactive approach to problem solving (2D), fire-fighting and expediting are common

(2) Containment and symptom treatment, such as rework, reset, repair, replace, return, reschedule, reissue (3D)

(3) Formal root cause analysis, disciplined use of fishbone and failure-analysis tools like FMEA by all managers (4D)

(4) Systematic root-cause elimination (5D) with recognition of prevention and evidence of reduced re-occurrence (6D)

(5) Problem prediction and prevention is management priority (7D); solutions translated into new standards (8D)

SOLVING/E/Tools

How well do people understand problem solving? What tools and techniques are used to eliminate root-causes?

(1) Problem solving methods unknown or not regularly practiced; no specific tools used, superficial knowledge

(2) Simple tools used, such as plan-do-check-act (PDCA) or 5-why template to address major failures or 10% of issues

(3) Standard problem solving procedure; people are trained and systematically address 50% issues, major and minor

(4) Problems thoroughly analyzed; FMEA, 8D, DMAIC, GROW are well understood and applied to address 90% issues

(5) Robust process from problem identification to problem prevention; most root causes eliminated on first attempt

SOLVING/E/Tracking

How well are problems tracked and solved? Consider non-conformances, process failures, customer complaints.

(1) Ad-hoc trouble-shooting or problems not logged
(2) Informal logging of problems, using uncontrolled notes or spreadsheets; reports not readily available
(3) System exists to record problems but inconsistently used or just used to track major customer complaints
(4) Central system used to address internal and external problems; robust and transparent process, reports posted
(5) Systematic solving of all customer complaints, quality alerts, and process failures; detailed action plans in system

Solving score = (sum of points) / 7 = ☐

STANDARDS

Standards checklists assess the effectiveness of procedures and systems to achieve consistency.

STANDARDS/E/Access

Where are standards stored? How quickly can users access them? Consider procedures, policies, drawings etc.

(1) Standards missing, hidden in drawers and computers, or accessible only by few people
(2) Standards not easily accessible, require searching or requesting from creator or manager
(3) Standards outside station, require several minutes walking or retrieving from computer
(4) Standards in station, accessible within one minute on computer or few steps of walking
(5) Standards accessible within 10 seconds, on the spot with minimal motion

STANDARDS/E/Authority

Who has the power to improve a process? Who has created and revised procedures in the past 12 months?

(1) Owner, director, or expert, three levels separated from the work team

(2) Manager or expert, two levels separated from the work team

(3) Supervisor or expert, one level separated from the work team

(4) Assigned member of the work team, under guidance of an expert

(5) Any qualified member of the work team; most team members have improved processes in the past 12 months

STANDARDS/E/Content

Which elements are included in the work standard? Check for steps, flow, timing, quality, skill, startup inventory.

(1) Basic user manuals from supplier or uncontrolled process documents; no evidence of standard work in use

(2) Basic process descriptions, such as quality manual or ISO handbook, mainly used for compliance purposes

(3) Simple procedures with pass-fail criteria; clearly describe what to do, how to do, and how to check the result

(4) Detailed procedures specify steps, flow, quantity, quality, and timing; used as basis for efficiency management

(5) Full standards specify steps, flow, quantity, quality, timing, inventory, min skills; serve basis for all improvements

STANDARDS/E/Degree

How many repetitive tasks follow standard procedures? System-guided activities are considered standard work.

(1) Employees mainly work by experience or without written instructions or system guidance

(2) Few activities or 10% of weekly tasks follow standards, mainly time and quality-critical tasks

(3) Main activities or 50% of weekly tasks follow standards; firm procedures in place for all direct labor work

(4) Most activities or 90% of weekly tasks follow standards; even managers can show their weekly standard agenda

(5) Most daily and all repetitive work follow standards; improvements are consistently translated into new standards

STANDARDS/E/Discipline

How consistently do people follow standards? What is the level of discipline?

(1) Standards are considered recommendations, while workers and supervisors follow their own methods of working

(2) Standards kept and processes followed when things run smoothly, and abandoned in times of stress and overload

(3) Standards generally followed, strict on external customer and compliance items, more lax on internal practices

(4) Standards for internal and external processes well defined, broadly understood and followed with few exceptions

(5) Standards strictly enforced, frequently challenged and continuously improved; consistently high level of discipline

STANDARDS/E/Timing

How well is timing defined? Check for cycle-times, pitch, and lead times.

(1) Processes lack time standards; the concept of standard work is largely unknown by supervisors and managers

(2) Limits set for few time-critical processes, such as response to customer requests or monthly financial closing

(3) Cycle times defined for core processes, but not well maintained or not effectively used for planning and manning

(4) Standard times set in system for most processes, understood by everyone and used for planning and manning

(5) Standard times continuously updated; used as foundation for costing, resource planning, efficiency management

STANDARDS/E/Update

How often are processes redesigned and new standards issued? Ignore cosmetic fixes, reissuing old procedures.

(1) Standards are outdated or dormant for 5 years or longer; many work practices differ from written procedures
(2) Standards are valid but stagnant; procedures are current but most processes unchanged for 3 years or longer
(3) Standards are improved after major problems and updated at least every 2 years, following a strict procedure
(4) Standards systematically updated; expiration dates enforce formal review every year to improve effectiveness
(5) Improvements consistently translated into new standards; the average standard is updated several times per year

Standards score = (sum of points) / 7 = ☐

TEAMWORK

Teamwork checklists assess the cooperative and coordinated effort for a common cause.

TEAMWORK/E/Atmosphere

Which statement best describes the team atmosphere? How do team members behave?

(1) Atmosphere is competitive and individualistic, not very open to suggestions; not-invented-here (NIH) syndrome
(2) General atmosphere of respect, but some have difficulties listening; others feel unheard, hesitate to ask for help
(3) Everyone treated with respect, all members listen to all ideas, feel free to seek help; contributions acknowledged
(4) Open discussions; build on ideas of others and recognize each other as legitimate contributors to shared goals
(5) Team encourages diverse views, openly tackles emerging issues; provide and accept feedback to build strength

TEAMWORK/E/Cohesiveness

How well do people work together? Consider all employees who are part of a team.

(1) People prefer to work by themselves, minimal interest in collaboration or idea sharing; closed doors are common

(2) People respect the perspectives of others but generally stick to their opinions; send email rather than talking

(3) People openly discuss problems and options, prefer face-to-face meetings over calling, and calling over email

(4) People reach out and actively seek advice, solve performance problems and also personality conflicts as one team

(5) People depend and trust each other, treat group interests over self-interests, open doors and virtually no politics

TEAMWORK/E/Meetings

How effective are cross-functional meetings? Consider meetings with representatives from all core functions.

(1) No regular team meetings; people get together mainly for special events, such as employee information meetings

(2) Meetings scheduled but time wasted from irregular attendance or unclear objectives, lack structure or discipline

(3) Meetings held regularly with good attendance but not always effective; they often take longer than expected

(4) Meetings well-structured and relevant to all team members, regularly held without exception, most are effective

(5) Daily meetings considered essential to everyone, participants fully engaged; no meeting is missed or delayed

TEAMWORK/E/Response

How quickly do people respond to requests from others?

(1) Do not respond or frustrating delay in response time; many pending items

(2) Respond sometimes or requires several reminders to get a response

(3) Respond as needed to agreed priorities, but slow on other items

(4) Respond as needed to all requests; consistently meet requirements

(5) Respond professionally at continuously improving speed and quality

TEAMWORK/E/Systems

What systems are in place to support teamwork?

(1) Team rules not defined, not posted, or not followed; no specific policies or procedures in place

(2) Team structure, group goals and ground rules are agreed and posted for everyone to see

(3) Team structure, goals, and timelines defined to meet critical path requirements; shared team schedules posted

(4) Work allocation, task prioritization, goal alignment, escalation and feedback process follow standard procedure

(5) Systems control activities and schedules, supporting people to meet group goals with clarity and efficiency

TEAMWORK/E/Workload

How well is workload defined and distributed within each team?

(1) Work not well defined, several people only pick the tasks they prefer to do; workload allocation is not fair or even

(2) Work defined but few people carry most of the load, do compensate for shortcomings and passiveness of others

(3) Activities clearly defined; willingness to share the load but uneven capability within team still burdens key people

(4) Everyone is doing their part, skilled people help each other, share the load; work allocation considered fair by all

(5) Team members synchronize their daily schedules to distribute work with strong effort on continuous balancing

Teamwork score = (sum of points) / 6 = ☐

TRAINING

Training checklist assess the effectiveness of the skills building process.

TRAINING/E/Amount

How many resources are available for training? How much time did the average employee spend in training over the past 12 months? Only consider formal workshops and seminars with individual feedback to each participant, and exclude informal lectures without competence test. Calculate: effective training hours / total work hours.

(1) 1 day per year or 0.5% of work hours or less spent on training
(2) 2 days per year or 1% of work hours spent on training
(3) 4 days per year or 2% of work hours spent training
(4) 6 days per year or 3% of work hours spent on training
(5) 8 days per year or 4% of work hours or more spent on training

TRAINING/E/Feedback

How do managers coach their people? Coaching refers to giving people professional advice to attain their goals.

(1) Managers expect people to learn by themselves; most interactions are focused on controlling, reporting, fixing
(2) Managers are busy and rarely have time to give specific feedback; spend time ad-hoc with people who need help
(3) Managers always give constructive feedback in response to a problem, providing suggestions on how to do better
(4) Managers offer on-the-spot coaching; all team members receive monthly feedback regarding their contribution
(5) Managers have fixed time slots reserved in their daily agenda for one-to-one feedback and coaching sessions

TRAINING/E/Process

How are skills developed? What is the process?

(1) Learning by doing; new employees gain skills through loose mentorship with experienced people
(2) Training based on simple process descriptions; skill requirements not well defined or skill scores missing
(3) Cross training ongoing; skills tracked against targets and skill matrices posted in most departments
(4) Cross training completed and people qualified per skill matrices; core skills doubled and deputies in place
(5) Continuous training and certification program; skill matrices cover all employees including senior level

TRAINING/E/Qualification

How capable are employees? How many are qualified?

(1) Most employees rely on tribal knowledge; can only perform the tasks they were assigned to do

(2) Most employees formally trained and capable to do multiple jobs in their area or department

(3) Most employees qualified per skill-matrix and able to perform all primary tasks in their area or department

(4) Most employees are qualified on all jobs in their area and able to perform critical tasks up and downstream

(5) Most employees gain experience in other areas through job-rotation; knowledge-transfer is fully institutionalized

TRAINING/E/Type

What type of training is provided?

(1) Training on the job; no formal training program defined or provided

(2) Generic training, basic job induction, or one-way presentations; not deep enough to build robust skills

(3) Specific training provided for selected people, well established and supported; firm training budgets allocated

(4) Structured training program with frequent updates improve skills; broadly rolled out and linked to business plan

(5) Strategic capability building program spanning several years, covers all departments and includes all employees

TRAINING/E/Versatility

How versatile are skills? Do people strictly work in one area or do they gain experience in other areas?

(1) Most people prefer to work in one area, the area they were assigned to work, and not interested in skill versatility

(2) Most people are willing to learn, taking the initiative to register for classes, order books, identify best practices

(3) Most people see value in broadening their skill base, assist in developing training programs, formed study groups

3. AUDIT

(4) Most people embraced skill flexibility as a personal goal; many participate in job rotations between departments

(5) People take pride in their capability and flexibility; most are certified at the master level in their respective jobs

Training score = (sum of points) / 6 = ☐

VISUALS

Visuals checklists assess the effectiveness of visual management.

VISUALS/E/Application

Where are visual management tools used?

(1) No visual tools beyond basic signs, such as marked aisles, rooms and offices, fire extinguisher, emergency exits

(2) Information boards display static information, such as company policies and organizational charts

(3) Departmental status displayed but insufficient for spot-review, requires printing reports or manager to explain

(4) Workflow visually controlled end-to-end; signals and charts allow spot review without reports and computers

(5) Cards, lines, bins, marks used to allocate resources, control workflow, balance load, and alert of abnormalities

VISUALS/E/Control

How effective are visual controls? Check how signals, bins, charts, marks and magnets trigger resources.

(1) Visual signals are missing, outdated or misleading; people rely on experience and reports to control work

(2) Visual signals trigger daily tasks, using scheduling and leveling boards, order tags, refill cards, repair tickets

(3) Visual signals control pacemaker process, monitor status of work, and trigger problem-solving activities

(4) Visual signals control pacemaker and pull processes, allocating resource hours and triggering corrections

(5) Visual signals control core processes and out-of-cycle work, including planning, controlling, reporting

VISUALS/E/Display

How well is status information displayed? Consider requirements and resources, schedules and abnormalities.

(1) Status information missing or outdated; informally documented, not openly displayed, or older than one month

(2) Status information posted at random locations; insufficient for spot review or too general to take action

(3) Boards installed at strategic locations, performance tracking is consistent but limited to few core processes

(4) Dedicated boards for each process and department; information is accurate and updated within reporting cycle

(5) Boards updated several times per day or real-time status display; key information transparent at all times to all

VISUALS/E/Locations

How many spaces are visually controlled? Consider physical storage locations for materials and information.

(1) Space freely used and most locations not marked; no visual management system in place or rules not defined

(2) Few locations demarcated (25%) for inbound or outbound items; need to ask someone from area to get status

(3) Key locations demarcated (50%) for inbound and outbound items, work in process, supplies, stores, and archives

(4) Most locations demarcated (75%) for in, out, process, supplies, stores, archives, exceptions requiring attention

(5) All locations demarcated (100%) for all items end-to-end; even visitors can quickly identify status, abnormalities

VISUALS/E/Signals

What types of status signals are used? Consider equipment, infrastructure, and information systems.

(1) Basic signals, such as fire alarm or unstructured notes on paper or email

(2) Error signals for some machines and systems, but status levels not standardized across the equipment installed

(3) Standard signals for major machines and systems; status displayed in three levels: running normal, alarm, off

(4) Standard signals consistently used on all systems, workstations, and departments: running normal, alarm, off

(5) Standard performance indicators show real-time status relative to requirements: on target, deviation, alarm, off

Visuals score = (sum of points) / 5 = ☐

Factory Questionnaire

The *Factory questionnaire* contains the 8 keys that are specific to manufacturing operations; they are required in addition to the 12 common keys from the Enterprise questionnaire to complete all 20 keys of the Lean Factory Audit.

EFFICIENCY

Efficiency checklists assess how well resources are used for the intended purpose.

EFFICIENCY/E/Control

How is efficiency measured and controlled?

(1) Indirect reporting, calculated from other metrics, such as revenue per person

(2) Labor time standards defined for main activities, first efficiency charts established

(3) Efficiency measured against standards in key areas; run charts show trend over several months

(4) Control charts established with firm efficiency goals for all departments and work centers

(5) Efficiency continuously tracked by system; deviations from targets trigger formal corrective actions

EFFICIENCY/E/Waste

What do most employees (80%) understand about value and waste? How well is waste identified and reduced?

(1) Little understanding of value and waste; most people are not able to identify the eight wastes (8W) in their area

(2) Concept of value and waste is broadly understood; most people have organized their area to reduce searching

(3) Waste analysis completed and projects started to tackle obvious wastes: wait, transport, error, double handling

(4) Broad waste reduction initiative ongoing, addressing inefficiencies around behavior, products, processes, systems

(5) Holistic waste reduction program, systematically addressing inefficiencies in strategy, structure, business model

EFICIENCY/F/Conservation

What method is used to conserve resources? Consider energy, materials, water, waste, and emissions.

(1) Resource conservation not actively pursued; no formal guidelines or conservation policies in place

(2) Company-wide conservation policy; high-level reduction goals defined without a structured program

(3) Conservation initiatives ongoing for key areas such as utilities; updated savings report published regularly

(4) Comprehensive conservation program with traceable reduction in energy, materials, water, waste, and emissions

(5) Full pursuit of resource conservation; going green is part strategy and culture, not just a marketing slogan

EFFICIENCY/F/Flow

How well do materials flow? How much process inventory (WIP) is required to keep the operation running?

(1) Large batches moved between warehouse and disjointed process areas, requiring many material handlers

(2) Batches held in standard inventory locations, only go back to warehouse after completion, not semi-finished

(3) Batches go from process to process, queue up until next process is ready; visual controls limit overproduction

(4) Batches flow without inventory buildup; max one batch in queue between two processes to balance cycle times

(5) Flow of units or batches is standard, processes fully connected; only inbound and outbound docks hold items

EFFICIENCY/F/Metric

How efficient is the factory? Consider overall equipment (OEE) and overall process efficiency (OPE) within plant operating hours. How many work orders are completed in the fastest possible way and right first time? Efficiency = Availability x Speed x Quality. Availability = actual / planned time. Speed = actual / optimal speed. Quality = units passed first time / total units made. Example: process is down for 2 of 10 hours; 60/h made while capacity is 100/h under perfect conditions; first-pass yield is 95%. Efficiency: 80% x 60% x 95% = 46%.

(1) Work disrupted by breakdowns and shortages; barely anything goes right first time, poor efficiency (<20%)
(2) Work planned and organized, but still characterized by waiting and double handling, low efficiency (20-40%)
(3) Processes and resources well managed, formal actions taken on defects and delays, average efficiency (40-60%)
(4) Most work completed at optimal speed, right first time, without extra effort; consistent good efficiency (60-80%)
(5) Processes are reliable and predictable, and pacemaker process performs at world-class factory efficiency (>80%)

EFFICIENCY/F/Setups

How well is setup time defined and controlled? Consider the time from the last item of the previous order to the first good item of the next order. Single minute exchange of dies (SMED) is setup below 10 minutes, at single digit.

(1) Setup time limits not defined or setup time not regularly measured
(2) First serious efforts to reduce and standardize setup time; team learns rapid changeover and SMED techniques
(3) Standard setup times defined and occasionally measured, but not well managed
(4) Standard setup times continuously tracked and control chart or report posted
(5) Setup process perfected and strictly controlled; SMED is standard or approaching the physical limit within 20%

EFFICIENCY/F/Value

How much value is created in the factory? Value-add (VA) refers to activities that are required and willingly paid by the customer. VA = total task time / total lead-time. Factory example: 150 minutes assembly time / 10 days lead-time = 1%. Shop example: 5 minutes to change a tire while customer waits 1 day to pick up the car, VA = 5 minutes / 1 day = 0.3%.

(1) Value-add is 0.1% or below
(2) Value-add is 0.1-1%
(3) Value-add is 1-3%

(4) Value-add is 3-9%

(5) Value-add is 10% or more

Efficiency score = (sum of points) / 7 = ☐

INVENTORY

Inventory checklists assess the capability of the inventory management process and system.

INVENTORY/F/Amount

How much inventory is in the system between receiving dock and customer? How often does the inventory turn per year? Calculate days of sales in inventory (DSI) = (inventory value / cost of goods sold COGS) x 365. Simpler but less accurate: (stock value / annual sales) x 365. Turns = annual COGS / average inventory value.

(1) Over 90 days of sales or less than 4 turns per year

(2) 30-90 days of sales or 4-12 inventory turns per year

(3) 7-30 days of sales or 12-52 inventory turns per year

(4) 2-7 days of sales or 52-183 inventory turns per year

(5) 1-2 days of sales or over 183-365 inventory turns per year

INVENTORY/F/Control

How is process inventory controlled? WIP refers to work in process.

(1) WIP not tightly managed, just basic controls such as cycle-counting

(2) WIP recorded on tally sheet or spreadsheet, monitored at least monthly

(3) WIP controlled by system; status-report available anytime from system

(4) Critical, fast, and large WIP items are visually controlled, using lanes, bins, cards

(5) Visual management is standard, no computer or reports required to control WIP

INVENTORY/F/Flow

How many work-in-process (WIP) items are waiting for the next step? Disregard items currently being worked on or loaded into machines. Calculate: items in queue / items shipped per day. WIP starts when picked from stock.

(1) Work centers managed separately, items pile up between stations, no limits defined; over 1 week WIP in queue

(2) Work orders carefully planned, but inventory still builds up between stations; 2-5 days WIP in queue

(3) Inventory controlled by visual or electronic system; items in flow used to balance load, 1-2 days WIP in queue

(4) Min-max levels strictly enforced; WIP items used to synchronize processes and cleared daily, few hours in queue

(5) Virtually no WIP in queue due to continuous flow; process inventory only present in supermarkets and flow lanes

INVENTORY/F/Locations

How many stock-keeping units (SKU) are stored in controlled locations? How many can be picked at first attempt and single touch, without searching? "Controlled" refers to meeting 5 checkpoints: location, amount, sequence, supplier, and replenishment frequency are defined. Check for labels on bins, containers, shelves, and other storage spaces. Consider raw material, work in process, finished goods, supplies and maintenance parts.

(1) Inventory stored where space is available; hunting for parts is common, only people from the area can find things

(2) First locations marked but not systematic, requires searching in multiple spots; 10% inventory is controlled

(3) Locations organized in clusters, requires searching within cluster locations; 50% inventory is controlled

(4) Locations defined on item level, occasional double-touch when picking items; 90% inventory is controlled

(5) All items stored in defined areas, picked at first touch and zero searching; 100% inventory is controlled

INVENTORY/F/Obsolescence

How much inventory is slow or dead? Consider all items that are expired, obsolete, useless, or without demand over the past 12 months. Calculate: value of slow and dead inventory / total inventory value.

(1) 10% is slow or dead, or obsolescence rate significantly higher than industry average

(2) 3% inventory is slow or dead, or obsolescence rate several times higher than industry average

(3) 1% inventory is slow or dead, or obsolescence rate at industry average

(4) 0.3% inventory is slow or dead, or obsolescence rate several times below industry average

(5) 0.1% inventory is slow or dead, or obsolescence rate at the leading edge within the industry

INVENTORY/F/Replenishment

How many inventory items have reorder points and safety stock levels defined? Check labels and central system. Consider raw materials, process inventory, finished goods, consumables, and spare parts. Note that even just-in-time (JIT) and buy-to-order systems have safety stock levels set, albeit at very low or zero level.

(1) Inventory managed by people; when something is missing, people go and get it

(2) 10% have safety stock levels defined; shortages and stock-outs frequently cause disruptions

(3) 50% have reorder points defined; occasional shortages and stock-outs cause some delays

(4) 90% kept between min-max levels, using reorder lines, return-bins, Kanban-cards or electronic system

(5) 100% strictly maintained between min-max levels, using visual control or fail-safe electronic system

INVENTORY/F/Sequence

How many inventory items follow first-in first-out (FIFO) sequence of withdrawal? Look for gravity-feeders, pipelines, guardrails, barcodes; any system that ensures that oldest or first-to-expire item is used first.

(1) FIFO is unknown or not practiced; sequence of withdrawal not controlled

(2) FIFO is rule-based and not systematic; relies on people to maintain FIFO sequence

(3) FIFO is systemized but weak design or issues with discipline; 50% withdrawals follow FIFO sequence

(4) FIFO system is fail-safe and covers most locations; 90% withdrawals follow FIFO sequence

(5) FIFO system is fail-safe within lots, no bypass without manipulation; 100% withdrawals follow FIFO sequence

INVENTORY/F/Structure

How is inventory organized?

(1) Inventory not clearly defined or not well maintained; inventory reports are incomplete or cannot be trusted

(2) Inventory defined by status of completion; raw materials (RM), work in process (WIP), and finished goods (FG)

(3) Inventory defined by status and purpose; buffers and safety stocks calculated based on demand and supply risks

(4) Inventory defined by purpose and velocity; inventory report available by runner, repeater, stranger (ABC classes)

(5) Inventory defined by status, purpose, velocity, and minimum amount required to balance cycles and meet takt

Inventory score = (sum of points) / 8 = ☐

LAYOUT

Layout checklists assess the physical configuration and workstation design in the factory.

LAYOUT/F/Design

How well are workstations designed? Check for excess motion caused by a suboptimal layout. Consider moving, walking, bending, stretching, reaching, lifting, and activities outside the workstation, like picking parts from store.

(1) Poor layout, designed with little consideration of ergonomics and workflow; heavy lifting or physical strain

(2) Outdated layout but with well-established locations; moving-bending-stretching are necessary but not very tiring

(3) Basic layout meets current industrial standards; still requires extra movements at comfortable range of motion

(4) Well-planned layout, all common items within reach; max two activities outside station per operator per shift

(5) Ergonomic layout, items accessible on the spot at minimal motion; workers only leave work stations for breaks

LAYOUT/F/Distance

Where are items stored relative to the point of use? How long does it take to fetch parts and documents?

(1) Scattered around or stored away, requires internal transportation or searching; takes over 10 minutes to fetch

(2) Designated areas might exist but not fully clear or not properly established; 5 minutes to find and fetch items

(3) Locations clearly established but require some handling or transport over short distances; 2 minutes to fetch

(4) Most items stored in the area and close to the point of use; few steps of walking or 1 minute to fetch items

(5) Most items stored within reach, accessible on the spot within 10 seconds from pick location at minimal motion

LAYOUT/F/Optimization

How well is the factory layout optimized? Consider recent improvements, changes over the past 12 months.

(1) Unplanned layout, evolved over time with little consideration of operating efficiency and information needs

(2) Team made small changes to improve flow, rearranged equipment and installed tables, shelves, service stations

(3) Layout updated based on scientific traffic analysis; evidence of higher efficiency, but structural issues untouched

(4) Plant redesign completed and structural issues solved, work flows without inventory build-up between stations

(5) Processes designed for continuous flow; quickly reconfigurable to changing needs; most hardware on wheels

LAYOUT/F/Structure

How well is the plant structured?

(1) Plant without clear structure, territories not defined or not demarcated, items stored where space is available

(2) Layout split into several buildings and clusters; structured around moving batches between disjoint areas

(3) Good layout but not utilized well; most processes under one roof but still separated by walls, rooms, stores

(4) Open plant design allows visual control; each supervisor can overlook his area from a single observation point

(5) See-through plant design allows visual control end-to-end; all machine and material storage spaces marked

LAYOUT/F/Transparency

How long does it take to get a complete overview of the entire operation? Consider the time to get a snapshot of customer demand, availability of people and machines, daily targets, and status of planned and completed work.

(1) Poor transparency, many walls and clusters, requires several people 1 hour or more to collect status information

(2) Low transparency requires 20 minutes pulling reports from system and walking around to get full status update

(3) Moderate transparency; few walls between processes and effective reports allow status review in 10 minutes

(4) Good transparency overall and full transparency in production and warehouse, status overview in 5 minutes

(5) Full transparency end-to-end, glass offices and real-time status displays allow overview within seconds

LAYOUT/F/Walking

How many people are working on product versus walking around to fetch or move items? Take photo and count.

(1) People walk around everywhere; many material handlers, 40% or more direct labor people fetch or move things

(2) Ineffective walk pattern, 30% direct labor people fetch or move items or 1 feeder serves 3 operators

(3) Moderate walk pattern, 20% direct labor people fetch or move items or 1 feeder serves 5 operators

(4) Good walk pattern, 10% direct labor people fetch or move items or 1 feeder serves 10 operators

(5) Optimized walk pattern, 5% direct labor people fetch or move items or 1 feeder serves 20 operators

Layout score = (sum of points) / 6 = ☐

MAINTENANCE

Maintenance checklists assess uptime control and maintenance effectiveness.

MAINTENANCE/F/Availability

What is the availability of key equipment in use? Calculate: available time / scheduled operating time.

(1) Equipment frequently unavailable; down for 1 hour average per shift, 90% available when needed, class-one

(2) Equipment occasionally unavailable; 5 minutes downtime per shift, 99% available when needed, class-two

(3) Equipment in good condition; 30 seconds downtime per shift, 99.9% available when needed, class-three

(4) Equipment is reliable; 3 seconds downtime per shift or 1 hour per year, 99.99% availability, class-four

(5) Equipment is highly reliable; 0.3 seconds downtime per shift or 5 minutes per year, 99.999% availability, class-five

MAINTENANCE/F/Data

How is maintenance effectiveness measured? Which metrics are used?

(1) Downtime not tracked or data not readily available

(2) Few data on downtime and none on overall equipment efficiency (OEE)

(3) Consistent downtime records, OEE chart posted, details on accidents, breakdowns, contamination, defects (ABCD)

(4) OEE reported with robust ABCD-analysis; meantime between failures (MTBF) calculated for main failure modes

(5) OEE, MTBF, and mean time to repair (MTTR) recorded, OEE target within operating hours firmly set above 80%

MAINTENANCE/F/Operators

Which maintenance tasks are delegated to operators? Ask them. What do they say about their responsibilities?

(1) I work the best I can until the equipment stops; I am calling maintenance when I cannot fix the problem myself

(2) I clean to inspect; I am cleaning my equipment daily at least up to head height and remove all foreign matters

(3) I inspect to detect; because I keep my equipment spotless clean, I easily see issues, such as leaks or loose screws

(4) I detect to repair; I am inspecting my equipment daily according to checklists and I fix potential issues right away

(5) I repair to prevent; I perform root-cause analysis and lead solution teams to implement preventive measures

MAINTENANCE/F/Response

How do people respond to breakdowns? What is the process?

(1) Response expected but no formal process defined; often takes hours until someone attends equipment failures

(2) Breakdown tickets issued; maintenance personnel take charge and sign-off tickets after repairs are completed

(3) Downtime metric owned by maintenance team; response process defined for critical and common failure modes

(4) Response process defined for 50% fail-modes on Pareto chart; formal root cause analysis for all downtime events

(5) Zero downtime goal; process for 90% fail-modes on Pareto; unplanned stops converted into improvement tasks

MAINTENANCE/F/Responsibilities

Who is responsible for maintenance? Check if standards for autonomous maintenance (AM) are in place.

(1) Maintenance responsibilities not clearly assigned; maintenance focus on restoring operating conditions

(2) Maintenance technicians responsible for machines; eliminating sources of contamination and major breakdowns

(3) Operators improve availability; handle basic maintenance or 30% of AM-tasks, such as cleaning and lubrication

(4) Qualified operators perform at least 60% of all maintenance tasks per AM-standard, validated by a technician

(5) Certified operators do all regular maintenance or 90% of tasks per AM-standard; technicians perform repairs

MAINTENANCE/F/Speed

What is the average response time to major breakdowns? How long until a qualified person attends the problem?

(1) Response time is a day and more; too many breakdowns or insufficient resources make response process slow

(2) Response time is several hours; breakdowns often unnoticed or operators are waiting for help

(3) Response time is 1 hour average; breakdown alert and response with some delay

(4) Response time is 10 minutes average; repeatable process and clear accountability

(5) Response within 2 minutes for 90% of all events; response time tightly controlled

MAINTENANCE/F/Stoppages

How many equipment stoppages were not planned? Consider technical downtime over the past 12 months.

(1) Unreliable equipment or infrastructure cause 80% unplanned repairs and 20% planned maintenance

(2) Frequent equipment issues reduce capacity at full load, 40% unplanned repairs and 60% planned maintenance

(3) Maintenance is well planned but breakdowns still cause delays; 20% unplanned repairs and 80% maintenance

(4) Equipment runs efficiently, stoppages rarely impact production; 10% unplanned repairs and 90% maintenance

(5) Defects are rare; max 1 of 20 stoppages or 5% due to unplanned repairs and over 95% planned maintenance

MAINTENANCE/F/System

Is there a process and system to prevent breakdowns? TPM refers to total productive maintenance.

(1) Maintenance plans not formalized or not posted; poor or missing downtime records

(2) Maintenance plans for critical equipment posted or controlled by system; inconsistent downtime records

(3) Maintenance plans in system for all tools and equipment, most are accurate; consistent downtime records

(4) Maintenance system fully deployed; machines tagged, schedules posted, checklists updated, disciplined reporting

(5) Maintenance effectiveness is continuously improved; efficiency charts show positive trend over several months

Maintenance score = (sum of points) / 8 = ☐

QUALITY

Quality checklists assess the capability of factory processes to meet customer requirements.

QUALITY/E/Level

How well do key processes perform? How well do they meet expectations of internal and external customers?

(1) Quality is below expectations, customer requirements not well understood or not fully met; frequent complaints

(2) Quality actively managed; meets expectations most times, but defects and instabilities still cause disruptions

(3) Quality consistently meets expectations, problems limited to occasional glitches; no major quality issues pending

(4) Reliable and repeatable processes, few issues quickly solved, quality and customer satisfaction consistently high

(5) Competitive advantage and improving market share due to superior quality and reliability

QUALITY/E/Management

How well is process and project performance understood and managed? ANOVA refers to analysis of variance.

(1) Management is more concerned about output than process; process performance data not readily available

(2) Simple tools used to monitor conditions and identify problems, such as tally charts, checklists, Pareto analysis

(3) Process performance analysis (PPA) regularly used to identify common and special cause variations (ANOVA)

(4) Critical-to-quality (CTQ) factors well understood; only minor issues, short-term variability within control bands

(5) Strong process focus; process noise and special cause variations understood and controlled within physical limit

QUALITY/E/Maturity

How mature are core business processes? Use the process capability model to assess the top ten processes.

(1) Initial state; processes are chaotic, ad hoc, reactive, undocumented, unstable, require continuous fire fighting

(2) Repeatable; processes are documented and some parts are repeatable, but inconsistent results or low discipline

(3) Defined; processes confirmed as standards with evidence of continuous improvement, best practices established

(4) Managed; processes are quantitatively managed according to agreed metrics; process capability is established

(5) Optimizing; processes are managed with a focus on perfecting performance through improvement and innovation

QUALITY/F/Capability

What is the rolled throughput yield (RTY) across the entire factory process chain? Consider the yields of the top five processes, such as planning, assembling, inspection, testing, and packing. First pass yield (FPY) refers to perfect output at single touch without backflow or rework. Example: a five-step process with 90% FPY at each step results in 0.9 x 0.9 x 0.9 x 0.9 x 0.9 = 59% RTY, requiring 41% items to be touched multiple times, reworked or discarded. Note: if yield is not measured or modeled, select the first answer.

(1) Persistent quality issues; 32% rolled throughput yield, or yield information not readily available, 1-sigma quality

(2) High variability; 63% rolled throughput yield, 37% in-process issues cause rework and delays, 2-sigma quality

(3) Quality is controlled but unstable; 93% rolled throughput yield, 7% items touched multiple times, 3-sigma quality

(4) Quality is stable; 99.4% rolled throughput yield, 1 of 167 items must be touched multiple times; 4-sigma quality

(5) Quality is approaching perfection; 99.98% rolled throughput yield, only 1 of 5000 touched twice; 5-sigma quality

QUALITY/F/Control

How is quality controlled? Consider inbound, outbound, and in-process quality, as well as supplier qualification.

(1) Ineffective controls; quality data are unreliable or missing, or not all items checked before shipment

(2) Basic controls focus on inbound and outbound quality, sorting and correcting; improvements mainly informal

(3) Yield and in-process controls, samples checked against standard; quality alerts trigger formal corrective actions

(4) Metric-driven product quality; capability indexes (Cpk) monitored and control charts posted in all factory areas

(5) Correlation between internal quality and external customer satisfaction, error traps and mistake-proof interface

QUALITY/F/Organization

How is quality organized and embedded in the company structure?

(1) Quality assumed in order; quality standards not well defined, or quality ownership not formally assigned

(2) Quality controlled by inspectors; most quality personnel are busy with testing, sorting, and correcting issues

(3) Quality department approves standards and shipments; focus on monitoring, sampling, and reporting quality

(4) Quality delegated and actively controlled within each team; quality personnel focus on reducing overall variability

(5) Quality is part of corporate strategy and executive agenda; expert teams deployed to drive process excellence

QUALITY/F/System

How mature is the quality system? Check for quality control plans (QCP) and statistical process controls (SPC).

(1) People generally not aware of quality standards; use buzzwords about quality without deeper meaning

(2) Big and stagnant quality manual for factory processes, updated before ISO audit or after major problem

(3) Simple containment system based on QCP with recognition of SPC; basic control charts posted in factory

(4) Correction and prevention system based on statistical data; all alerts on charts trigger formal root-cause analysis

(5) Quality system orientation and fully deployed; robust quality standards for all core and support processes

Quality score = (sum of points) / 7 = ☐

STRUCTURE

Structure checklists assess 5S organization, the level of housekeeping and cleanliness in the factory.

STRUCTURE-5S/E/Audit

How often is the housekeeping level (5S) audited?

(1) No formal audit; people are expected to keep things organized

(2) No regular audit or just before events, such as customer visits

(3) Regular audit in most areas; scores reported at least monthly

(4) Weekly audit and scores posted for everyone to see, reports not hidden in desks or computers

(5) Daily cleaning and checking by each team, consistent tracking on run-chart, weekly scores posted for all areas

STRUCTURE-5S/E/General

How well is the physical workplace organized?

(1) Areas look messy, dirty, neglected, and chaotic; disorder goes along with safety issues, such as cables on floor

(2) Sorting completed; clutter and unnecessary items have been removed; only items required for work are kept

(3) Organized level; items stored in optimal locations, areas spotless clean, equipment in perfect working order

(4) Standardization completed; all spaces marked and items kept in assigned places and returned after each use

(5) Structure and discipline consistently high, organization is culture and housekeeping is part of daily activities

STRUCTURE-5S/E/Knowledge

How many employees truly understand 5S rules and process? How many are able to teach 5S and perform audits?

(1) 1 of 5 or 20% of people or fewer understand 5S; superficial knowledge

(2) 2 of 5 or 40% of people can perform 5S audits; weak knowledge

(3) 3 of 5 or 60% of people can perform 5S audits; developing knowledge

(4) 4 of 5 or 80% of people can perform 5S audits; good knowledge

(5) 5 of 5 or 100% of people can perform 5S audits; solid knowledge

STRUCTURE-5S/E/Process

How well is the housekeeping process defined and followed? Look for 5S procedures and 5S checklists.

(1) Process not defined or 5S procedures not posed in work areas

(2) Basic process for cleaning and organizing; basic checklists and housekeeping procedures for frequently used items

(3) 5S procedures and organizational rules well defined and posted in all active work areas, but not always followed

(4) 5S standards for all areas, but performance not yet automatic; some anomalies require managers to follow-up

(5) 5S process fully institutionalized and organization is culture; automatic performance, no supervision required

STRUCTURE-5S/F/Safety

How safe is the factory?

(1) Poor safety; accidents repeat, hazardous spots freely accessible, exit doors blocked, or moving parts unsecured

(2) Basic safety; compliant with local regulations, but cables unsecured on floor or items stored in high traffic areas

(3) Average level; machines with modern safety features, hot spots contained, protective equipment worn all times

(4) Good level; safety above industry average everywhere; equipment and behavior meet high safety standards

(5) Safety culture; everyone is conscious of potential risks, has improved safety standards in own area over past year

STRUCTURE-5S/F/Standards

How well are locations defined? Can everyone recognize abnormalities, such as excess or missing items?

(1) No identification of territory; unclear what is needed and what not; items stored where space is available

(2) High-traffic and safety-relevant areas are free of waste and demarcated, such as aisles and emergency exists

(3) Cluster locations defined on surface level, such as cabinets and drawers labeled outside but unstructured inside

(4) Locations defined and labeled on item level inside clusters; over 90% parts and tools kept in standard locations

(5) A place is defined for each item; abnormal conditions such as missing or excess items are visible to anyone

STRUCTURE-5S/F/System

How many factory areas are under housekeeping control? Calculate 5S-controlled space / total factory space.

(1) Organizational system not defined (0%); people are expected to keep factory, warehouse, and offices organized
(2) Organizational system deployed in few critical areas (25%); daily cleaning and organizing of work items and tools
(3) Organizational system deployed in key area (50%); only items used daily kept in stations, others moved to stores
(4) Organizational system deployed in factory and warehouse (75%), some areas excluded, such as offices or parking
(5) Organizational system fully deployed everywhere (100%), includes plant, stores, offices, basement, parking

STRUCTURE-5S/F/Tagging

How often is tagging used to determine usefulness of items? Tagging marks physical items with stickers to make their status visible. Red tags indicate items that are not useful, defective, questionable, or without demand.

(1) Tagging not known or not practiced
(2) Basic repair and removal tags, or occasional tagging without formal actions
(3) Tagging performed at least quarterly, red tag disposal areas defined and actively used
(4) Monthly tagging event or when 5S score below level 4.0 (80%); formal corrective actions defined
(5) Weekly tagging process or when 5S score below level 4.5 (90%); formal corrective actions defined

Structure score = (sum of points) / 8 = ☐

TECHNOLOGY

Technology checklists assess technical capabilities and the degree of automation in the factory.

TECHNOLOGY/E/Benchmarking

How advanced is site technology relative to that of competitors? Consider infrastructure, equipment and systems.

(1) Benchmarking data not available or capabilities of competitors not monitored

(2) Benchmarking report compiled or competitors with better capabilities identified

(3) Benchmarking regularly performed and capabilities kept up with industry average

(4) Benchmarking identifies technology one step above industry average; technology trends diligently monitored

(5) Benchmarking identifies technology among best in the industry; quick adaption of new methods and systems

TECHNOLOGY/E/Capabilities

How well is technical capability developed and utilized? Consider technology in business-critical areas.

(1) Core technology in place for many years; technical contractors used to perform maintenance and upgrades

(2) Core technology upgraded in recent years, but still not very modern; internal specialists keep systems running

(3) Technology considered up-to-date; internal resources dedicated to maintain and improve technical capabilities

(4) Modern technology in all key areas; advanced capabilities allow quick deployment of new methods and systems

(5) Cutting-edge technology designed in house; tech team highly valued by customers for breakthrough innovations

TECHNOLOGY/E/Computers

How are computers used? What systems and devices are in place to automate workflow and support people?

(1) Mainly manual system; managers and administrative people process papers and move documents

(2) Stand-alone computers assist people in basics tasks, such as email communication and accounting

(3) Computers integrated into networks; shared folders and databases simplify daily planning and reporting

(4) Computers used to control key processes; routings and cycle-time standards maintained in central system

(5) Electronic workflow from order to delivery, automatic monitoring, and status versus plan is displayed in real time

TECHNOLOGY/F/Monitoring

How much monitoring is required to keep the team and operation running? What is the degree of automation?

(1) Watching machines is normal and necessary; most processes are shut off or idling during breaks
(2) Monitoring considered waste; first attempts to increase efficiency through installation of new technology
(3) Key processes or 10% run autonomously, while 90% require dedicated people to keep them running
(4) Many processes or 50% run autonomously, do not require dedicated people to load, watch, and prevent failures
(5) Most processes or 90% run on one-cycle automation; operators just start processes without need for monitoring

Technology score = (sum of points) / 4 = ☐

TIME

Time checklists assess how effectively time is planned, used, and controlled.

TIME/E/Absenteeism

How many people are expected to work but absent? What was the absenteeism rate in the past 12 months?

(1) 10% or among highest in the industry or not measured
(2) 5% or above industry average
(3) 3% or at industry average
(4) 2% or half of industry average
(5) 1% or a quarter of industry average

TIME/E/Control

How well is rhythm established, time controlled, and discipline managed?

(1) Attendance is unstable; some critical areas unstaffed during core times; break times left to employee discretion
(2) Attendance recorded but not strictly managed; social breaks are common; work and meetings often start late
(3) Attendance controlled and schedules regularly updated; work starts promptly and meeting time well managed
(4) Everyone is conscientious about time; no early stops and next day targets are clear; long days are exceptions
(5) Time considered valuable resource by all; strictly managed and effectively used, high discipline is part of culture

TIME/E/Planning

How well are regularly performed activities planned, assigned, and managed?

(1) Difficult to predict how long steps take, periods of stress and breakdowns, people always seem in catch-up mode
(2) Schedules loosely defined, high variations between people and days, long days and overtime considered normal
(3) Solid plan defined but frequently updated, issues with discipline, some variations, occasional overtime expected
(4) Weekly plan with few variations and some rescheduling, work hours occasionally adjusted, extra hours are rare
(5) Daily plan with predictable and balanced workload, high execution discipline, minor variations barely noticeable

TIME/E/Schedule

How well are schedules defined and commitments met? Consider promises to internal and external customers.

(1) Schedules and deadlines not well defined; time management considered difficult; commitments regularly missed
(2) Schedules loosely defined; team makes special efforts to meet commitments, but still missing important dates
(3) Schedules frequently adjusted, while team is able to contain slippage within the customer tolerance range
(4) Schedules closely tracked and deviations quickly addressed; critical deadlines met with only minor variations

(5) Schedules with firm deadlines for all planned activities, timing based on standards, performance consistently top

TIME/E/Tracking

How well are processes and projects tracked against the target? Check manual boards and electronic system.

(1) Processes and projects not systematically tracked against targets, or tracking information missing or outdated
(2) Tracking started with focus on bottlenecks and critical path, but data not yet consistent or not readily available
(3) Key processes and projects consistently tracked against standards and schedules; data available on demand
(4) Processes and projects consistently tracked against schedule and cycle time standards; status updated daily
(5) Continuous tracking of total actual cycle time (TACT) or cycle time ratio (CTR), full transparency in real time

TIME/F/Pace

How is pace of production set and adjusted? Takt refers to the rate of customer demand, time per unit.

(1) Pace is assumed fixed by equipment capacity; using inventory buffers, overtime, rescheduling to meet demand
(2) Pace set by central system and standard flow; using inventory buffers and occasional overtime to meet demand
(3) Capacity resource planning based on forecasts; people assigned to plan, not easy to adjust when demand changes
(4) Actual demand pattern used for assigning resources; pace adjusted to match demand, pace is close to takt time
(5) Pace in sync with takt time through entire plant; resourced adjusted daily with effort on continuous balancing

Time score = (sum of points) / 6 = ☐

Office Questionnaire

The *Office questionnaire* contains the 8 keys that are specific to service and office operations; they are required in addition to the 12 common keys from the Enterprise questionnaire to complete all 20 keys of the Lean Office Audit.

EFFICIENCY

Efficiency checklists assess how well resources are used for the intended purpose.

EFFICIENCY/E/Control

How is efficiency measured and controlled?

(1) Indirect reporting, calculated from other metrics, such as revenue per person

(2) Labor time standards defined for main activities, first efficiency charts established

(3) Efficiency measured against standards in key areas; run charts show trend over several months

(4) Control charts established with firm efficiency goals for all departments and work centers

(5) Efficiency continuously tracked by system; deviations from targets trigger formal corrective actions

EFFICIENCY/E/Waste

What do most employees (80%) understand about value and waste? How well is waste identified and reduced?

(1) Little understanding of value and waste; most people are not able to identify the eight wastes (8W) in their area

(2) Concept of value and waste is broadly understood; most people have organized their area to reduce searching

(3) Waste analysis completed and projects started to tackle obvious wastes: wait, transport, error, double handling

(4) Broad waste reduction initiative ongoing, addressing inefficiencies around behavior, products, processes, systems

(5) Holistic waste reduction program, systematically addressing inefficiencies in strategy, structure, business model

EFFICIENCY/O/Flow

What degree of flow is realized in the office? How many items flow naturally from person to person without interruption? And how many need to be pushed or require special attention? A good indication is how managers spend their time. Do they work on developing new opportunities or are they busy handling exceptions?

(1) Processes not well defined; most work items or 80% need special attention to avoid delays and quality problems

(2) Processes defined but managed individually, many work items or 40% need special attention to keep moving

(3) Processes scheduled with attempts to synchronize, 20% items need intervention and 80% flow per standard

(4) Interfaces defined, processes synchronized but not yet integrated; 90% follows standard flow, 10% exceptions

(5) Processes fully integrated, teams organized around value streams; 95% follows standard flow, 5% exceptions

EFFICIENCY/O/Metric

How efficient is the office? Consider overall process efficiency (OPE) within business hours. How many requests are fulfilled in the fastest possible way and right first time? Efficiency = Availability x Speed x Quality. Availability = 100% - absenteeism% - sickness%. Speed = average speed / max speed under perfect conditions. Quality = items right first time / total items completed. Example: 90% employee-hours available for work; 2 items per day completed versus 3 per day peak performance; 20% needs to be touched twice while 80% is perfect at first time. Efficiency: 90% x 75% x 80% = 48%.

(1) Flow disrupted by variations, absenteeism, issues; barely anything goes right first time, poor efficiency (<20%)

(2) Work planned and organized, but still characterized by waiting and double handling, low efficiency (20-40%)

(3) Processes and resources well managed, formal actions taken on defects and delays, average efficiency (40-60%)

(4) Most work completed at optimal speed, right first time, without extra effort; consistent good efficiency (60-80%)

(5) Processes are reliable and predictable, and pacemaker process performs at world-class office efficiency (>80%)

EFFICIENCY/O/Simplification

What method is used to reduce complexity? Check if guidelines exist to drive simplicity.

(1) Processes allows high degree of freedom and many choices; no measures defined to limit or reduce complexity

(2) Rules with soft criteria, often bypassed to serve customers or win business without considering consequences

(3) Design-to-cost (DTC) criteria control customization of services, complexity of processes, proliferation of variants

(4) Formal process to systematically reduce complexity; tools like contradiction matrix (TRIZ) regularly applied

(5) Strict complexity control; standardization, modularization, delayering contributes to a competitive advantage

EFFICIENCY/O/Value

How much value is created in the office? Value-add (VA) refers to activities required by the customer. VA = hours willingly paid by the customer / total hours spent. Back office example: 5 minutes to enter an order while customer waits 1 day for a confirmation, VA = 5 minutes / 1 day = 0.3%. Administration example: 2 days to respond to an email with a decision that took 0.5 hour to make, VA = 0.5/48 = 1%. Engineering example: 12 hours development time under optimal conditions, while standard lead time is 30 calendar days under normal conditions including time for waiting, approvals and corrections, VA = 12 hours / 30 days = 1.7%.

(1) Value-add is 0.1% or below

(2) Value-add is 0.1-1%

(3) Value-add is 1-3%

(4) Value-add is 3-9%

(5) Value-add is 10% or more

Efficiency score = (sum of points) / 6 = ☐

INFORMATION

Information checklists assess the accessibility of information and quality of data.

INFORMATION/O/Accessibility

How accessible is essential information?

(1) Information controlled by few people and not openly shared, or tribal knowledge

(2) Information controlled by few managers and experts, shared with others upon request

(3) Information shared freely within departments, but little exchange between teams and functions

(4) Information stored in central location, but access not always easy due to restrictions or complex systems

(5) Information available on demand; teams configure their own systems, first communities evolve

INFORMATION/O/Asset

How strong is the enterprise information architecture? To what degree is information treated as an asset?

(1) Information not recognized as an asset and no clear stewardship of data

(2) Data management concepts are intuitively understood and practiced ad-hoc with focus on applications level

(3) Additional value drawn from data, organized along the lines of business and senior level, stewardship by experts

(4) Data treated as strategic asset to be exploited and reused, strong stewardship of data at senior and expert levels

(5) New products and services derived from data; all staff seen as knowledge workers, empowered to steward data

INFORMATION/O/Quality

How many files are accurate and current? How many are junk or outdated? Check cabinets, desks, computers.

(1) Undefined locations and unclear rules make it difficult to find useful information; lots of time wasted searching

(2) Cleanup started, people are responsible for their own information, basic rules, but weak process or low discipline

(3) Information standard defined and ownership assigned, but files still lost or misplaced, 50% correct and current

(4) Information regularly audited and updated, 75% correct and current, 25% need minor update, zero invalid files

(5) Information continuously updated and issues quickly resolved, no file older than 3 years, 100% meet file standard

INFORMATION/O/Reports

How effective is the existing reporting system? Consider key information required by managers and experts.

(1) Lack of solid data and weak reports; decisions based on guesses or data must be collected before making decision

(2) Data collected but only 25% of standard reports are truly helpful; data not always available at the time of decision

(3) Reports generally effective; 50% of decisions based on standard reports and no need for collecting additional data

(4) Most or 75% of decisions based on standard reports; format is regularly reviewed and continuously improved

(5) Virtually all decisions based on standard reports; well-defined requirements ensure that reports are effective

INFORMATION/O/Storage

Where is information stored?

(1) Stored in personal locations, causing major problems when a computer fails or someone leaves the company

(2) Both, central and personal storage locations used in parallel, multiple systems, often unclear where to search

(3) Central storage enforced, general policy but weak process, documents still duplicated and misplaced

(4) Personal storage fully replaced by central storage, maintenance process followed with few exceptions

(5) Highly reliable system and disciplined maintenance process keeps information organized and accessible

INFORMATION/O/Systems

What types of information systems are used to support people?

(1) Low awareness of information systems; workflow mainly based on paper

(2) Isolated computer terminals for basic administrative tasks, such as email and accounting

(3) Most computers connected into networks; shared folders and databases simplify daily tasks

(4) Office workflow monitored by computers; systems trigger activities and measure work against standard times

(5) Company-wide automation policy, electronic workflow is standard, status of work displayed in real time

Information score = (sum of points) / 6 = ☐

LAYOUT

Layout checklists assess the physical configuration and effectiveness of the office design.

LAYOUT/O/Communication

(1) How well does the office layout and infrastructure support people? How easy is it to communicate?

(2) Office islands; teams work primarily in isolation with little exchange between them, talking rarely or irregularly

(3) Offices disjointed, people need several minutes walking or setting up conference calls to exchange information

(4) Offices grouped together, infrastructure allows quick exchange; few steps to walk to an office or conference room

(5) Office layout allows quick exchange face-to-face or everyone can be reached via videophone with a single click

(6) Open layout and modern systems enable continuous communication; eye contact and real-time video streaming

LAYOUT/O/Distance

Where are items stored relative to the point of use? How long does it take to fetch documents and supplies?

(1) Scattered around or stored away, requires internal transportation or searching, over 10 minutes to fetch

(2) Designated areas might exist but not fully clear or not properly followed, 5 minutes to find and fetch items

(3) Locations clearly established but require some handling or transport over short distances, 2 minutes to fetch

(4) Most items stored in the area and close to the point of use; few steps of walking or 1 minute to fetch items

(5) Most items stored within reach, accessible on the spot within 10 seconds or 10 clicks at minimal motion

LAYOUT/O/Ergonomics

How well is the office designed? How often do people have to get off their chair and leave their place to fetch or move something? Disregard meetings and breaks; only consider items that are out of reach and require movements, such as going to a printer, archive, or other office.

(1) Layout with little consideration of workflow, more than 10 movements per person per day

(2) Layout outdated but locations well defined; requires 1 movement per hour or 10 per day

(3) Moderate layout, but still requires extra motion every other hour or 5 movements per day

(4) Good layout, critical items within reach; required gross movements do not exceed 2 per day

(5) Ergonomic layout with all required items within reach; people only leave their place for breaks

LAYOUT/O/Optimization

How well is the office layout designed and optimized? Consider recent improvements, changes over the past year.

(1) Layout unplanned or evolved over time with little consideration of workflow and information requirements

(2) Team made small changes to improve flow, rearranged equipment and installed tables, shelves, service stations

(3) Scientific analysis of traffic patterns, layout updated; evidence of higher efficiency, but structural issues remain

(4) Office redesigned and workstations changed from dedicated to flexible use, reconfigurable to changing needs

(5) Office cells allow continuous flow between people, spaces reconfigurable to changing needs; hardware on wheels

LAYOUT/O/Transparency

How long does it take to get a complete overview of the business? Consider the time it takes to get a snapshot (real-time) of customer demand, available resources, and status of planned and completed work.

(1) Poor transparency requires several people one hour or more to collect status information

(2) Low transparency requires 20 minutes pulling reports from system and walking around to check status

(3) Moderate transparency; few walls between processes and effective reports allow status review in 10 minutes

(4) Good transparency overall and full transparency in key areas; status review possible within a few minutes

(5) Full transparency end-to-end, glass offices and real-time status displays allows overview within seconds

Layout score = (sum of points) / 5 = ☐

QUALITY

Quality checklists assess the capability of office processes to meet customer requirements.

QUALITY/E/Level

How well do key processes perform? How well do they meet expectations of internal and external customers?

(1) Quality is below expectations, customer requirements not well understood or not fully met; frequent complaints

(2) Quality actively managed; meets expectations most times, but defects and instabilities still cause disruptions

(3) Quality consistently meets expectations, problems limited to occasional glitches; no major quality issues pending

(4) Reliable and repeatable processes, few issues quickly solved, quality and customer satisfaction consistently high

(5) Competitive advantage and improving market share due to superior quality and reliability

QUALITY/E/Management

How well is process and project performance understood and managed? ANOVA refers to analysis of variance.

(1) Management is more concerned about output than process; process performance data not readily available

(2) Simple tools used to monitor conditions and identify problems, such as tally charts, checklists, Pareto analysis

(3) Process performance analysis (PPA) regularly used to identify common and special cause variations (ANOVA)

(4) Critical-to-quality (CTQ) factors well understood; only minor issues, short-term variability within control bands

(5) Strong process focus; process noise and special cause variations understood and controlled within physical limit

QUALITY/E/Maturity

How mature are core business processes? Use the process capability model to assess the top ten processes.

(1) Initial state; processes are chaotic, ad hoc, reactive, undocumented, unstable, require continuous fire fighting

(2) Repeatable; processes are documented and some parts are repeatable, but inconsistent results or low discipline

(3) Defined; processes confirmed as standards with evidence of continuous improvement, best practices established

(4) Managed; processes are quantitatively managed according to agreed metrics; process capability is established

(5) Optimizing; processes are managed with a focus on perfecting performance through improvement and innovation

QUALITY/O/Capability

What is the rolled throughput yield (RTY) across the entire office or service process chain? Consider the yields of the top five processes, such as proposal, planning, design, validation, and delivery. First pass yield (FPY) refers to perfect output at single touch without backflow or rework. Example: 70% work meets requirements at first submission, budget overrun is 10%, and the average project takes 25% longer than scheduled = 0.7 x 1/1.1 x 1/1.25 = 0.7 x 0.9 x 0.8 = 50% RTY. Note: if office yield is not measured or modeled, select the first answer.

(1) Persistent quality issues; 32% rolled throughput yield, or yield information not readily available, 1-sigma quality

(2) High variability; 63% rolled throughput yield, 37% in-process issues cause rework and delays, 2-sigma quality

(3) Quality is controlled but unstable; 93% rolled throughput yield, 7% items touched multiple times, 3-sigma quality

(4) Quality is stable; 99.4% rolled throughput yield, 1 of 167 items must be touched multiple times; 4-sigma quality

(5) Quality is approaching perfection; 99.98% rolled throughput yield, only 1 of 5000 touched twice; 5-sigma quality

QUALITY/O/Control

How is quality controlled? Consider office processes such as quotation, planning, design, reporting, service, etc.

(1) Ineffective controls; quality data are poor or missing, not all work checked against standards before submission

(2) Basic controls; inbound and outbound quality measured, such as forecasting accuracy and service variability

(3) In-process controls; work checked against standard, quality data posted, alerts trigger formal root-cause analysis

(4) Metric-driven process quality; capability indexes (Cpk) monitored and control charts posted in all departments

(5) Correlation between internal quality and external customer satisfaction, error traps and mistake-proof interface

QUALITY/O/Organization

How is quality organized? Consider quality of office processes, such as service variability or forecasting accuracy.

(1) Quality assumed in order; quality standards not well defined or quality ownership not formally assigned

(2) Quality aspects in procedures and job descriptions; people are expected to evaluate their work against standards

(3) Quality controlled centrally to ensure compliance with standards; management focus on monitoring, reporting

(4) Quality delegated and actively controlled within each team; strong focus on reducing variability and failures

(5) Quality is part of corporate strategy and executive agenda; expert teams deployed to drive process excellence

QUALITY/O/System

How mature is the office quality system? Quality control plans (QCP) and statistical process control (SPC) used?

(1) People generally not aware of quality standards; use buzzwords about quality without deeper meaning

(2) Big and stagnant quality manual for office processes, updated before ISO audit or after major problem

(3) Simple containment system based on QCP with recognition of SPC; Pareto analysis and basic control charts posted

(4) Correction and prevention system based on statistical data; all alerts on charts trigger formal root-cause analysis

(5) Quality system orientation and fully deployed; robust quality standards for all core and support processes

Quality score = (sum of points) / 7 = ☐

ROLES

Roles checklists assess how well responsibilities are defined and assigned.

ROLES/O/Definition

How well are roles and responsibilities defined?

(1) Jobs not formally defined; managers expect people to know their jobs

(2) Simple job descriptions; definitions are rather soft due to generic specifications or broad requirements

(3) Detailed job descriptions, firmly defined and based on measurable standards, specific to each position

(4) Job standards linked to job metrics, skill matrix and training plan; skills regularly assessed against standards

(5) Capability index defined for each team and individual; actual level tracked against target and used for feedback

ROLES/O/Flexibility

How flexible are employees in their daily work? How is flexibility improved?

(1) Work practices defined around individuals; people work mainly by experience and prefer to stay in one area

(2) Org chart, job profiles, and process descriptions are current; willingness to learn, formal training program started

(3) Ongoing initiative to improve flexibility; skill targets firmly set; teams defined and posted their own training plans

(4) Cross-training completed; at least two people qualified per process; fluid and transparent handover process

(5) Everyone qualified on all processes within their area; possess solid knowledge of up and downstream processes

ROLES/O/Leveling

How is work assigned and leveled within departments? What happens if someone is absent, sick or on vacation?

(1) People firmly assigned to one area, work stops when someone is missing; high variance between people and days

(2) People can work several processes in same area, but assigned to one; delays are common when someone absent

(3) People work several processes in same area, reassigned to level load; most work continues when someone absent

(4) People move freely to balance load without being reassigned by supervisor, all work continues when one absent

(5) People qualified on all processes; teams responsible for manning and delivery; managers handle exceptions only

ROLES/O/Process

How are roles and responsibilities defined? What is the process?

(1) Roles evolved over time; responsibilities are more assumed than defined

(2) Roles defined top-down with little discussion; more imposed than aligned

(3) Roles discussed between manager and team; some issues around standards: too rigid or generic, or not binding

(4) Roles defined and aligned with few exceptions; all key responsibilities linked to goals and performance metrics

(5) Responsibility assignment matrix (RASCI) for all processes, updated at least once per year to meet changing needs

Roles score = (sum of points) / 4 = ☐

STRUCTURE

Structure checklists assess 5S organization, the level of data keeping and cleanliness in the office.

STRUCTURE-5S/E/Audit

How often is the housekeeping level (5S) audited?

(1) No formal audit; people are expected to keep things organized

(2) No regular audit or just before events, such as customer visits

(3) Regular audit in most areas; scores reported at least monthly

(4) Weekly audit and scores posted for everyone to see, reports not hidden in desks or computers

(5) Daily cleaning and checking by each team, consistent tracking on run-chart, weekly scores posted for all areas

STRUCTURE-5S/E/General

How well is the physical workplace organized?

(1) Areas look messy, dirty, neglected, and chaotic; disorder goes along with safety issues, such as cables on floor
(2) Sorting completed; clutter and unnecessary items have been removed; only items required for work are kept
(3) Organized level; items stored in optimal locations, areas spotless clean, equipment in perfect working order
(4) Standardization completed; all spaces marked and items kept in assigned places and returned after each use
(5) Structure and discipline consistently high, organization is culture and housekeeping is part of daily activities

STRUCTURE-5S/E/Knowledge

How many employees truly understand 5S rules and process? How many are able to teach 5S and perform audits?

(1) 1 of 5 or 20% of people or fewer understand 5S; superficial knowledge
(2) 2 of 5 or 40% of people can perform 5S audits; weak knowledge
(3) 3 of 5 or 60% of people can perform 5S audits; developing knowledge
(4) 4 of 5 or 80% of people can perform 5S audits; good knowledge
(5) 5 of 5 or 100% of people can perform 5S audits; solid knowledge

STRUCTURE-5S/E/Process

How well is the housekeeping process defined and followed? Look for 5S procedures and 5S checklists.

(1) Process not defined or 5S procedures not posed in work areas
(2) Basic process for cleaning and organizing; basic checklists and housekeeping procedures for frequently used items
(3) 5S procedures and organizational rules well defined and posted in all active work areas, but not always followed
(4) 5S standards for all areas, but performance not yet automatic; some anomalies require managers to follow-up
(5) 5S process fully institutionalized and organization is culture; automatic performance, no supervision required

STRUCTURE-5S/O/Computers

How well are computers organized? What is the level of digital 5S?

(1) Folders look messy and file names are inconsistent; disorder goes along with incorrect and incomplete data

(2) Sorting completed; outdated, incorrect and incomplete files removed; only essential information is kept

(3) Organized level; all files have been moved to optimal locations with clear structure, no questionable files left

(4) Standardization completed; dedicated folders for all information needs, file and folder names follows standards

(5) Structure and discipline consistently high; digital organization is culture and data keeping part of daily activities

STRUCTURE-5S/O/Information

How well is information organized? How long does it take to find and retrieve specific files from past 12 months?

(1) No clear structure; takes 10 minutes searching in multiple locations, some files cannot be found, seem missing

(2) System not well defined or not strictly followed; takes up to 5 minutes to locate files that have been misplaced

(3) System is loosely defined; takes up to 2 minutes searching in several folders and directories to find specific files

(4) System is well defined and kept; takes up to 1 minute to retrieve any file from past 12 months at first attempt

(5) System is organized at world-class level; takes 10 seconds or less to find and retrieve any file by any qualified user

STRUCTURE-5S/O/System

How many office areas are under housekeeping control? Calculate 5S-controlled space / total office space.

(1) Organizational system not defined (0%); people are expected to keep office items and computer files organized

(2) Organizational system deployed in few areas (25%); daily cleaning and organizing of documents and office items

(3) Organizational system deployed in key areas (50%); only items used daily kept nearby, others moved to storage

(4) Organizational system deployed in offices (75%), but not yet all archives, common areas, outside buildings

(5) Organizational system fully deployed everywhere (100%), includes all spaces inside and outside buildings

STRUCTURE-5S/O/Tagging

How often is tagging used to determine usefulness of information? Tagging marks computer files to make their status visible. Red tags indicate information that is not useful, files that are outdated, incomplete, or misleading.

(1) Digital tagging not known or not applied

(2) Some files tagged and folders for invalid and outdated information exists, but not consistently used

(3) Digital tagging performed at least quarterly, invalid and outdated files moved to red or exit folders

(4) Monthly digital tagging event or when digital 5S score below level 4.0 (80%); formal corrective actions defined

(5) Weekly digital tagging process or when digital 5S score below level 4.5 (90%); formal corrective actions defined

Structure score = (sum of points) / 8 = ☐

TECHNOLOGY

Technology checklists assess technical capabilities and the degree of automation in the office.

TECHNOLOGY/E/Benchmarking

How advanced is site technology relative to that of competitors? Consider infrastructure, equipment and systems.

(1) Benchmarking data not available or capabilities of competitors not monitored

(2) Benchmarking report compiled or competitors with better capabilities identified

(3) Benchmarking regularly performed and capabilities kept up with industry average

(4) Benchmarking identifies technology one step above industry average; technology trends diligently monitored

(5) Benchmarking identifies technology among best in the industry; quick adaption of new methods and systems

TECHNOLOGY/E/Capabilities

How well is technical capability developed and utilized? Consider technology in business-critical areas.

(1) Core technology in place for many years; technical contractors used to perform maintenance and upgrades

(2) Core technology upgraded in recent years, but still not very modern; internal specialists keep systems running

(3) Technology considered up-to-date; internal resources dedicated to maintain and improve technical capabilities

(4) Modern technology in all key areas; advanced capabilities allow quick deployment of new methods and systems

(5) Cutting-edge technology designed in house; tech team highly valued by customers for breakthrough innovations

TECHNOLOGY/E/Computers

How are computers used? What systems and devices are in place to automate workflow and support people?

(1) Mainly manual system; managers and administrative people process papers and move documents

(2) Stand-alone computers assist people in basics tasks, such as email communication and accounting

(3) Computers integrated into networks; shared folders and databases simplify daily planning and reporting

(4) Computers used to control key processes; routings and cycle-time standards maintained in central system

(5) Electronic workflow from order to delivery, automatic monitoring, and status versus plan is displayed in real time

TECHNOLOGY/O/Paper

How many admin papers does an average employee consume each day? Ignore legal, shipping, hygiene papers.

(1) 10 or more sheets consumed per head per day

(2) 5 sheets consumed per head per day

(3) 2 sheets consumed per head per day

(4) 1 sheet consumed per head per day

(5) Less than 1 sheet consumed per head per day

Technology score = (sum of points) / 4 = ☐

TIME

Time checklists assess how effectively time is planned, used, and controlled.

TIME/E/Absenteeism

How many people are expected to work but absent? What was the absenteeism rate in the past 12 months?

(1) 10% or among highest in the industry or not measured

(2) 5% or above industry average

(3) 3% or at industry average

(4) 2% or half of industry average

(5) 1% or a quarter of industry average

TIME/E/Control

How well is rhythm established, time controlled, and discipline managed?

(1) Attendance is unstable; some critical areas unstaffed during core times; break times left to employee discretion

(2) Attendance recorded but not strictly managed; social breaks are common; work and meetings often start late

(3) Attendance controlled and schedules regularly updated; work starts promptly and meeting time well managed

(4) Everyone is conscientious about time; no early stops and next day targets are clear; long days are exceptions

(5) Time considered valuable resource by all; strictly managed and effectively used, high discipline is part of culture

TIME/E/Planning

How well are regularly performed activities planned, assigned, and managed?

(1) Difficult to predict how long steps take, periods of stress and breakdowns, people always seem in catch-up mode

(2) Schedules loosely defined, high variations between people and days, long days and overtime considered normal

(3) Solid plan defined but frequently updated, issues with discipline, some variations, occasional overtime expected

(4) Weekly plan with few variations and some rescheduling, work hours occasionally adjusted, extra hours are rare

(5) Daily plan with predictable and balanced workload, high execution discipline, minor variations barely noticeable

TIME/E/Schedule

How well are schedules defined and commitments met? Consider promises to internal and external customers.

(1) Schedules and deadlines not well defined; time management considered difficult; commitments regularly missed

(2) Schedules loosely defined; team makes special efforts to meet commitments, but still missing important dates

(3) Schedules frequently adjusted, while team is able to contain slippage within the customer tolerance range

(4) Schedules closely tracked and deviations quickly addressed; critical deadlines met with only minor variations

(5) Schedules with firm deadlines for all planned activities, timing based on standards, performance consistently top

TIME/E/Tracking

How well are processes and projects tracked against the target? Check manual boards and electronic system.

(1) Processes and projects not systematically tracked against targets, or tracking information missing or outdated

(2) Tracking started with focus on bottlenecks and critical path, but data not yet consistent or not readily available

(3) Key processes and projects consistently tracked against standards and schedules; data available on demand

(4) Processes and projects consistently tracked against schedule and cycle time standards; status updated daily

(5) Continuous tracking of total actual cycle time (TACT) or cycle time ratio (CTR), full transparency in real time

TIME/O/Flow

How much time do knowledge workers spend in uninterrupted concentration? Consider managers and experts.

(1) 5% or few minutes each day; frequent demands make it nearly impossible to concentrate on important tasks

(2) 10% uninterrupted time allows completing basic tasks such as emails, but stop-and-go for more demanding tasks

(3) 20% uninterrupted time is sufficient for planning and monitoring; still difficult to keep up with demanding tasks

(4) 40% uninterrupted time allows completing demanding tasks, such as root-cause analysis and executing change

(5) 80% time spent in flow state, working on complex tasks such as strategy with a strong sense of accomplishment

TIME/O/Pace

How is work in the office paced and synchronized with demand?

(1) Office pace not defined or not controlled, many pending items in queue, stress and delays are common symptoms

(2) Drumbeat and deadlines set for core activities, but not closely followed; variations cause delays and idle times

(3) Resources planned based on forecasts and people assigned to plan; but not easy to adjust when demand changes

(4) Actual demand pattern used for assigning resources; office work hours adjusted monthly with effort on balancing

(5) Workload continuously balanced; flexible office work hours adjusted daily or weekly to match changing demand

Time score = (sum of points) / 7 = ☐

Lean Audit Templates

Scores from the questionnaires are best graphed using a radar chart. Five concentric circles represent the five maturity levels, crossed by twenty lines, one for every assessment key. The Lean Audit chart is generated with the following steps: (1) copy the blank audit charts from the book or download templates, (2) enter scores of individual keys in the table and calculate the average score, (3) transfer scores to the radar chart, one dot per key, (4) connect dots to draw the profile, and (5) add reference information, such as assessment scope and date. You can download the Lean Audit templates from www.leanmap.com/tools.

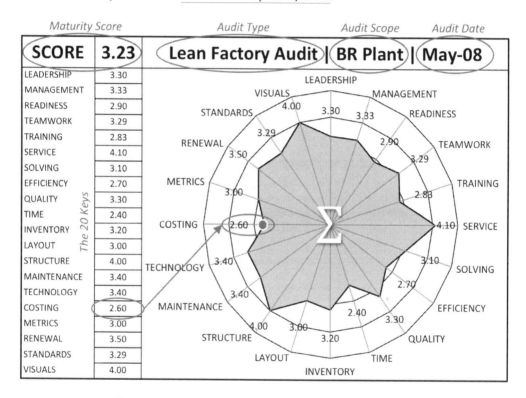

Figure 3.2 - Example of a completed Lean Factory Audit (LFA)

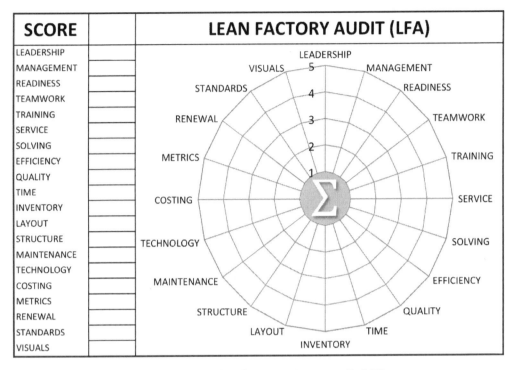

Figure 3.3 - Template for a Lean Factory Audit (LFA)

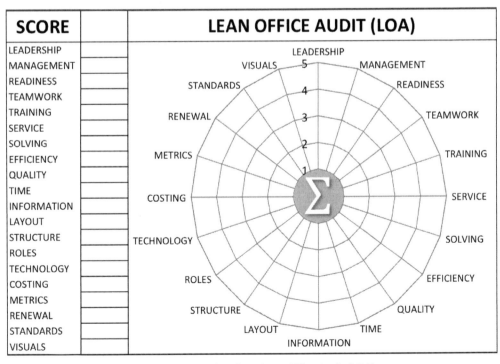

Figure 3.4 - Template for a Lean Office Audit (LOA)

4. RESULTS

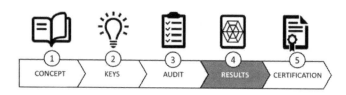

This chapter shows how to turn the Lean Audit scores into tangible benefits. It describes analysis methods and the results from our research—how manufacturers and service providers have applied the concepts described herein to their own operations, what challenges they faced, and the results they achieved.

Interpreting Results

After answering the diagnostics questions and completing the questionnaires, it is time to analyze and interpret the data, which is the most interesting and rewarding part of the Lean Audit. During the audit process—and this is common with all of our audits—you probably gained new insights and ideas. In particular, when working through the questionnaires, you likely identified multiple areas with significant, untapped value-creation opportunities. We will now organize the twenty measurements and create a unique profile that describes the audited organization in terms of maturity, balance, and agility. This is a seven-step process, from assessing maturity to setting an improvement goal.

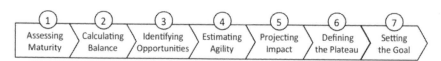

Figure 4.1 - Analysis and goal-setting process

Step-1: Assessing Maturity

The *maturity score* is derived directly from the checklist responses. It represents an evaluation of current practices against established benchmarks. The score is calculated by averaging the results from all twenty keys and serves as a base for further analysis. It assumes that all keys are equally important and similar in strength, so the remaining variability between individual keys is low and insignificant. Using the grand average is straightforward, and despite its simplicity, is fully sufficient to discover opportunities and initiate improvement actions, which is the main goal of the Lean Audit.

Understanding the Lean Audit Score

The Lean Audit score represents the *maturity level* of the organization it assesses. However, some people argue that no organization is perfectly balanced, so its varying strengths and weaknesses will have an impact on the overall result (maturity level). This is true. Each key impacts the Lean Audit score by 1/20 or 5%, but its effect on operating performance could be much higher. In practice, we have seen that weak spots (as identified by low scoring keys) are often the barriers that limit an organization from performing at the assessed level, so it can't reach its full potential as the average score suggests; we will therefore examine, in more detail, the impact of *balance* on maturity.

Average Score versus Effective Score

To get a good feel for the maturity score, imagine it as the *weight* of a chain. Since all chains consist of both strong and weak links, the weight of a chain is not proportional to its strength. In a similar fashion, the Lean Audit score does not perfectly reflect the true maturity level of the organization; due to vulnerabilities caused by low-scoring keys; they make up the "Achilles heel" of the operation. The difference between the Lean Audit score and the true maturity level, however, is only relevant once the organization has successfully addressed major deficiencies to bring its key processes under control.

In some instances, to account for imbalances in the profile, an adjustment is warranted. This score correction is determined by reducing the audit score by one standard deviation:

Effective Score = Average Score – 1 Standard Deviation

The adjustment is a valid approach because the Effective Score more accurately reflects the correlation between maturity level and operating performance than the unadjusted Lean Audit score. As discussed previously, this method is only recommended for mature organizations because the introduction of a correction factor opens the door for endless discussions about formulas and mathematics, and this takes away time and energy that should be spent on improvements. A good practice is to use the raw audit score to initiate improvements and then, over time—once major issues have been addressed and processes are stable—change the approach and use the Effective Score to drive improvements towards perfection. By then, with growing maturity, companies are naturally more balanced anyway, so the average score approaches the Effective Score, and the need for a correction factor is eliminated. To keep things simple and practical, we use the raw, unadjusted score for all our discussions in this book.

Baseline Maturity from our Research

The Lean Audit uses a broad scope, making it effective for most manufacturing and service companies, but given the widely varying target population, it is impossible to create a test sample that is representative for the entire population. As such, we relied on non-probability sampling for our research. Even with this limitation, the results provide tremendously useful insights into the process of assessing and improving any operation. Here's what we found.

The companies included in our research were all well-established—some even industry leaders—but all operating at different levels of maturity. The spectrum ranged from a basic sorting plant and an unstructured service provider on the lower end (Iron level) to a modern electronics assembly plant and a sophisticated customer support center on the upper end (Gold level). Despite differences in maturity, they all had a management team with high ambitions and all had embarked on an improvement program or were poised to start one. During the study, we worked closely with these clients to support their journey and monitor their progress over several years. The following histogram represents the distribution of subject company baseline scores at the outset of this study.

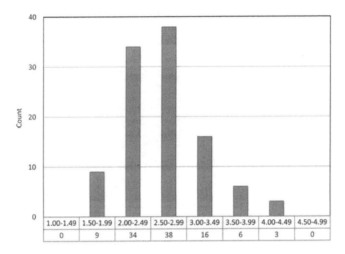

Figure 4.2 - Distribution of baseline maturity scores

The initial maturity scores of the 106 subject companies were broadly distributed between 1.7 and 4.2, with an average of 2.67 and a standard deviation of 0.52 around the mean.

Repeatability and Bias

An important characteristic of any diagnostics tool is the repeatability of the measurement process and the reproducibility of results when different assessors perform the audit. In our research we have found a notable difference between internal and external assessment scores. One reason for this is human nature: most of us have a tendency to see our own performance in a more positive light than others do, so scores from a self-assessment (internal) are usually higher than those from an assessment performed by an external auditor. Company employees are biased and this can lead to assessment errors.

Assessment errors can also be introduced by external auditors since judgments are based on limited observations during a limited time span, which is not a perfect reference point. To determine the significance of this factor, we measured gauge repeatability and reproducibility (GRR) and found that when the same auditor repeats the same audit multiple times within a few days, variations never exceed 0.5%. When you consider all the audits we have performed to date, the score difference between any pair of qualified auditors auditing the same company has typically been within 0.6% (1 sigma) and has never exceeded 1.3% (worst case). This indicates that the Lean Audit process is repeatable and robust.

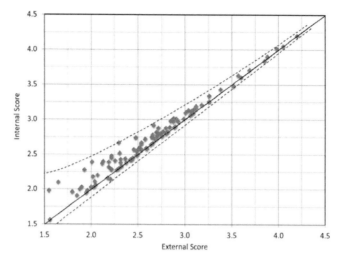

Figure 4.3 - Internal versus external scores

Figure 4.3 maps internal with external scores, comparing the results from the unguided self-assessments to those from the external auditors. Because there was no training and no expert-guidance provided, the difference between scores represents the worst case. Members of the internal audit team were free to select whatever rating they felt was appropriate. When in doubt, they usually selected the more favorable answer (human nature) to attain a higher score. The chart reflects this. The differences between internal and external scores (0.45 peak) are smaller at lower levels of maturity and diminish with increasing maturity levels. The delta between both scores averages 0.09 points at the lower half and 0.03 points at the upper half of the scale, with a variability of 5.5% (1 sigma) at the Bronze level (2.0 maturity) and 0.8% at the Gold level (4.0 maturity).

Is this significant?

We can answer this question by considering the most extreme difference of 0.45, which occurs at 1.87 maturity, causing an error of 24%. This makes the unguided self-assessment almost useless—in stark contrast to the guided self-assessments, with differences averaging 1.6% respectively and peak at 6% for a few outliers. Those extremes were caused by less-mature teams who felt they were the "best", despite the shocking low score they received from their first audit. The presence of an external auditor in such cases is invaluable since it provides the required support to keep the team honest and the results accurate.

But even for a well-guided audit, differences remain. How do we deal with them? By definition, an external expert is more experienced and less biased than a company employee, so the external score more closely reflects reality. But because an error is introduced by either, we found that the most accurate scores are produced by simply averaging both. This way, when all voices are considered in the assessment, people feel treated fairly and are more willing to accept the result. This "buy-in" is much more important than achieving a more precise score, since it leads to the dedication and commitment required to drive improvements post audit.

Reported score = (internal score + external score) / 2

Now, how accurate and precise is the Lean Audit? *Accuracy* has to do with repeatability and reproducibility, which we have already discussed (typically 0.6% and 1.3% peak). *Precision* refers to the difference between the audit score and the "true" level of maturity, which depends on the quality of research we have done in developing the checklists. Our assumption is that our research is solid enough to get at least 95% of the definitions correct (5 of 5 levels) with a potential shift by one level (1 of 5 levels) at 5% of the checklists. Under this assumption, the audit score could be off by 5% x 1/5 = 1%, making the Lean Audit 99% precise.

Step-2: Calculating Balance

Plotting scores of individual keys on a radar chart provides another useful piece of information: the balance between individual keys. An unbalanced profile looks jagged, whereas a perfectly balanced profile is circular. The following matrix shows profiles at two levels of maturity: 1.6 (low maturity, small area) and 3.6 (high maturity, large area), and at different degrees of balance: 80% (low balance, jagged outline) and 100% (high balance, circular outline). Balance is simply calculated by deducting the "unbalance" from 100%, which is the ratio of one standard deviation to the maturity score.

Balance = 1 – (Standard Deviation / Maturity Score)

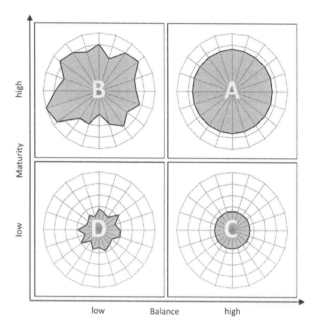

Figure 4.4 - Maturity-balance matrix

The four quadrants reveal four distinct profiles:

(A) High maturity in a balanced profile is the result of consistently making good decisions over many years backed by solid capability; it is a typical profile for strong performers within their respective industries.

(B) High maturity in an unbalanced profile indicates significant strengths in some areas (the spikes) that are offset by significant weaknesses in other areas; it is a typical profile for specialists, such as technology firms.

(C) Low maturity in a balanced profile indicates a careful optimization over many years at a low level of maturity; it is a typical profile for small businesses, domestic niche players, and government institutions.

(D) Low maturity in an unbalanced profile indicates instabilities and dysfunctions that may lead to business failure, unless the profile belongs to a specialist or monopoly (the only shop in town) that is not under pressure do do better.

Compiling results in this fashion begs several questions: *How much balance is actually needed? What is healthy and what not?*

Our research indicates a typical balance of 86% with 5% variation (1 sigma) around the mean. Less mature organizations, especially those scoring below two (Iron level), tend to have less balanced profiles than those operating at a higher maturity (Silver level and above). We found that variability between keys is not an issue when the standard deviation is below 10%, at a single digit percentage relative to the maturity scores. Variability becomes an issue when the standard deviation is in the double-digit range. In the previous chart, profiles A and C are perfectly balanced (100%), while profiles B and D are strongly unbalanced (80%), with a standard deviation of 20%. Here is a three-level breakdown on the possible variations, from healthy to dysfunctional:

- 0%...9% indicates a healthy balance
- 10%...19% is moderately unbalanced
- 20% and greater indicates dysfunctions

How to deal with Imbalances?

Imbalances are not a problem per se as long as weaknesses do not affect areas of competitive importance. A premium provider for example cannot afford to be weak in *Quality* and *Service*; the same is true for an engineering firm, which must be strong in *Information* and *Technology*.

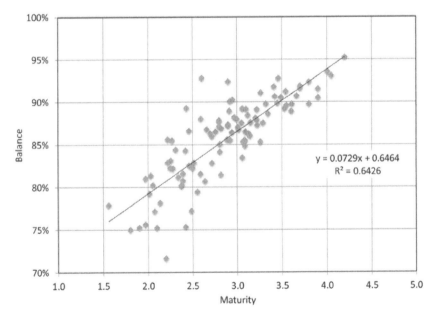

Figure 4.5 - Balance as a function of maturity

The good news is that balance tends to improve as maturity increases; we found a moderate but noteworthy correlation of 64% between these dimensions. Extending the line in the chart intercepts nicely with the point of 100% balance at level 5 maturity, which underscores our hypothesis that companies get naturally more balanced as they progress on their journey to perfection.

Step-3: Identifying Opportunities

So far, we have discussed the higher-level features of the Lean Audit, evaluating *maturity* (small versus large area) and *balance* (circular versus jagged outlines). We will now go deeper to read the "fingerprint" of the organization assessed by the Lean Audit. By identifying strong and weak keys and considering their position and relationships, we can better understand how the organization is configured and run, its state of operational health, and its fitness to compete. Let's consider two profiles and see what we can read from the charts:

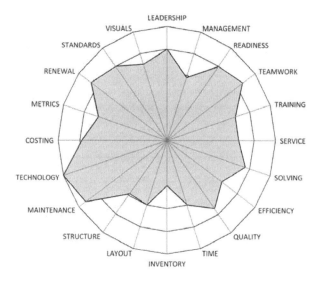

Figure 4.6 - "Fingerprint" of a manufacturer

Figure 4.6 shows the profile of a factory that is using advanced *Technology* in an older plant with a rather outdated *Layout*, limiting overall *Efficiency*. The team is taking good care of its assets, as indicated by a high score in *Maintenance*; the operation is likely run by an engineer or technical-minded team with a long-term perspective since the *Leadership* and *Renewal* dimensions are also strong. The low score from *Inventory* is a sign that many items are kept in stock to meet deliveries at just an average level of *Service*. This indicates a weakness in the inventory management process or system. The high score in *Solving* and *Teamwork*, in combination with a weaker score in *Management*, are signs of a reactive approach to meeting requirements, which is common when in-line process controls are missing so that issues appear at the end of the line. The score in *Readiness* indicates the team has recognized the shortcomings of their current model and is up for a change.

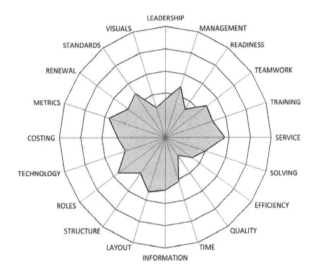

Figure 4.7 - "Fingerprint" of a service provider

Figure 4.7 shows the unbalanced profile of an office operation with relative strengths in assigning *Roles* and responsibilities. This might be a structured and possibly hierarchical and conservative organization, as the low score in *Readiness* and *Renewal* suggests. The above-average level of *Service* seems to be achieved through a combination of robust *Training* and *Teamwork*, an effective *Layout*, and the focus on performance management (as indicated in the *Metrics* and *Management* keys). Operating *Efficiency* is low despite available *Information* and *Standards*, making those keys a target for immediate improvement. Visual tools should be added to make status transparent and help people in the daily management process. The lower Leadership score might be caused by an aging business model as the overall profile suggests; it is an area that must be addressed to succeed in the long run.

It is important to remember that reading a Lean Audit profile—as reflected by the radar chart—alone is never enough to make definitive conclusions. The profile merely provides hints about underlying issues; the initial findings must always be substantiated by focused investigations and "deep dives". The diagnostics are more precise when they include information from multiple sources: (a) how key indicators are trending, (b) subjective observations and objective scores from the audit, and (c) the insights gained from the deeps dives. The Lean Audit functions like a fitness test, providing an assessment of the current state, which in turn allows for the formulation of specific plans that increase maturity.

Step-4: Estimating Agility

Once the maturity score is published, the next question is by how much the score can be improved. The expected gain in maturity is strongly correlated to the team's *agility*. In this section, and the following one, we make reference to the results obtained from a two-year study of a global manufacturer with 12 sites in nine countries.

Our experience from performing the audit indicates that under optimal conditions, a company can gain in maturity by +0.5 point per year before the curve flattens out and approaches a plateau. We consider this number a benchmark and the optimal rate for world-class companies. This gain is dictated mostly by existing limitations in configuration, capability, capital, mindset, and operating environment. For most companies, this rate is not easily attainable and exceeds what can be gained in the 12 months immediately following the Lean Audit. We use a linear approximation to estimate the improvement trajectory based on the agility score of the audit team. The agility checklist encapsulates our experience over many years into a simple checklist.

Looking Beyond the Data

During the Lean Audit, we take detailed notes to record what we hear and see. Our results indicate that several patterns repeat over and over again across many companies and industries. Our notes not only include details about how the hardware is configured and how processes and systems perform, but they also outline how people *respond* to the self-assessment questions. These responses typically produce many vital cues about the future performance of the operation. For example, weak or less mature teams often place an excessive amount of emphasis on scoring high. They inflate the numbers, which in turn induces a noticeable amount of stress when they are prompted to justify each answer to the moderator and fellow team members. In stark contrast, mature improvement teams stay calm and focused during the self-assessment, selecting the accurate answer again and again after a short alignment discussion. This is the case no matter how high or low the maturity score of the organization might be. Mature teams are less interested in the absolute score and instead focus their attention on gaining a deeper understanding to translate insights into opportunities—and ultimately those opportunities into realized benefits.

Our Lean Audit database indicates that certain traits separate the good teams from the average performers. To better reflect the underlying reality, during each audit we assign ten agility factors. This allows us to estimate the improvement rate during the 12 months immediately following the audit. A team is considered fully agile when all items on the below checklist are answered with a "yes":

- Do team members quickly align on scores after short discussions?
- Do they think critically and challenge each other's views?
- Do they possess solid knowledge about their area of control?
- Do they clearly understand up and downstream processes?
- Do they enjoy the self-audit and the insights gained from it?
- Do people feel they are in control of their own destiny?
- Do they look back to a track record of delivering strong results?
- Do they apply their knowledge by developing best practices?
- Do they make educated decisions based on facts rather than opinions?
- Do they drive systematic, continuous improvement beyond spot fixes?

The greater the number of agility points (answers in the affirmative), the closer the expected improvement rate is to the world-class benchmark of +0.5 points per year. Every agility point adds 0.05 to the total, and fractions are possible. For example, when a team meets 8 agility points, the expected improvement is 8 x 0.05 = 0.4 points per year, or 0.4/0.5 = 80% of the world-class rate. With a baseline audit score of 2.8, the operation is expected to improve +0.4 points to 3.2 in maturity within the next 12 months.

The following graph shows the results from the two-year study of a global manufacturer with 12 sites in nine countries. Even though the plants belong to the same company, the demographics vary drastically. When the Lean Audit was performed, the oldest plant had been in operation for over a century, while the newest had been running for just two years. Despite differences in setup, capability, and age, the improvement rate was nearly linear for all sites within the assessed population, fitting a straight line to 96% (R-square), at a low of 79.1 and a high of 99.9, and a standard deviation of 5.2. The average gain of the twelve plants was 0.301 per year or 60% of the world-class rate at a standard deviation of 0.092. This fit between projected and achieved improvement confirmed the validity of the underlying maturity model in the medium term, before reaching the plateau.

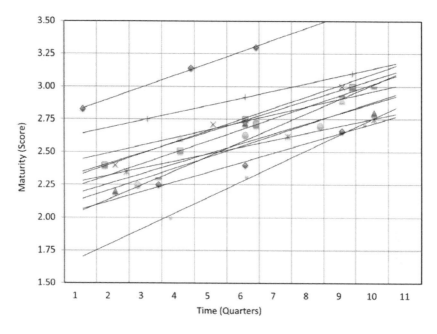

Figure 4.8 - Maturity gain of pilot group

You might wonder how accurate our predictions were on this small pilot group. The following graph shows the expected improvement rate (as determined by the agility score, where 10 points equals 100%) versus the realized or actual improvement rate, where a world-class gain of +0.5 points per year equals 100%. Ideally the actual performance would follow the line on the diagonal.

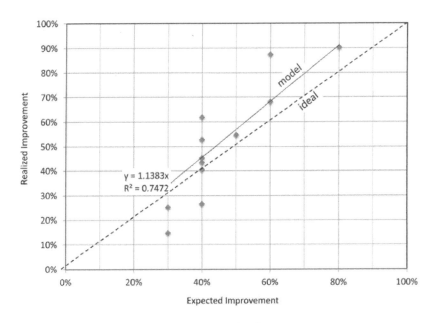

Figure 4.9 - Expected versus realized improvement rate

The agility model certainly helps to estimate the improvement post audit, but it must be used with caution. The model at this point is simply too simplistic and there isn't much data available to fully prove its validity. Nevertheless, we are publishing it here to encourage auditors to make predictions and measure against it. Feedback from auditors like you will help us refine the model so we can publish an updated version of the agility checklist in the near future. Please share your experience to keep this research going by sending an email to: audit@leanmap.com

Step-5: Projecting Impact

At this point, you might be thinking: *"Maturity is interesting but what can it do for me?"* So far we have discussed the maximum advancement rate of +0.5 points per year and methods to forecast the actual improvement rate. We are now able to estimate the impact on the bottom line. Translating maturity into money is "where the rubber meets the road". The process is not straightforward, as there is no single formula that fits all configurations and business models. There is however a notable relationship between maturity level and operating performance, measured in quality, delivery, and cost.

To project the bottom line impact, we use productivity as our key result variable since any improvement—in any dimension—has a positive impact on productivity. The following graph of the 12 sites shows productivity gain (reduction of conversion cost per output unit) versus advancements in maturity. Results are organized into four clusters, A, B, C and D, and indicate that the 12 companies improved productivity on average by 25.3% at a standard deviation of 9.5%; the highest gain was 38.6% and lowest 8.4%, normalized to one year.

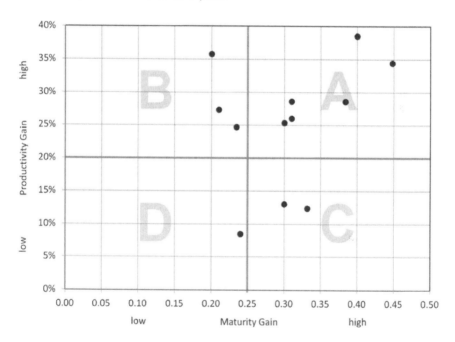

Figure 4.10 - Productivity-maturity matrix

Figure 4.10 indicates the following:

Group-A: The upper-right quadrant contains six sites, or half of the sample. These showed the highest gains in both operating margin and maturity. The common denominator of this group was a strong top-down commitment and an open-minded management team, willing to challenge conventions and try new things. Note that the teams in group A were not the most experienced but they were the most committed, which is the reason they outperformed their peers.

Group-B: The upper-left quadrant contains three sites that benefited from a solid productivity gain despite a lackluster change in maturity: one new plant (Greenfield) was in ramp-up mode and two legacy sites (Brownfields) were going through a structured cost reduction program. Despite very different operating conditions, results were similar as the management teams focused on the same things: reducing yield losses and balancing resources to increase volume in the Greenfield plant and reducing overtime in the two Brownfield operations, hence they attained a productivity gain similar to group-A.

Group-C and D: The lower half of the chart contains one quarter of the population, three sites that moved only a little in productivity and maturity. The difference between these and those in groups A and B was in the perspective of their management teams, which generally took a long-term approach to strengthening skills and capabilities first before driving productivity. The three companies were all located in a favorable growth environment in Asia, so they could afford this different focus. They made lower cost (through higher productivity) a desirable side effect but not a target of their improvement program; they focused on building capacity instead.

Of the 12 sites, all but one improved productivity at double-digit rates, up to 39% rolling monthly average and 65% weekly peak. This was a great result at the process level, but senior management was more interested in the bottom line impact at the site level, measured in *cost per output unit*. The financial analysis showed that operational improvements netted a 1.3% to 5.6% reduction in cost base (3.9 average at 1.4 standard deviation), even after offsetting an unfavorable change in product mix and a smaller average batch size. The average gross gain was estimated to be roughly double the net, or close to 8% before adjusting for labor cost increases, higher energy prices, and market-driven effects.

These numbers might seem small, but let's put them into perspective. To simplify the math, we apply those gains to an imaginary company that sells $100 million worth of goods and services, making an operating margin of $15 million or 15% of sales. The 3.9-point reduction in cost base increases operating margin from $15.0 to $18.9 million, which is equivalent to a benefit of 26% in incremental sales or $126 million in revenue.

Let's go now from our imaginary to the real companies that used the Lean Audit to improve their competitive position; here are the results they have proudly presented on their annual performance report:

- 50% productivity gain from lean-transforming liquid compounding in Brazil
- 43% shorter lead time increased service level from 92 to 97% in Ohio, USA
- 30% labor efficiency gain from converting assembly lines to cells in Mexico
- 28% shorter lead time from connecting lines to achieve flow in Japan
- 16% throughput gain from rapid changeover and de-bottlenecking in Holland
- 15% productivity gain from standardizing customer service in Switzerland
- 79% lower water consumption from 15.9M to 3.4M gallons in New Jersey, USA

Since the results and conditions vary so widely, how can we accurately project impact?

The environment is dynamic: every site is configured differently and runs differently; market conditions are shifting; new competitors are emerging; teams and capabilities are changing; strategic updates are being implemented; disruptive technology is at work. There is not a single formula that fits all. Behind every point on the chart, there is a story. Therefore it makes most sense to look at stratified (organized) data, one chart per organization with one data-point per site, instead of mixing all the data of many companies on a single chart.

There is no single formula to determine the impact, but our research suggests that a year-on-year productivity gain of at least 6% is feasible under any focused improvement effort. For each of the sites in the Lean Audit research, this assumption held true, so we can summarize that

- at a world-class improvement rate,
- maturity grows +0.5 points per year,
- improving productivity >6% per year,
- until the maturity plateau is reached.

Step-6: Defining the Plateau

Until now we have assumed the possibility of linear growth and never-ending improvement, which would lead to a maturity level exceeding the five-point rating scale in a matter of years. This is not realistic of course. What we can expect though is a slow start caused by the initial inertia to overcome (i.e., wherever there is change, there is resistance to it), followed by strong performance gains as more and more people get convinced and join the improvement effort, which levels off later on as the organization approaches its plateau. Of all the companies monitored over more than three years, about half of them moved up in maturity at a rate consistent with world-class. About half of the "fast movers" or one quarter of the audited population reached their plateau after a period of strong linear improvement, leveling off between 3.2 and 3.7 points on the maturity scale. Something systemic seemed to cause this "glass ceiling", a factor that could not be explained with the available data. Auditing those companies more granularly on the departmental level revealed not a single deficiency but an entire weak link in the value chain that prevented the company from going further.

For example, a consumer electronics manufacturer got in trouble not because they had poor products, but because they didn't know their true cost when participating in a reverse auction, where the lowest bidder gets the order. They made a huge loss when accepting a price below total cost, basing their decision just on the bill of materials (BOM) without understanding their non-performance costs (NPC), as explained in the "Quality" key.

We learned that we had to include all functions in the diagnostics—in this case Finance—to get a better understanding of the obvious and hidden constraints. A second thing we learned: the companies with the most experienced people or the best equipment did not achieve the highest marks; rather, it were those companies operating under permanent pressure to perform that showed the highest rate of improvement. The pressure kept them motivated to push boundaries all the time, and when approaching a plateau through continuous improvement (kaizen), they looked at new ways to radically change the way they operated (kaikaku). You can read more about it in the "Renewal" key section in chapter 2. The essence of what we learned was that stability caused complacency and a low ceiling, whereas constant pressure and the burning desire to do better lifted the ceiling higher and higher.

We discovered that companies mature following an S-curve, slowly in the early stages of implementation, and then more rapidly, and they eventually resume the slower rate again. The following graph illustrates a scenario we have encountered in several companies we worked with: they reached their maximum improvement rate within 1-1.5 years after starting their journey, followed by 3-5 years of linear improvement, and finally leveling off at their plateau after another 3-5 years. Those companies willing to adapt their operating model and structure to meet changing conditions were able to use their current plateau as a launch pad to start another renewal cycle, pushing their ceiling even higher. An example of such radical change takes place when moving from a manual—paper-based—to an electronic workflow.

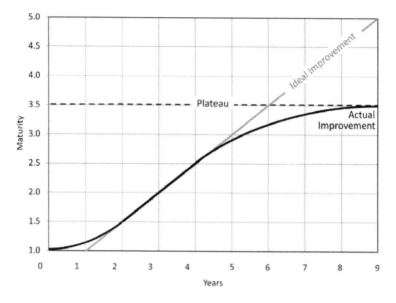

Figure 4.11 - S-curve improvement with plateau

Related to the plateau, there is another common scenario that we have encountered many times during our audits: a disharmony exists between the *commercial* side of the business (the office – LOA) and the *manufacturing* side (factory – LFA). The effects of this separation, caused by organizing the value chain into departmental silos, then appear in the Lean Audit results. A sales-driven company often views their manufacturing plant as a "capital-hungry beast", i.e., more as a necessary evil than a source of competitive advantage. On the other hand, people from an engineering-driven company often look down at the commercial function as being full of "day dreamers" who are unable to sell what exists, while they are viewed as being in "deep love" with their own technology and "missing the boat" on what customers really want. In reality, both business components (factory and office) affect each other dynamically, and in ways that are not readily apparent. Due to the nature of manufacturing, most issues surface at the end of the value-chain, and many of these are introduced upstream. The marketing side will launch a new product, often prematurely to short-cut lead times from an overambitious schedule, while engineers are tempted to reschedule due dates as "things are not perfect yet". At the end, the product is pushed to market with instabilities, and the factory has to rectify them during normal production runs. It's a balancing act and an optimum can only be attained when optimizing cross-silo, taking into consideration all individual parts of the value chain.

In one such scenario, the factory scored 4.2 in maturity, while the entire company was assessed at 3.4. Taking a simplistic view and imagining the value chain to consist of only two links, the maturity level of the office must have therefore been: 3.4 − (4.2−3.4) = 2.6. Even though, or because of the fact that, the commercial side of the business was the driving force, its maturity score was more than one and a half levels behind the manufacturing side. For the same company, we compared different keys to better understand the gap between factory and office maturity. For one, we looked at the degree of standardization in place, the policies and procedures that are meant to ensure reliable processes and predictable outcomes. In the office functions, the conditions that led to accepting or rejecting an order were either undefined or the decision was made at the discretion of a sales representative, which prompted a low score in "Standards". In the factory functions, for each single production defect, there was a formal root-cause analysis protocol to follow, which prompted a high score in "Standards", while, ironically, a lost bid or a failed product launch that cost the company millions triggered nothing more than a short notification email from the commercial or engineering team.

From our audits we learned that for any company to improve beyond its saturation point, the entire value chain must be addressed. Thus, to overcome the plateau, all functions and interfaces must be included in the diagnostics to optimize the operating model overall.

Step-7: Setting the Goal

With the information collected from the audit and the agility assessment, we are able to calculate the trajectory of maturity level, the number of years and the required rate to attain the targeted maturity level. When creating such a model we must keep the targeted improvement rate within the sustainable limit of +0.5 points per year, all the while remaining mindful of the conditions that constrain the improvement to a level that makes up the plateau. The critical relationships are embodied in the following equations:

- Required Improvement Rate = (Target − Baseline) / Years
- Projected Maturity = Baseline + (0.5 x Years x Agility)
- Required Years = (Target − Baseline) / (0.5 x Agility)

These simple equations can be used to develop a company-specific improvement model, to set goals, and even to estimate the monetary benefit that can be attained from the improvement program—considering the examples from Step-5 "Projecting Impact".

Lean Audit Journey

You might wonder how your results compare to those of other companies. But before we can judge any data and use them for comparison, we must have a good understanding of the "mechanics" of the Lean Audit system, the sampled population, the data collection and analysis process, as well as the conditions and limitations of our research. Let's start by reviewing how the audit method and system evolved over the years.

The Lean Audit journey began in 2006 with a simple Excel spreadsheet, which was the original checklist that gave rise to those presented in chapter 3 of this book (see the questionnaires). It was used to monitor the progress of efficiency improvements using a lean approach. The first data collected suggested a noteworthy correlation between audit score and operating performance: plants that performed well on the audit also scored higher in the composite index, comprised of quality, delivery, and cost. This insight led to the hypothesis that operating performance can be predicted to a certain degree by measuring observable characteristics, which are scored by the Lean Audit. To collect more data, the Lean Factory Audit was made available online and was thus accessible to a broad audience. This open approach generated plenty of new data. The results tabulated from over 1000 records were interesting but not conclusive due to (1) the narrow scope of the audit, which focused solely on factories, (2) variations in assessment capability due to the limited experience of junior auditors, and (3) auditor bias, introduced by internal auditors (company employees) performing the assessment, which skewed the results. These three factors called for a more controlled and better organized audit format.

Narrowing down the Data

We sorted the available data, separating the useful from the questionable. Two-thirds of the records came from auditors who we didn't even know, and therefore we couldn't judge their capability and expertise. We removed these data and focused on the remaining 324 records that came from 62 certified auditors. These audits covered a broad range of companies, manufacturers and service firms, large and small, including electronics assembly, food ingredients, consumer goods, automotive, research and development, executive search, hotels, a call center, a hospital, metal forming, logistics, accounting services, waste sorting, business administration and a central service center.

The smallest organization had 15 employees and the largest over 6000 in a single location, with the median size site being 283. The data were interesting, but the sampled population was simply too diverse for a meaningful analysis. To create more homogeneous groups, we allocated audit records to strata by company, scope (factory, office) and configuration (project, job, batch, repetitive, continuous), and looked at each cluster separately. For our study we selected only those audit records from companies that (a) were operating at least five sites, (b) employed at least fifty people per site, (c) were audited at least twice by a qualified, external auditor within (d) a time span of at least two years between the first and last assessment, and also (e) were reasonably stable during the observation period, i.e. not going through a merger-integration, management change, or restructuring phase. As a result, we had 106 solid data sets available that stem from 5 global companies, operating 45 sites in 23 countries and from 18 regionally operating companies located in 5 countries. Most plants were assessed on both the manufacturing (factory audit) and the administration side (office audit). The data collected created the groundwork for the Lean Audit, and ultimately this book.

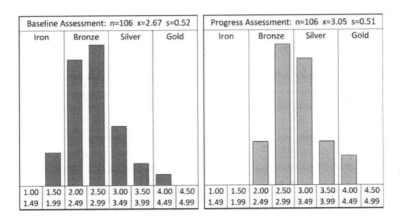

Figure 4.12 - Histograms of baseline and progress audits

The initial assessment set the marker at 2.67 points on the five-point maturity scale. Improvements "moved the needle" to 3.05 within the first year, representing a 0.38-point gain over the baseline or 76% of the +0.5 points per year world-class improvement rate.

Evolutionary Triangle

For each of the 45 sites, we created a "company passport" that captured key information such as cost of goods and services sold, number of employees, organizational units, performance measures etc. The data revealed a pattern: at each stage of maturity, a specific, dominant style is evident in the way companies are organized and how teams prefer to work. At that point in the evolution of the Lean Audit, there was not enough data to support a general statement, but nearly three-quarters of the audited organizations followed a very similar pattern as they matured, making the model an interesting starting point for further research. Between maturity levels 1.5 and 3.5, these companies passed through the same evolutionary stages, regardless of their size and setup—from regional companies to multi-national corporations.

At stage 1, the "Iron" stage, they set their focus on solving breakdowns and bottlenecks, thus removing constraints to respond to requests in a timely manner. At stage 2, "Bronze", the organization follows a traditional silo structure where managers focus on their departmental objectives and "improvement" is narrowly defined as reducing costs. At stage 3, "Silver", the structure shifts from *functions* to *processes*, and focus shifts from cost reduction to customer support excellence and operating efficiency. At stage 4, "Gold", processes are being connected and interfaces optimized, thus organizing people around value streams, and setting the focus on changing operating concepts and growing market opportunity. At stage 5, "Diamond", focus shifts from internal to external entities, partnerships and transplants (knowledge transfers), creating a lean enterprise that maximizes value-add from supplier to consumer, following the leading examples of McDonalds, Amazon, Toyota, Walmart, Ikea, and FedEx.

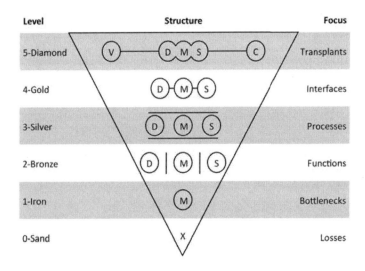

Figure 4.13 - Evolutionary triangle, structure follows maturity

The reverse pyramid chart in Figure 4.13 shows five evolutionary stages, from "Sand" to "Diamond". Functions in this model include (E) engineering, (O) operations, (S) sales, (V) vendor, and (C) customer. Setup and structure change with growing level of maturity, managing bottlenecks at the Iron stage, functional silos at Bronze, process clusters at Silver, value-chains at Gold, and networks at the Diamond level.

Next Stop: World-Class

Following the words of Vince Lombardi, who said, "Perfection is not attainable, but if we chase perfection we can catch excellence", the development and improvement of the Lean Audit never ends. World-class is therefore a *destination* not a starting point. Like a toddler passing through several maturity stages—crawling-walking-running—most companies pass four maturity phases on their journey to world-class. At the initial stage, the focus is on *Quantity*, eliminating bottlenecks and breakdowns to make deliveries and meet commitments. Once major shortages and barriers have been addressed, the priority shifts to *Quality*, reducing defects and controlling variability to get things right the first time. Once processes are stabilized, the focus shifts to *Efficiency*, increasing run rates, reducing labor content and machine hours, while balancing resources to demand. At the final phase leading to world-class, the focus shifts to new *Concepts* of products and services, revamping the value chain to provide more variety in shorter lead times while integrating customers and suppliers into the extended value chain.

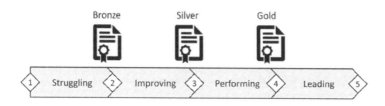

Figure 4.14 - Maturing phases and certification levels

Each of these four phases is different and characterized by specific activities; the following list describes them for a journey to World-Cass, from a *struggling* to a leading position, passing through the Bronze, Silver, and Gold stages.

Activities during the "Struggling" phase, between maturity level 1 and 2, focus on solving bottlenecks to meet basic commitments and deliveries.

- Set standards for processes, machines, behavior
- Provide information and education
- Address bottlenecks
- Reduce breakdowns and failures
- Define and maintain basic conditions
- Reduce waste from walking and errors
- Establish basic flow, remove excess inventory
- Stabilize lead times and quality rates
- Establish basic teamwork practices
- Engage everyone to one change agenda

Activities during the "Improving" phase, between maturity level 2 and 3, focus on reducing costs by tackling defects, delays, and disconnects.

- Simplify and refine core activities
- Eliminate causes of recurring problems
- Get process performance under control
- Achieve zero rework and zero backflow
- Reduce variability to meet committed deliveries
- Refine layout to enable continuous flow

- Define required inventory, implement strict controls
- Set planning parameters to reflect true demand profile
- Compress internal lead times
- Establish high performance teamwork

Activities during the "Performing" phase, between maturity level 3 and 4, focus on customer support excellence while maximizing overall efficiency.

- Transfer and delegate all routine activities to teams
- Develop and deploy expert resources to address variations
- Extend time between interventions towards zero unplanned interventions
- Achieve single-touch processing
- Connect processes, optimize interfaces
- Establish service level agreements
- Install low cost automation
- Compress total supply lead times
- Create positive team culture, remove cross-functional barriers
- Establish flawless introduction of new products and processes

Activities during the "Leading" phase, between maturity level 4 and 5, focus on changing the business model and structure, and growing market opportunity.

- Condition the way of working to sustain process optimization
- Create value from reduced variations in quality and delivery
- Redeploy expert resources to renewal activities
- Create value from market-leading innovations
- Achieve seamless flow and automatic excellence
- Reduce new product time to market
- Foster critical thinking and challenge current methods and models
- Develop strategic partnerships, integrate suppliers and customers
- Create value from big data and real-time information
- Increase customer loyalty and growth

Each stage removes several layers of waste and cost from the business, creating an operations-led competitive advantage from five sources:

- *Quality* – making things right based upon customer needs,

- *Speed* – making things fast and in shorter amounts of time,
- *Delivery* – making things on time with dependable lead times,
- *Flexibility* – offering a variety with the ability to adapt to changes, and
- *Cost* – making things fit for the purpose over life at lowest cost.

The Lean Audit results get you started but the scores alone are not enough to guide people from the trigger to the target. Numbers in general are only powerful when they are linked to actions, and are part of an overall improvement program, which is the topic of the next paragraph.

How does this work in practice?

Here is an example. An electronics manufacturer was in deep trouble but is now leading its industry only seven years later. Back then, their defect rate was extreme; the operation was constrained by major bottlenecks; work in process piled up to the roof, tying up money and drying up cash flow. It almost killed the company, so the new leadership team embarked on a lean transformation program focusing on manufacturing to turn the company around. It worked and the transformation story is nothing short of amazing. During seven years, maturity level increased at a steady pace of +0.31 per year, from a 1.6-point baseline to level 3.8, while productivity rose 1100% (eleven-fold!) during the same period.

Let's digest the numbers: an employee who originally made 13 units per day is now producing an incredible 143 units per day representing a 41%-gain in productivity, year by year, over the past seven years already. They must have automated or outsourced some processes to achieve this, right? They did not. The breakthrough in productivity was achieved by systematically applying lean principles to manufacturing and the supply-chain, creating (almost) seamless flow from planning to shipping, rather than tinkering around with departmental spot fixes.

And, where is the plateau? No plateau yet, as the team is still pushing boundaries (within the factory) wherever and whenever they appear. They change processes and build new capabilities as they are required to achieve targets. To go even further, the team must now go beyond manufacturing and focus on the entire value chain, addressing upstream processes with their interfaces to commercial and engineering. Only then will they be able to boost productivity by an additional 70% within the next three years which is required to achieve their ambitious target for producing 241 units per employee per day, an amount that is 18 times over what was done at the baseline.

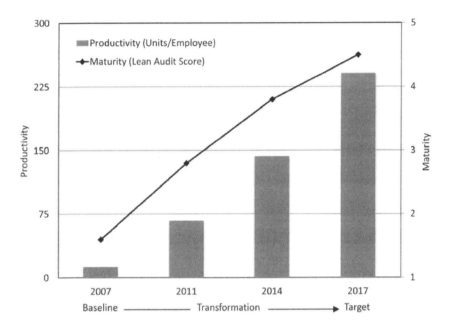

Figure 4.15 - Lean transformation case study

Each transformation, regardless of its goal and scope, starts with taking a reference point that (1) defines how well the operation performs relative to world-class benchmarks and (2) reveals improvement opportunities. The results from the Lean Audit get you started in the right direction and give you the ability to see the end goal. However, the results alone will not take you by the hand and lead you from the trigger to the target step-by-step. The audit provides you with the insight and shows you the goal, but you have to implement the improvements and take action to attain that goal. To be effective, you must go through the audit and embrace the results: make them—and the insight they provide—a driving force that links scores to strategy to actions. In essence, you will use the audit to establish a "perpetual improvement machine" in your organization, one that keeps you moving closer to world-class with each stroke of the engine.

The Leanmap Performance Cube™

Many of our clients ask for further guidance, what to do post audit. Two frequently raised questions relate to (1) which method to apply and (2) how to link different frameworks together so they complement instead of contradict or cannibalize one another. So we decided to merge some proven management concepts into one easy-to-apply framework, which we call the Leanmap Performance Cube™ (LPC).

The graphic below displays the basic logic behind the performance cube. The model consists of three sides. The top of the cube, the *Foundation Plane*, establishes strategy and structure, objectives and ownership. The left side, the *Assessment Plane*, scores the health and maturity level of people, processes, setup, and system. Results from the Assessment plane are used for baselining and benchmarking. The right side, the *Improvement Plane*, builds capabilities and improves performance levels, following the Deming cycle (PDCA). All three planes must be interconnected for the performance cube to work as a system.

The two common entry points into the cube are top-down and bottom-up. During a strategic review for example, the senior team initiates a benchmarking exercise to discover improvement opportunities (top-down). Or, during a self-assessment, the work team identifies weak areas that need to be addressed with the help of senior management (bottom-up). Both entry points set the Deming-wheel (PDCA) in motion: analyzing the opportunity and planning the improvement (plan), implementing the change (do), validating its effectiveness (check), and acting on the outcome (act) by either standardizing the new way of working or starting another improvement cycle. The cube is continuously in motion, turning from side to side, acting as the engine of perpetual improvement.

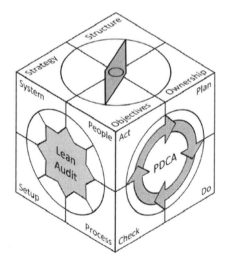

Figure 4.16 - Leanmap Performance Cube™ (LPC)

The Cube in Practice

Over the past five years, we have implemented the performance cube at client companies around the world, helping their management teams address operational challenges.

Scenario 1: A large injection molding plant in South China was heavily constrained by electricity shortages. We used the cube to drive improvements in "Inventory" and "Management", enabling the plant to compress its production load from 5.5 to 4 days so people could go on a "holiday break" during forced shutdowns (when the government scheduled the electricity off).

Scenario 2: After the launch of a new product series, replacing analog with digital control units, the central customer service department in Europe was unable to keep up with the flood of incoming calls because they did not have enough skilled people to deal with the complex installation and configuration issues. Service technicians were stressed out and customers frustrated. Using the cube, we identified "Standards" and "Solving" as the two keys to focus on. Three years later, the same service representatives are now handling close to 4 times the call volume with a fraction of the original complaint rate.

Scenario 3: A plant manager in Scandinavia was trying to gain approval for building a new warehouse because "there isn't enough space" to store all the incoming material (industrial waste) waiting for manual sorting. The team used the performance cube to gain further insight and focused on "Structure" and "Efficiency". Eighteen months later, solely by organizing processes and rearranging workflow, the team reduced inventory by 82% and increased labor productivity by 31% (tons per man-hour), while shortening throughput time from 2 months to 1 week. The same site that was inundated with excess inventory was now able to absorb additional volume from another division's plant—in so doing, it became the internal benchmark and model for other plants to follow.

In all three scenarios, these companies leveraged additional insight gained from the performance cube in unique ways to address specific business problems. In practice, it turns out that roughly one quarter of the performance cube's applications are related to solving resource shortages—water, energy, machine capacity, or skilled labor. More common applications target profitability by reducing costs or by increasing throughput to absorb growth.

Here are more examples of performance cube applications that led to significant benefits. Over a 12-month period, three sites in Latin America improved productivity of their compounding processes: 65% in Mexico, 19% in Argentina, and 50% in Brazil. In addition, the Brazil location nearly tripled labor efficiency from 9 to 26 units per man-hour (unfortunately, there wasn't enough demand to fully utilize the newly gained capacity). In addition, the largest operation in the US reduced lead-time by 43%, while bringing service levels from 92% to 97%. In Japan, production and bottling processes at one plant were connected to work in sync, reducing lead-time by 28%. In China, a Telecom supplier used the cube's insight to merge two assembly lines into one, reducing double-handling, lead-times, and working capital.

These gains are great achievements, but can we expect to repeat such success stories year-by-year?

Every turn of the cube creates new insights and builds new capabilities that make metrics move. Success will repeat year on year as long as you keep moving at the pulse of the market and faster than your competitors.

The individual tools and techniques comprising the Leanmap Performance Cube™ are not new, but together they function in a new way, creating a "lean machine" that propels you forward. The Leanmap Performance Cube™ is a proven system that effectively and consistently creates a competitive advantage for both manufacturers and service firms. The Leanmap Performance Cube™ integrates best practices into a ready-to-use package. It builds a solid foundation with a focus on Strategy, Structure, Objectives, and Ownership (SSOO); it provides feedback on People, Process, Setup, and System (PPSS); and it also drives the Deming wheel Plan-Do-Check-Act (PDCA), reducing waste and variability, while improving productivity and competitiveness with each turn. And finally, the Leanmap Performance Cube™ promotes a performance culture that lifts the organization above its competitors.

5. CERTIFICATION

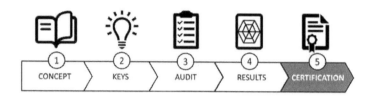

About Lean Certification

Any product and service company that falls within the scope of the Lean Audit can be measured and certified in Lean. Becoming "Lean Certified" involves passing a physical certification audit by a certifying agency such as Leanmap. But why would any company want to be certified? Lean standards offer the strategic tools and guidelines companies need to tackle some of the most demanding challenges of modern business. Lean standards ensure that businesses operate as efficiently and effectively as possible. They increase productivity and help companies capture new customers and access new markets using strategies and techniques such as just-in-time delivery performance (see the *Inventory* Key in chapter 2).

Benefits of Certification:

Certified companies at Silver level and above have the structures and processes in place to ensure work is done right first time every time, thus enabling a more efficient operation in a more effective configuration. Those companies understand that delivering quality products and services at the pace of demand increases customer satisfaction and makes customers desire more. Companies use their lean certification as a marketing tool to promote a customer-centric mode of operation to end-users, and their value-driven management philosophy to investors. This makes it more likely that third parties will engage a lean-certified company than one lacking certification. Inside the organization, across all levels and functions, becoming certified to lean standards raises awareness among employees and motivates them to apply the principles in the areas they are responsible for, building the foundational skills that enable systematic, continual improvement. And, of course, one of the most compelling benefits of adopting lean strategies as a consequence of the Lean Audit is that reducing waste and increasing productivity leads to greater profits for certified companies.

Certification Process

Certification requires at least two measurements to confirm that the audited organization has truly achieved the level of maturity as assessed by the Lean Audit score. The certification process is an extension of the auditing process, which provides both the baseline and subsequent progress measurements.

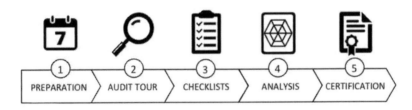

Figure 5.1 - Assessment and certification process

How does this work in practice?

Suppose an organization measures 2.7 on the first assessment. This initial measurement does not warrant a certificate; rather, it establishes the baseline for a certificate. Several months later, the audit is repeated to determine progress relative to the baseline. As an example, consider the case study discussed earlier. Post-audit, the team was able to move the needle by +0.4 to 3.1 on the maturity scale, which justifies awarding a Silver certificate.

Step 1-4: Assessment

The first four steps are identical to the auditing process, which does nothing more than establishes the baseline of maturity, balance, and agility. Once progress is confirmed and a new level of maturity has been achieved, the company is ready for the next step.

5. CERTIFICATION

Step 5. Certification

After the progress measurement is established, the team compares it against the goal they have defined during the previous audit. Two things must occur for certification: (1) the target maturity has been attained at (2) an advancement rate of +0.15 per year or higher.

When certification occurs, the event should be formally communicated and celebrated in the same (or similar) fashion that a company celebrates when they meet a significant financial goal or capture a new valued client. Why celebrate? Because more mature companies do better than less mature ones, so an improving score in the Lean Audit—along with certification—suggest better operating results in the near future. Tracking maturity is like tracking atmospheric pressure with a barometer: it provides a clear indication of improving weather. Maturity gain, as established by the 20 Keys, is therefore a leading indicator that complements financial reports in an ideal way because they are comprised solely of lagging indicators. What does this mean? If a company makes fundamental changes to its setup or structure affecting capability, it will quickly be reflected in the maturity score, but it may take months or years for it to affect financial reports. The 20 Keys are therefore a kind of weather forecast for future operating performance.

Figure 5.2 - A silver-certified company

So, what can you do with this certification?

You can use your lean-certified status in your marketing. The fact that you measure your performance shows that you care about quality and customer service. This alone will differentiate you from many competitors, and will reflect your image in a positive fashion. Your capabilities, your management system, and its processes have been certified to the standard of Lean Manufacturing or Lean Service. You can also use the certificate as an acknowledgment of what has been achieved to date. Like a compass, it guides you to the next phase of the journey. It motivates people to continue building the capabilities (the 20 Keys) that move you closer to world-class.

What can't you do?

You can't use or modify the Leanmap logo (sigma), as it is the Leanmap brand and intellectual property. You can't say "Lean certified"; you must spell out the level and scope, e.g.

> "Lean Manufacturing, Level 3.0 (Silver) for
> Bronsfield Industries Inc, Dorado location"

Make sure that your description properly depicts your certified activities and geographic location. The stamp of "Lean" certifies a level of maturity relative to established benchmarks; it can't be listed on your products or used in literature to imply product certification, as it certifies a level of maturity that does not warrant a certain outcome for customers. It's like the multiple choice test at a driving school attests a level of proficiency; it does not indicate how well someone can drive a car.

When to Issue a Certificate

In the Olympics, only the top three levels—Bronze, Silver, and Gold—are acknowledged. And if your organization were like most others, starting at 2.5 and leveling off around 3.5 in maturity, you'd only have one chance in your company's life cycle to celebrate—the Silver certification at level 3.0. Acknowledging only full levels (2.0, 3.0, and 4.0) would be too infrequent to keep people interested in the journey. What works better is celebrating smaller steps, so we use every quarter-point. If your company has great ambitions but is also limited in capability or is constrained in resources, the advancement rate will be less than world-class, for example 50% of the benchmark rate or +0.25 points per year. Getting a new, updated certificate for every quarter-point gained would mean that your company receives a formal evaluation with positive feedback once a year—moving from Silver* (3.25) to Silver** (3.50) for example. Such positive feedback keeps people engaged and motivated, which in turn prompts them to expend a little more effort, moving the company forward by a small step, every single day.

What's Next? Getting Help

To learn more about improving operations, attend the latest Lean Auditor Class by coming to our Lean Consulting offices. You can download Free Procedure Templates to see how easy it is to diagnose your operation and build your first Lean Standard Operating Procedures (SOPs).

If you have taken the time to read this book, you are obviously concerned about improving performance. You must also have the ability to understand the concepts outlined in this book, some of which go beyond basic business. The next step is simple: contact us. Allow us to guide you on your journey to World Class. We look forward to speaking with you. If you want to start this process on your own, we have made the tools and templates available. Take the audit online or download the tools and look them over at your leisure. Or drop us a line. We are glad to hear from you.

Here is our contact information:

- Download tools and templates: www.leanmap.com/tools
- Do the audit online: www.leanmap.com/benchmarking
- Need help to do an assessment: audit@leanmap.com
- Contact the author: joerg@leanmap.com

CONCLUSION

Corporate Longevity

Some business leaders choose to run their operation in a narrow-minded fashion. Year after year they focus largely on the budget. Company resources are devoted to making the numbers and not much else: *Meet the revenue goals! Cut expenses!* In the sporting realm, this is comparable to playing in games but never practicing. At game time, players lack the endurance and skills needed for prolonged athletic competition. Instead of a tactical approach developed from long hours of training and practice, they are relegated to using haphazard, get-lucky finesse. They kick their soccer balls at the goal from mid field, shoot their basketballs without attempting layups, and swing their bats for home runs only, no base hits.

In the business world we also need practice, assessment and feedback. Products and services must be properly developed *before* they are deployed in the marketplace. Skills must be assessed and improved, services practiced and refined, and processes streamlined. Business leaders must proactively measure the viability of their operation—and implement the necessary programs to improve performance—or they risk losing in the game of business. Lacking a good regimen of fitness assessment and performance improvement, they might as well be out-of-shape quarterbacks, tossing Hail Mary passes with 10 seconds on the clock, hoping for a lucky catch, an easy win. It's only a matter of time before something bad happens—a change in product demand, a new technology, an economic pullback, an aggressive competitor, or anything that might cause a budget hiccup too big to address with tinkering ...and then, in the blink of an eye, cash flow is disrupted, payroll looms large, vendors are pounding at the door for payment, and the company is teetering on failure. It happens that fast, especially in today's rapidly evolving, global marketplace...

In business, as in sports, practice is necessary—and practice should start with an accurate assessment of business strengths and weaknesses. The Lean Audit provides this assessment and gives business leaders all the insight they need to make the necessary changes and implement the strategies and programs required to improve—programs that lead to long-term strength and viability, and ultimately World Class. Those businesses that ignore the rapidly changing business world and continue operating blindly, without using powerful self-assessment tools like the Lean Audit, are destined to fail, sooner or later; their demise is imminent.

> The Lean Audit provides a fast, effective framework to help business leaders uncover untapped opportunities and formulate the changes needed to attain significant performance improvements. Start your journey to WORLD-CLASS now.

The Lean Audit targets operational competitiveness, but transforming operations is only one component of the success formula. Here are the key activities that significantly increase corporate life expectancy: (1) focus on customers to understand what they really need beyond what they ask for and what they are currently working on, (2) engage key suppliers in joint problem solving and waste removal activities to streamline the value chain, (3) avoid introversion and actively seek to understand broader trends outside the organization and industry, (4) challenge legacy thinking and legacy mindsets, encouraging internal competition while accepting "healthy cannibalization" to reallocate resources to high potential projects, (5) avoid hubris by creating a culture of dissatisfaction with current performance, no matter how good, and (6) proactively seek ways to change the mode of operation in times of fundamental and disruptive change.

And let me finish this book with the same words as it started: "Perfection is not attainable, but if we chase perfection we can catch excellence." Start your Lean Journey now!

REFERENCES

Bicheno, Holweg: "The Lean Toolbox""" – Picsie Books, 2008
Covey: "The Seven Habits of Highly Effective People" – Simon & Schuster, 1992
Davis: "Reflections on Corporate Longevity" – McKinsey Quarterly, 2014
Davis, Aquilano, Chase: "Fundamentals of Operations Mgmt" – McGraw-Hill, 2003
Deming: "Leadership Principles from the Father of Quality" – McGraw-Hill, 2012
Deming: "Out of the Crisis" – MIT Press, 2000
Duncan, Ritter: "The next Frontiers for Lean" – McKinsey Quarterly, 2014
Goodson: "Read a Plant – Fast" – Harvard Business Review, 2002
Gladwell: "The Tipping Point" – Little, Brown and Company, 2002
Goldratt, Cox: "The Goal" – North River Press, 1992
Hayes & Wheelwright: "Restoring our competitive edge" – Wiley & Sons, 1984
Juran: "Quality Control Handbook" – McGraw-Hill, 1988
Kobayashi: "20 Keys to Workplace Improvement" – Productivity Press, 1995
Liker: "The Toyota Way" – McGraw-Hill, 2004
Mann: "Creating a Lean Culture" – Productivity Press, 2005
Masaaki: "Kaizen" – McGraw-Hill, 1997
Metters: "Successful Service Operations" – South-Western College Publishing, 2007
Nakajima: "TPM: Total Productive Maintenance" – Productivity Press, 1988
Ohno: "Workplace Management" – McGraw-Hill, 2007
Pande, Neuman, Cavanagh: "The Six Sigma Way" – McGraw-Hill, 2000
Pine: "Mass customization" – Harvard Business School Press, 1993
Schneider, Bowen: "Winning the Service Game" – Harward Business Press, 1995
Schonberger: "World Class Manufacturing" – Simon & Schuster, 2010
Todd: "World-class Manufacturing" – McGraw-Hill, 1995
Womack: "Lean Thinking" – Simon & Schuster, 1996
Womack, Jones: "The Machine that Changed the World" – Rawson Associates, 1990

QUESTIONS & ANSWERS

Q: *Who should use the factory audit and why?*

A: The Lean Factory Audit (LFA) is designed for product companies to assess the process of converting raw materials into finished goods.

Q: *Who should use the office audit and why?*

A: The Lean Office Audit (LOA) is designed for service companies to assess the process of converting consumers into satisfied customers.

Q: *Who should participate in the audit?*

A: Representatives from core functions, such as commercial, operations, quality, service, and technical must take part; optional are representatives from support functions, such as HR and IT.

Q: *How long does it take to do the audit?*

A: Answering 120 questions takes 2 hours at a (fast) rate of 1 question per minute, while scheduling 3 hours is recommended to allow some time for alignment discussions.

Q: *Are all 20 keys relevant to any company?*

A: Yes, but to various degrees. Dependent on the company and industry, some keys are always more critical and some are of lesser importance, but still relevant and worthwhile to be assessed.

Q: *What happens if multiple answers are correct?*

A: Select the "normal" case that represents 80% of all situations and occurrences; never select favorable exceptions to prevent skewing the results.

Q: *Is a single score a valid indicator for an entire organization?*

A: Yes, for small and homogeneous organizations led by the same leader or leadership team. For large corporations, no, as each entity must be audited separately to accurately assess the differences between them.

Q: *How often should the audit be repeated?*

A: Audit at least once and ideally twice per year to get frequent feedback on progress.

Q: *How is the audit report used?*

A: Select 3 to 12 priority areas to be tackled over the next 3 to 12 months, strengthening keys to compete and reducing weak spots.

Q: *How fast can a business evolve and mature?*

A: Under best conditions maturity level increases by +0.5 points per year, while most companies improve at 60-80% of this benchmark level (+0.3...0.4 points per year).

Q: *Is there a limit to improvement? What is the maximum score?*

A: Yes, each company can improve until reaching its "natural" plateau, while the limit on the measurement scale is 5 points.

AUTHOR AND COMPANY

Author

Joerg Muenzing is an international efficiency expert and interim operations executive who designs and leads industrialization, rationalization and turnaround programs for multi-national corporations. He holds degrees in business and engineering, and he is a frequent speaker on the topics of lean transformation, rapid innovation, and sustainable cost reduction. He has successfully applied lean principles in over 20 countries for companies such as Mercedes Benz, Givaudan, Franke, Landis-Gyr, Detroit Diesel, Eltek, Navico, Gategourmet, and Techtronic Industries, among others. He lives with his family in Switzerland and can be contacted at joerg@leanmap.com.

Company

Leanmap helps clients achieve world-class operations. With targeted consulting advice, benchmarking audits, training seminars, and interim management services—all centered on lean principles—the Leanmap team of experts prepares companies for a better, more productive future. They not only analyze current conditions and develop the transformation program, but also play an active role in the implementation, until goals are achieved and skills and systems are in place to sustain them. By solving operational constraints, streamlining processes, rationalizing structures, and by bringing mission-critical projects back on track, they help leaders to move organizations to a higher level of performance – *Navigating to Results*.

Printed in Poland
by Amazon Fulfillment
Poland Sp. z o.o., Wrocław